The Book of
BRIDESTOWE

Gleanings of a Devonshire Parish

D. Richard Cann

HALSGROVE

This book is dedicated to the people of Bridestowe past, present and future.

First published in Great Britain in 2002

Frontispiece photograph: *White Hart, 1920s.* (Doug Gale)

British Library Cataloguing-in-Publication Data
A CIP record for this title is available from the British Library

ISBN 1 84114 196 8

HALSGROVE

Halsgrove House
Lower Moor Way
Tiverton, Devon EX16 6SS
Tel: 01884 243242
Fax: 01884 243325
email: sales@halsgrove.com
website: www.halsgrove.com

Printed and bound by
Bookcraft Ltd, Midsomer Norton

Whilst every care has been taken to ensure the accuracy of the information contained in this book, the author disclaims responsibility for any mistakes which may have inadvertently been included.

FOREWORD

Incomers say that Bridestowe people are very welcoming and this is probably true, they in turn being responsive to fit into village life. Bridestowe is not a big parish; the nucleus of the population, which is less than 500, live in the village whilst the remainder are spread around outlying farms. During the mid-nineteenth century, at the height of the lime quarries and with the short-lived mining industry boom in the area, the population was at its largest at 1500 people. Bridestowe was, and still is in the main, a rural economy.

Of the large families, only the Calmady-Hamyns on their Leawood Estate are still in being and it is to the Leawood Estate that the Cann family became tenants in about 1935. They initially settled in a cottage towards the top of Poole Hill before moving to East Bridge in 1956, being resident in the village for some 60 years. Their son, Richard, had plenty of time to absorb the atmosphere of the place even though he left the village as a permanent resident at the age of 15 for he frequently visited his parents at Bridestowe until their demise. When his interest inspired him to write his manuscript, *Royal Blood in the Village*, he spent many years researching the archives held in Exeter and Plymouth and wrote knowledgeably about the principal estates, families and inhabitants of the area.

I am very pleased and honoured to have received a copy of the manuscript and even more so to be asked to write a foreword to the Halsgrove edition of his account of Bridestowe, complete with numerous pictures to illustrate the text. I have been in the village for rather more than 40 years but the family has been here for some four centuries so perhaps I have some small claim to the privilege of writing this tribute to a well-researched publication.

JOAN CALMADY-HAMLYN, LEAWOOD ESTATE, JANUARY *2002*

Poole Hill. (Doug Gale)

Bridhayes, 1920s. (Doug Gale)

Fore Street, 1920s. (Doug Gale)

CONTENTS

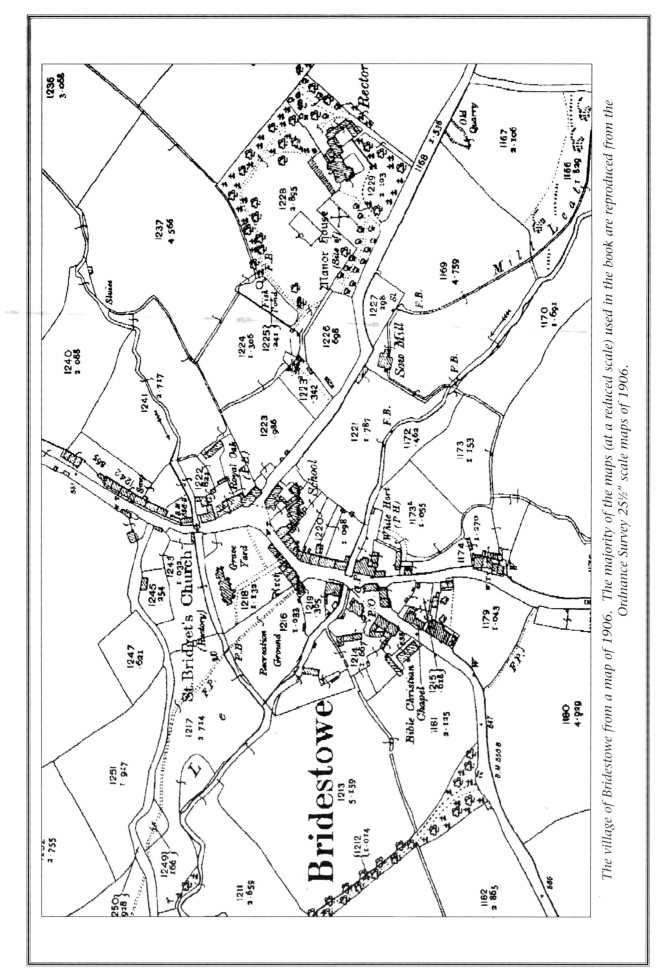

The village of Bridestowe from a map of 1906. The majority of the maps (at a reduced scale) used in the book are reproduced from the Ordnance Survey 25½" scale maps of 1906.

ACKNOWLEDGEMENTS

The fascinating selection of photographs in this volume represents a wonderful community effort. There are many people who supplied treasured pictures in order that they might be preserved in published form. The addition of their postcards and photographs to my text has added interest to Bridestowe's past and brought events and people of the past to life; knowing that cattle fairs were once held in Bridestowe I was certainly surprised when Brian Maddaford produced a photograph of the event.

As well as Brian I must thank Howard Barkell, Sam Ball, Brian Lavis, George Lavis, Derek Northcott, Norman Gale, Joan Calmady-Hamlyn and Bridestowe School for allowing me access to precious photographs. There is also Alan Pearn, who would expect someone to produce old glass plate negatives of Bridestowe other than the Dawlish photographer, Chapman. My thanks go to John Stredwick of Exmouth for taking prints off the plates. Then there is Douglas Gale; his large collection of postcards is unbelievable – one would never have imagined that there could really be 100 cards of such a small place as Bridestowe.

Thanks are also due to the staff of the Devon Record Office, the West Country Studies Library and the main Exeter Library for their help over the years. My next-door neighbour, Peter McMillan, must also be thanked for drawing my attention to the Halsgrove Community History Series by putting their flyers through my letter box; if I had not seen the flyer this book would still be on the hard disk of my computer. Finally I thank my wife for putting up with my history, history, history...

RICHARD CANN, EXMOUTH, JANUARY 2002

Views of Bridestowe. (Alan Pearn)

Bottom of Poole Hill with Devon Constabulary sign above doorway, 1920s. (Doug Gale)

Looking towards Bridestowe from the Launceston Road, 1920s. (Alan Pearn)

INTRODUCTION

Although not a place of great note or importance, Bridestowe Parish, situated on the north-western edge of Dartmoor, is a place with a long and varied history. Through the ages the village has never been other than a farming community where some families were in residence on their farms over hundreds of years, others disappearing long before their farms were swallowed up by the events of time. Inhabitants provided for their own self-sufficiency whilst performing an administrative role in every aspect of parish life. In the not-so-distant past industry took place in a small way with the development of local resources. The remains of a fortification exist and battles have been fought nearby. During the Civil War Royalist and Parliamentarian causes were both supported. The church had a major role to play in the village, the rector being lord of a manor. Before the bypass was constructed the main London to Falmouth road ran through the village and a distant railway station served the needs of a traveller.

Bridestowe might appear insignificant but when you commence researching a history of such a place you begin to realise that a vast subject is being uncovered. Disappointment looms however whenever questions seem impossible to answer after many a lunch hour has been spent studying the numerous archives deposited by Bridestowe families and other sources from which much of this book has been written.

I saw you at Bridestowe but couldn't see your face. Postcard postmarked 1909.
(Doug Gale)

This is not a scholarly edition of the history of Bridestowe but perhaps a starting point for someone who may wish to achieve such a history. Doubtless someone upon reading this book will notice that certain items are not covered; the Methodist Chapel comes to mind but information is not always readily available – we apologise in advance for these regrettable omissions (also for any inadvertent errors which may have crept in). The one thing I hope is that readers of this book will gain an insight into the past by forming conclusions of their own about village life in bygone days, by visualising how our (often less well off) predecessors lived and contributed to the rich tapestry of life in our rural community.

'Seek peace and ensue it in what you may, for to live peaceably with all men maketh a man and woman long to seem young.'

(John Bidlake 1613)

Town Farm, 1920s. (Doug Gale)

Bridestowe view, 1920s. (Doug Gale)

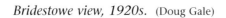

Chapter 1

THE DEVELOPMENT OF BRIDESTOWE

FIRST VIEW

Whilst Dean of Exeter Cathedral between 1762 and 1784 Jeremiah Milles had question-naires sent out to the clergy of Devon and from the answers returned he was hoping to produce a history of Devon. Although Milles did not achieve his goal, much of the material upon which he was going to base his work has survived, and it is this that provides our initial insight into Bridestowe. The form of the original manuscript has been changed to facilitate understanding, but the core of the text remains, as does the spelling of the place names.

Briddistow is a Rectory in the Hundred of Lifton and Deanery of (Totnes), situated on the high road from Exeter to Launceston, about six or seven miles distant from Okehampton, ten from Tavistock and 28 from Exeter. Its present name is evidently a derivation of Bridgetstow to which saint this church is dedicated and so it is called in a deed 300 years old in a dispute between this parish and Sourton. The parish is about five or six miles long from east to west and about two miles broad from north to south.

The church is situated in the north east part of the parish in a bottom not far from the river Thrussel. It stands in a very large churchyard, which is well planted with trees. The building consists of a nave, two aisles divided by two pillars, the roof arched but not ceiled. There is a square tower at the west end in which is three bells. There is a painting of our Saviour's resurrection. The Communion table is not bad. In the windows of the south isle are the following coats. [Here follows the description of various heraldic badges.] Against the north wall of the chancel there is a square monument over which is the following. 'Here lieth the body of John Wrey Esq. who died the 3rd day of March 1576.' [Again a description of the heraldic badges.] There is a likewise monument in memory of Lady Honor Calmady who died in 1663 and whose two husbands are said in the inscription to have laid in the bed of Honour.

The Rectory with the daughter church of Sourton,

which is joined in the same presentation, is worth about ... per annum and is in the gift of the Bishop of Exeter. The Parsonage house stands near the church but is in an indifferent building. There is a glebe of between 40 or 50 acres belonging to it. There are two manors in this parish. That of Comb Wyke or Cobham Wyke now belonging to Mr Harris of Hayne and formerly Lord Cobham, and the Parsonage manor lying near to the church belonging to the Rector who pays a yearly rent of £6.13s. to the auditor of the Crown, which is the amount of the high rents he receives. Mr Calmady has a house at a place called Leywood about half a mile west of the church. There is a likewise house called Bidlegh about a mile west of the church belonging to a family of the same name.

The villages in this parish are the church farm, Fearnworthy, south of the church and Ebbisworthy, north west of the church, which gave name to an ancient family so called. The face of the parish is in general hilly and not very fruitful, more open than enclosed, chiefly stony with some clayey soil. There is a good limestone quarry at a place called Comb Bau a mile west of the church of the same nature and colour with that of Digport. There is more pasture than arable land in the parish and the meadows are generally course. There are a few orchards and the cider in general not extraordinary. There are about 200 acres of woodland in the parish. Two rivulets rise in the parish and running through it empty themselves into the river Lyd; one of them is called Crandford.

This parish has the privilege of Fenfield man, for which they do suit and service at the Prince of Wales Court at Lidford for the forest of Dartmoor and have a right of Turbary and feeding cattle by day. They have besides several commons adjoining to the moor within their own parish.

Although the early history is lacking from this eighteenth-century account of Bridestowe, much of the parish's essence is conveyed in just a few lines, and much of what it describes is still true today. It tells us that Bridestowe then

Unveiling of the Parish Map, 1996. Left to right, back: *Ann Palmer, Vera Whiting, Carol Whiteley, W.I. Visitor, Kath Tudge, Elsie Barkell, Beatrice Pritchard;* front: *Rosie Pritchard.*

(Howard Barkell)

incorporated a church with rectory, houses, farms and a lime quarry; Bridestowe on the face of it has never really been much more than its eighteenth-century description. It may be thought that we only need to add a school, a chapel, some shops and a couple of inns to bring the parish up to date, as with these additions Bridestowe remains a small, insignificant place to the north-west of Dartmoor with farming its main source of living.

However, Dean Milles has only laid the foundation stone when it comes to looking at Bridestowe's past. What about the Red Lion inn – are many people aware of it? What of William Smith, a schoolmaster in 1662? What about the many other small industries besides farming? There is much to explore.

THE PLACE NAME BRIDESTOWE

The first question most people ask regarding Bridestowe is usually concerned with why the name is pronounced 'Bridd-is-tow', rather than 'Bride-stowe'. The simple answer is that nobody seems to know! It is fair to say that in Devon we are lazy with our speech. (For example, we often drop 'th' from a word, so that 'three' would become 'dree'.) However, if this is the case, then it is reasonable to assume that Bridestowe would be pronounced as 'Bridstow', or even 'Bristow'. To complicate matters further, Risdon, the Devonshire historian and antiquarian writing in the early-seventeenth century, stated that 'Bridestow' was 'corruptly so called for Brithrickstow'. It seems most sensible to simply follow tradition and accept the way things are.

From Risdon we may deduce that many variations on the form and spelling of Bridestowe have occurred over the years, so we need to have an understanding of how the name arose. The first half of the name is linked with St Bridget, the famous Irish saint (450–525) to whom the parish church is dedicated. 'Stow' usually attests to a church of ancient origin, going back to the missionary days of Christianity. It means 'a holy place, a place of gathering'. Ravenhill is of the opinion that Celtic scholars agree that ancient churches dedicated to a Celtic saint were either established by the saint himself or by one of his immediate disciples. Christianity arrived in Britain by AD200, from which time on the saints flourished. How then, did the Stow, the place of St Bridget, come into being?

Some clues are offered by the earthworks at Burley Wood, the tentative origins of which stem from around 100–200BC during the Iron Age 'A' culture. In accordance with other hill-forts in Devon there is no indication of a church within the bounds of the Burley Wood site. Indeed, the earliest works constructed at Burley Wood were used primarily for containing herds of animals for short periods during bouts of cattle raiding by a warrior society in which wealth was counted in terms of the number of cattle one owned. The people who made use of Burley Wood in times of trouble almost undoubtedly took possession of the land around the River Lew and the Crandford Brook during peaceful times. This came to represent the nucleus of a community waiting for a saint to come into their midst and set up a Stow.

If we accept Ravenhill's opinion the particular missionary coming to Bridestowe would have been St Bridget or one of her disciples, and the church at Bridestowe was established around the end of the fifth century.

Initially, a cross was erected as a permanent testimony to the religious dedication of the saint. The Stow, as well as being used as a place of religion, became a place to inter the dead. As the population of the settlement increased the Stow also became a place where many aspects of life would be developed and cultivated. The tithing-men would convene, courts would be held, trading would take place, and sports and games would be played. As culture improved, a holy house was built, probably in wood, on the part of the Stow where the cross once stood.

In light of the unusual pronunciation of 'Briddistow' it seems fair to deduce that various spellings have been used throughout history. The Domesday Book entry of 'Bridestou' gives us our first easily traced version of the name. After this, many different spellings have appeared in various documents, some of which are listed below:

Bridestowe, 1221-30, Book of Fees;
Brydestou, 1259-79, Episcopal Registers of the Diocese of Exeter;
Byrightstowe and **Brightesstowe**, 1242, Book of Fees;
Brithtestawe, 1249, Assize Rolls;
Briztetsowe and **Brigidestowe**, 1259-79, Episcopal Registers of the Diocese of Exeter;
Stow Sce Brigide, 1299, Assize Rolls;
Biritestowa, 1300s, G. Oliver, Monasticion Diocesis Exoniensis;
Brittestowe, 1303, Feudal Aids;
Brithstowe, 1350, Calendar of Patent Rolls;
Briddestowe, 1391, Ep. Reg. Exr.;
Bristow, 1428, FA;
Breddestawe, 1539, Letters and Papers Foreign and Domestic.

BRONZE AND IRON AGE

Perhaps the earliest that we may go back in a quest to trace the roots of Bridestowe is to the period 2400–700BC, the Bronze Age. Ring cairns, stone hut circles and a round barrow dating from this period lie on Dartmoor within the common land that is shared with the neighbouring parish of Sourton. There is more evidence of the Bronze-Age period within the bounds of Bridestowe that do not straddle Dartmoor.

In a field by the road leading to the now redundant railway station, opposite the road leading to Watergate, a ploughed down long mound has been tentatively identified as a long barrow. The mound is about 60m long, 27m wide at its east end, 18m wide at its west end and 1m high. There are no traces of side ditches and the date remains uncertain. To the south of Burley Wood a round barrow of stone and earth, 15m in diameter and 0.3m high, lies on an east–west ridge.

For evidence of the Iron Age, 700BC to AD43, we return to Burley Wood. *The Victoria County History, Devon, Vol. 1*, contains the following entry:

Upon the verge of a bold spur of hills of great height, at the foot of which flows the River Lew, is one of the strongest fortifications on the West Side of Dartmoor. Within the dense growth of Burley Wood, north of Woodhead and east of Foxcombe Wood, we find not only a mount and bailey, but other extensive works.

This entry refers to earthwork fortifications of two periods. The first consists of an 'Iron-Age promontory fort and hill slope enclosure' which is 'one of the best and most elaborate of the "wide-spread defence" type'. The second, an earthwork castle, was constructed by the Normans.

The earliest earthworks were built on a cramped point on the northern end of a ridge. The rampart constructed in the most southerly position is up to 3.5m in height with a ditch 2.2m in depth. It contains two breaks that are probably original entrances. The second inner rampart with an outer ditch is up to 1.2m high. This has a gap near its centre for an entrance, which may have been altered through time. A broad natural cross-ridge that may have been scarped lies behind the two ramparts.

The main area of settlement comprises an irregular oval enclosure of 1.5 hectares in area with a south-west facing entrance. This entrance is approached through a bank and ditch annex with an inturned entrance on its west side. The annex, 0.75 hectares, has a small pen of 0.25 hectares constructed in the north corner, with an entrance linking the two. The earthworks were set out in this way in order to allow for separate enclosures in which to contain animals and to provide grazing and water. A bronze palstave and a flat axe in poor condition have been found on this site.

These earthworks are an Iron-Age 'A' plateau camp, probably occupied by the earliest Iron-Age

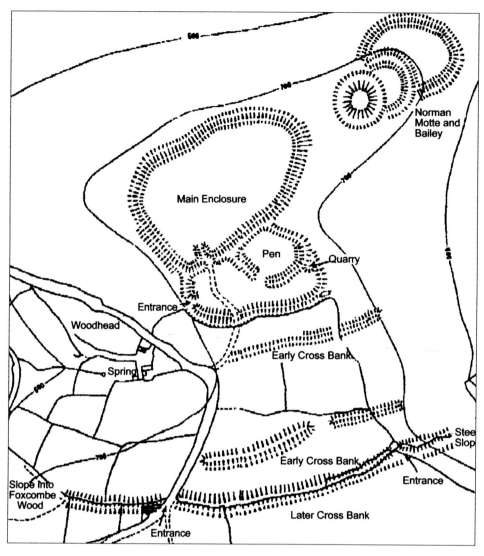

Map of Burley Wood Earthworks.

invaders. They were small groups of peasant farmers whose culture involved the use of iron alongside a bare subsistence economy. Later occupation of the area was by Iron-Age 'B' people who turned the hill into a promontory fort. Originating in Brittany, they had probably brought their culture to South-West England by AD100. It is these people who, on overcoming the Iron-Age 'A' culture, mainly constituted the 'Dumnonii' the 'people of the land'.

It is unclear how long the hill-fort remained occupied before the medieval period. The earthworks lie close to Galford Down in the parish of Lewtrenchard, which may possibly be linked with the Gavulford mentioned in the Angle Saxon Chronicle, where, in AD823, the Britons made a last-ditch stand against Egbert and his Saxons.

To the north-east of the hill-fort lies the Norman castle (also mentioned in *The Victoria County History)* that was probably built soon after the Conquest. The new Norman landlords built motte-and-bailey earthworks at many places in Devon, as much of the English population was hostile. The earthwork at Burley Wood, of which there is no documentation, was probably constructed by a member of the Norman family, Pomeroy, who held the manor of Bridestowe. In all probability this site was not used after the Civil War during Stephen's reign; as with many other motte-and-bailey earthworks, it was not converted into a castle of stone because manor houses were found to be more conducive to a comfortable life.

The motte at Burley Wood has a diameter of 21.3m and is 3m high. The crescent-shaped inner bailey is 15.2m wide whilst the outer bailey is 35m wide. It has been said that the remains of iron smeltings have been found on this site.

In conclusion, it seems reasonable to say that a settlement, which later developed into the village of Bridestowe with farmsteads scattered around it, was established at the very latest with the arrival of the Bronze- and Iron-Age people. With Christianity came the Stow and the cross, which was later replaced with a wooden building. In turn this was replaced with a Saxon church. The roots of Bridestowe had been laid.

THE MANOR OF BRIDESTOWE

To understand fully the manor of Bridestowe we need to take a brief look at general events in Devon between the time of the Romans and the arrival of the Normans. The Romans made little impact in Devon (except in Exeter) although there have been many references to the existence of Roman roads to the west of the River Exe. There is as yet little evidence of Roman occupation of land beyond this point. The Devon County Ancient Sites and Monuments Register records a Roman road at the Ordnance Survey grid reference of SX 5100 8910. This refers to a site on the road (the old A30) that runs through Bridestowe neighbouring the cricket field.

It seems that the Celtic kingdom of Dumnonia carried on with its own culture, although it was very thinly populated, until the beginning of the Saxon occupation of Devon in about AD658. There was little opposition to the Saxons and they over-ran Devon rapidly and took control of tracts of land alongside the Celtic people. The county was at this time in English hands.

It was during the Saxon period that Devon was incorporated into the political organisation of Wessex and became recognised as a shire that was divided up into small districts known as hundreds. Bridestowe was placed in the hundred of Lifton for the purpose of taxation, the keeping of law and order and the settlement of local pleas.

After the Saxons, the Danes came to Devon in AD851; they were defeated but later returned. After a number of battles over a very long period of time Devon passed into Danish rule under Cnut in 1016.

We can only assume that the manor of Bridestowe, along with its village and surrounding farms, was left to develop at its own pace throughout the Bronze Age and the Norman administration. The Domesday Book, written during this period, at last offers firm evidence of the existence of Bridestowe.

The manorial system was in place before William I came to England although the term 'manor' came with the Conquest. Historians debate as to whether it was the Roman system of land-holding adopted by the English or the Teutonic school of thought whereby Saxons settled in free village communities, lost their freedom and developed into the villeins of the Domesday Book, that formed the basis upon which the manor was formed.

Once William was crowned, the majority of land held by members of the English aristocracy was soon given to his retinue. A survey was carried out 20 years into the reign of William I, which resulted in the Domesday Book. The survey

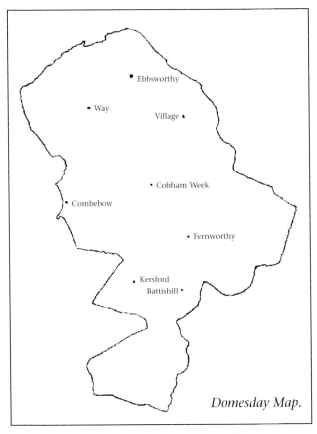

Domesday Map.

looked back to the time when Edward the Confessor was on the throne and is a remarkable attestation to the extent of settlement in Devon at the time of the Norman Conquest. The Domesday Book is not only a tax appraisal but also a dependable register of rightful possession; every 'man should know his right and not usurp another's.' The Saxon Chronicle records in 1085 that:

at Gloucester at midwinter... the King William had deep speech with his counsellors... and sent men all over England to each shire... to find out... what or how much each landowner... held in land and livestock, and what it was worth...

They were to ask:

The name of the place. Who held it, before 1066, and now? How many hides? How many ploughs, both those in lordship and the men's? How many villagers, cottagers and slaves, how many free men and Freemen? How much woodland, meadow and pasture? How many mills and fishponds? How much has been added or taken away? What the total value was and is? How much each freeman or Freeman had or has? All threefold, before 1066, when King William gave it, and now, and if more can be had than present.

From these questions it might be thought that

great detail would be gleaned but not all the available information was recorded, some places were missed completely or perhaps included with others. The extract from the Domesday Book for Bridestowe shows that:

Ralph of Pomerai held Bridestowe from Baldwin de Brionne, Sheriff of Devon. Before the year of 1066 when William came to power, Edmer the Saxon held Bridestowe. It paid tax for ½ a hide (a hide being a land unit reckoned as 120 acres) and ½ a furlong. There was land for six ploughs. In lordship there were two ploughs and eight slaves. There were nine villagers and four smallholders with four ploughs. The land consisted of 12 acres of meadow, 30 acres of pasture and 40 acres of woodland. The livestock held was one cob, six cattle, 10 pigs, 135 sheep and 20 goats. The value was formerly £3 but it was now valued at £4.

Baldwin also held with the manor the land of six thanes who did not belong there before 1066. It paid tax for ½ a hide and 1½ furlongs. There was land for six ploughs. The value was formerly 30s. but it is now valued at 60s. less 20d. The six thanes were Saewin Tuft, Doda, Doda, Godwin, Godwin and Abbot Sihtric.

Apart from the above extract from the Domesday Book itself, which is known as the Exchequer DB, there exists the Exeter Book, which appears to be a preliminary draft but it contains more information than its successor. We find the 'thanes held the land jointly' and that they 'could go with this land to which ever lord they would'. The Exeter Book names the thanes' lands as Carsforda (Kersford, 'Cress ford'), held by Saewin Tuft; Batesilla (Battishill, probably held earlier by 'Baetti' therefore 'Baetti's hill') held by Doda; Comba (Combebow, where 'Bow' may refer to a bridge over the Lew), held by Doda; Etbolduswrda

(Ebsworthy, 'Ecgbeald's clearing'), held by Godwin; Ferneurda (Fernworthy, 'Bracken clearing'), held by Godwin; Weia (Way, there seems to be no definition for this place name) held by Abbot Sihtric.

We cannot always accept that all persons holding thane land were indeed thanes – for example, the person holding Way was Sihtric, an abbot of Tavistock. Way was probably a Tavistock Abbey manor. Another of the thanes, according to Sir Roper Lethbridge, was Saewin Tuft, presbyter to Queen Matilda. Although the names Godwin and Doda each appear twice, it is likely that this refers to two thanes each holding two thane lands.

There are no entries for freemen, mills or fishponds, probably because there were none. Cottagers are not mentioned; they were similar if not identical to smallholders and may have been included in their number.

Other points to note are that manors in Devon were underrated due to the poverty of many in the county. The entry of 'land for six ploughs' is an estimate therefore a convenient way of giving the arable extent without the complexities associated with the hide. Devon had the highest proportion of slaves compared to other categories of population; about one in five.

In order to arrive at any conclusion about Bridestowe at the time of the Domesday survey we need to look at the nature of the manorial system itself. The manor may be described as an estate owned by a lord and occupied by dependent cultivators. The land assigned to the lord, the 'demesne', constituted the home farm. The manorial tenants worked to cultivate the land of the demesne, which contained a manor house. The lord usually resided here, controlling the affairs of the villagers and holding court. It constituted a centre where the cultivators of the land were subject to legal and economic sanctions.

Bridestowe Valuations

BEFORE 1066, during the time of Edmer, Bridestowe was valued at £3.

At the time of Domesday when Ralph of Pomeroy held Bridestowe of Baldwin the Sheriff, its value was £4. Ralph also held Way, Ebsworthy, Fernworthy, Combebow, Battishill and Kersford valued at £2.8s.4d.

In 1291 the Benefice of Bridestowe was assessed at £12. This assessment came about in order to finance a crusade to the Holy Land by King Edward I. The crusade did not however, take place.

In 1535 the Benefice of Bridestowe was assessed at £32.17s.9d. This assessment, as that of 1291, consists of the value of church land, offerings, tithes, rectorial and victorial remunerations etc.

In 1692 Bridestowe was assessed at £104.8s.1d. for a tax known as the Land Tax. The usual rate for this particular tax was four shillings in the pound.

In 1837 the Tithe Commutation, rated at about 2s.6d. in the pound on the rateable value of land, was assessed at £975.

During the year 1882-3 the Poor Law assessment amounted to £4357. The acreage of the parish was given as 5661.

First in social importance of manorial tenants were the villeins; their holdings were hereditary. Villeinage, often called a virgate or yardland, usually of 30 acres, consisted of a bundle of strips dispersed in the open fields amongst other tenants. Every tenant shared with the lord the use of the meadow and wasteland but also had rights of pasture and possessed a homestead (messuage) surrounded by a farmyard. Villeins were required to cultivate the lord's demesne two or three days of the week. Other customary practices included contributions to the lord in money and kind, such as poultry at Christmas, eggs at Easter, grain at Martinmas, honey, ale and multure payments for grinding of corn at the mill. The tenant was not allowed to fell timber, whomever cut down oak or ash unless it was perhaps to repair his house, plough or cart received punishment which was exacted in the lord's court. However, if the tenant suffered from the encroachments of his neighbour, he could seek a remedy in his lord's court where custom of the manor had a formality and strictness distinctive of law proper.

The cotters (or cottagers), the cottage tenants, occupied a lower place in the manorial hierarchy. They were known as bordars in some locations, including Bridestowe. Cottagers were recruited from the younger sons of the villeins and from slaves whom the lord of the manor had settled on the soil with the improved status of manorial tenants. Their holdings were about five acres and their obligations less. They worked for the lord one day a week only, usually on a Monday, the term 'Monday men' being applied to them. As cottagers were generally without oxen of their own they did not share in the principal task of ploughing. They hired themselves out to the lord and to the wealthier villeins at busy times of the year such as at harvest time.

The slaves who were possibly members of the conquered race were the most dependent class in the manorial community. They were probably employed about the lord's household being entrusted with the charge of the plough team. By 1086 they had begun to disappear – most likely they had been completely absorbed into the cottager class.

Free tenants were attached to the manor mainly by the relatively slight services that they owed to the lord in recognition of his authority over them. They usually helped out at harvest time but their main obligation was rent. A freeman could go with his land where he would, dissolve at will the ties that connected him with the lord and go to another for protection.

The authority of the lord over his manor was exercised through a ministerial body, which formed an important element in the rural population. Where the lord owned several manors the charge of their administration was entrusted to the seneschal or steward, and the bailiff was responsible for the management of the estate. The reeve, who was chosen by the village, supervised the work done by the tenants. As to the lessor administrators, the hayward looked after the wood, corn and meadows, whilst the auditor saw to the accounts and complaints of the tenants. The ploughmen were to drive the oxen, while the waggoners were concerned with the carrying done by the horses. Lastly there were the cowherds, swineherds, shepherds and dairymaids.

In light of this, it is possible to form a picture of Bridestowe in 1086. It should be safe to assume that Ralph de Pomeroy who held 60 lordships in all did not personally manage Bridestowe as it was such a small estate. As such he probably did not live in the village. The Domesday Book tells us that there was enough land cleared of wood for six ploughs, so around 700 to 750 acres had been brought into use. Ralph kept about 240 acres for himself as a home farm with slaves in attendance, supported by the other classes carrying out their customary duties. There were also a further 82 acres of meadow, pasturage and woodland. The livestock mentioned, with the exception of the plough oxen, belonged to the lord's farm; villagers' beasts were not recorded. We do not know for sure the exact location of the home farm but it is probable that the farm known as Cobham Week, which belonged to later lords of the manor, was the demesne farm. We have seen that the manor was enlarged by the addition of the land of six thanes. With Ralph de Pomeroy being described as 'rapacious' this land may have been seized unlawfully but we know for certain where the thanes' lands lie.

As for the location of the farms of the nine villagers and four smallholders, it is likely that they formed some of the scattered developments whose names appear much later than Domesday, even though they may well have been in existence at the time of the survey. These farms would have been worked by their occupiers, the tilling of the land and tending of their livestock being carried out with the aid of their immediate family, while the wealthier among them employed the lower classes to aid them. As for a church, it is not unusual to omit the presence of such in the survey, which is the case for Bridestowe.

In 1086 then, Bridestowe comprised the nucleus of a small village, probably with a church, and if we include the home demesne, a total of 20 farms consisting of some 1580 acres. If the number of people mentioned in the survey is multiplied by Hoskin's figure of 3.5 it is possible that Bridestowe had a population of 90 people.

There was also another manor in Bridestowe – that of the church or rectory, commonly known as the Sanctuary Manor. Details of this will be discussed later.

LATER LORDS OF THE MANOR

In 1166 'Henry de Pomerai' held the manor of Bridestowe for one fee of Robert the King's son. The manor then came to Hugh de Boulay or de Bolley, as did many estates that 'Pomerai' held. In 1228 Hugh de Boulay and his wife Muriel held the manor. In 1241 after the death of her husband Muriel de Boulay was in possession. She held one fee in Brightestowe of John le Curtenay of the honor of Okemeton. James de Boulay was the son and heir of Hugh and Muriel de Boulay. His heir was his daughter, Amicia. In 1303 John de Cobeham had succeeded to the manor in right of his wife Amicia and held Brittestowe, as it is written in the Fine, for one fifth of a fee. John de Cobeham died in 1337 and he was succeeded by James Cobham who held Brydestouwe, for one third of a fee in 1346. The manor was known as Cobham's Wick.

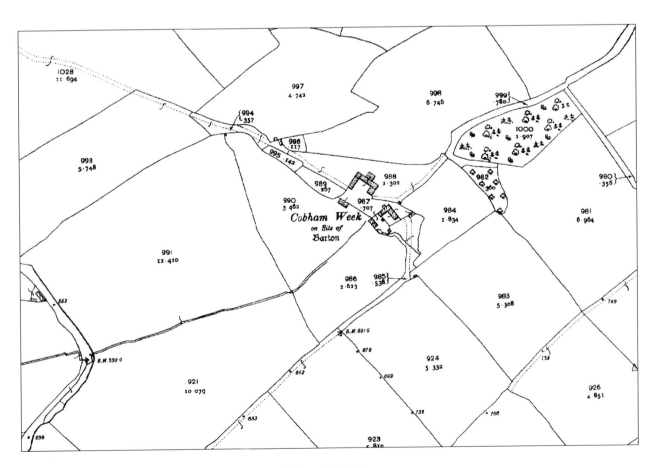

During the time that the de Boulays and Cobhams held the manor of Bridestowe the manorial system began to break up. The lord preferred hired labour and began to dispense with his officials, which of course reduced his expenses. The tenants, being emancipated from their customary duties were able to concentrate their energies on their own holdings and raise produce for the urban market, which in turn provided money with which to pay their rents. The cottagers became wage earners by working for the lord.

The Cobham male lineage failed during Richard II's reign. Elizabeth, the heir of the Cobhams, married William Charleton who died without an heir during the reign of Henry IV. The manor thus descended to general heirs. In 1428 Walter Hungerford, William Talbott, John Hyll and John Bampfeld each held a quarter fee as freeholders in Bristowe.

Bampfeld sold the manor to Arundel of Lifton who in turn sold it to Albany Saville MP, in 1790. His son sold the manor to various people around 1840.

Cobham Week Map.

Emerging Place Names of Bridestowe & Possible Origins

Bidlake: Bydelak(e) 1238 (Assize Rolls) from 'Bid(d)a's streamlet' – a stream name.

Millaton: Millenton in 1238 (Assize Rolls) from 'Milla's farm' – a personal name.

Crandford: Craneford in 1238 (Assize Rolls) from 'Heron-ford'.

Shortacombe: Sortecumb in 1270 (Assize Rolls).

Woodhead: 1270 (Assize Rolls) from the home of Nicholas de la Wode.

Churndon: Cherendon in 1279 (Assize Rolls) may be from the Welsh 'cern', meaning 'side of a steep hill'.

Blackabroom: Blakebrom(e) in 1319 (The Episcopal Registers of the Diocese of Exeter).

Beara Down: 1330 (Lay Subsidy Rolls) from the home of Jordan atte Beare.

Stone: 1330 (Lay Subsidy Rolls) from the home of Richard atte Stone.

Brambleham: Bremilham in 1330 (Lay Subsidy Rolls) probably the place lying in a bend on the River Lyd.

Sprighill: Sprighill in 1378 (Court Rolls) probably the home of Richard Sprygg, 1414.

Leawood: Lywode in 1500 (Calendar of Inquisition Post Mortem).

Woodfordham: Woodford in 1504-15 (Early Chancery Proceedings).

FURTHER DEVELOPMENT OF THE PARISH

The areas of Bidlake, Millaton and Crandford occur around 150 years after the Domesday Book whilst Leawood appears much later (in 1500) followed by Woodfordham. Above is a list of some emerging place names, and their possible origin.

It was during the development of the names in the chart that families emerged. Among the most important were the Ebsworthys of Ebsworthy, the Millatons of Millaton, the Bidlakes of Bidlake, the Shilstons of Leawood and the Calmadys (later Calmady-Hamlyns) of Leawood. They, it would seem, could all put the term 'Gent.' to their name.

In 1332 a Devonshire Lay Subsidy was imposed. This was a tax exacted in 1181 on a person's movable items rated at one-tenth their value. It was later only paid by laypeople at one-tenth for townsfolk and one-fifteenth for country people. In connection with this tax, 15 names are linked with Bridestowe:

John de Cobeham, taxed at 6s.8d.
John Biddelake, 12d.
Richard Thorndon, 16d.
John of the same [Weye], 8d.
Andrew de Eboldesworthi, 12d.
William atte Stone, 12d.
Geoffrey Schonke, 12d.
William de Combe, 2s.
John Toker, 16d.
John de Thorndon, 14d.
Geoffrey atte Waye, 12d.
Roger Toker, 14d.
Richard Vppehulle, 12d.
Richard of the same [Stone], 8d.
James Mulward, 12d.

Two centuries on the number of people being taxed had increased at least four-fold: 59 people were listed for the Lay Subsidy of 1543 but there were 'a few lost by mutilation' so a complete figure is not known. The Muster Roll for 1596 *(overleaf)* shows the men of Bridestowe and Sourton who were part of a 'home defence force' preparing to repel a threatening Spanish invasion during the reign of Elizabeth I.

The year 1641–2 saw the Protestation Returns that had been organised as a signed protest against the possibility of 'an arbitrary tyrannical government'. The return for Bridestowe listed 110 names, all male. The Hearth Tax for 1674, just 32 years later, shows 66 people being levied. If there was more than one occupier of a house, each person paid for the hearths in his particular part of the dwelling. The house with the most hearths, a dozen, was Leawood, followed by Bidlake with eight. Next came Honor Pengelly with seven, Edward Fortescue and Walter Mitchell each had six hearths whilst the Parsonage house had five. Two people had four hearths, four people had three, and twelve had two. The remaining 36 people had one hearth. It is not possible to say where the named people lived except for the Calmady, Bidlake and the Parsonage entries, but doubtless the properties with the larger number of hearths were farmhouses.

Moving on 140 years to the Land Tax Assessment of 1781 we can see the extent to which Bridestowe had expanded. Many smallholdings were in being by this time but the majority of the property in the parish was held between three proprietors. The Tithe Commutation Schedule of 1836 offers a view of the growth of farms and smallholdings.

View from the Launceston Road towards Poole. (Doug Gale)

Tithe, a render of one-tenth of the produce of land, was payable to the local church from early-medieval times as village churches were established by private landholders. These landowners would assign the tithes of the land to the parson, who was responsible for the cure of souls in the parish. Although tithe income was originally assigned to the parson of the church, the 'advowson' of the living was granted in the twelfth or thirteenth century to religious houses and with the advowson went the tithes. The religious house might at first appoint one of its own officials to serve a church thus appropriated, although the later practice was to appoint 'vicars' (from the Latin 'deputy') to live in the parish and serve the church. The vicars were remunerated by a share of the tithe income, usually about a third of the total, the 'small tithes', whilst the 'great tithes' went to the rector (ruler) of the church (a religious corporation not an individual). In the modern church the difference between vicars and rectors is purely titular.

The Bridestowe and Sourton Muster Roll for 1596

PRESENTERS SWORN: Henry Bidlake, Robert Lyllycroppe, Walter Lyllycroppe and William Blacheforde (prominent parishioners), who do presente as afforsaid: William Yeo, Henry Walter, John Browne, Thomas Rise, John Boroughe, Henry Bidlake (as wealthier citizens they provided their own armour and weapons).

ARCHERS: William Yeo, William Harrye, Roger Gowscott, George Crosseman, Henry Walter, John White, Richard Ebbesworthy, Michael Yoldon and John William.

HARQUEBUSIERS: Henry Bidlake, William Cudlye, John Yoldon, Henry Steven, Robert Wortham, Richard Rowe, Thomas Crossman, Roger Lyllycroppe, Roger Rowe, John Williams, William Barber and John Draper.

PIKEMEN: William Rise, John Horn and John Browne.

BILLMEN: Walter Frinde, John Lyllycroppe, Edmond Lange, Edmond Prigge, John Rokefilde, John Raddon, William Harrye and Martin Haywood.

During the early-nineteenth century a campaign for tithe reform was concerned with the arbitrary nature of tithe payments, which were traditionally payable in kind but often rendered in cash. In order to standardise the payments the Tithe Commutation Act was passed in 1836. It provided for the conversion of tithe from a payment in kind or cash to a 'rent charge' on land, the amount to vary according to the way in which the land was cultivated and the price of corn. Whoever received the tithes would instead receive a tithe rent charge.

The Act of 1836 set up a Tithe Commission in London whilst in each parish assistant commissioners held public meetings and drew up an agreement to be confirmed by the commissioners in London. This resulted in a map showing every parcel of land, and the rent charge associated with it. Each tenant was listed alphabetically along with the landowner's name. Occupiers are not always listed in full, especially for cottages, where the entry 'John Smith and others' is often given. Other details include the acreage and state of cultivation of each parcel of land (the Act demanded a variable rent charge for arable, meadow and pasture) along with field names and the amount of rent charge payable to the tithe owner.

The Commissioner held his first meeting at the White Hart Inn in Bridestowe on 6 April 1841. Mr Edward Luxmoore appeared for the rector and Messrs Hawkes and Burd for the landowners. It seems that the tithes of Bridestowe and Sourton had been received in a mixed manner; the averages were ultimately settled at £264.7s.6d. Upon the rent charge in lieu of tithes settled land surveyors were required to map the parish, which contained about 32,400 acres exclusive of common and moorland. Upon the eventual completion of the Tithe Map and Apportionment the Tithe Commissioners confirmed the award on 22 September 1841.

Estimated quantity in statute measure of all lands in the parish except Glebe (63 acres) amounted to 3682 acres, of which there were 2130 acres of arable land, 192 acres of meadow and pasture, 296 acres of woodland, 15 acres of orchards and 1049 acres of commons and moors. Exempt from the tithe were 73 acres of land, which belonged to Calmady Pollexfen Hamlyn. This land included Burley Wood and Burley Wood Quillets with 45 acres of Watergate. Hamlyn nevertheless paid 13s. 4d. annually to the rector for Leawood (215 acres). The Leawood estate was omitted from the Tithe Map as Christopher Hamlyn appears to have settled his rent charge by way of an agreement whereby he paid £180 to Coryndon Luxmoore. John Gubbins Newton, owner of Cobham Week (1022 acres, three roods and 27 perches) paid £1.6s.8d. annually to the

rector in lieu of tithes. Lands in the manor of Cobham Week consisted of Little Yellands, Brambleham Estate, Great Yellands, Little Cross Park, Long Park alias Bramble Brook, Rundle Brook alias Buddle Brook, Bear Down, One forth of Sprig Hill, Oxen Parks, Winkhill, Lower Stone, Water Leats, Shallaford, Fern Park, Quint's Tenement, Broom Ball, Cross Parks and Raddon Estate.

The following is an extract taken from the Tithe Apportionment, showing property with approximate acreage and the name of the owner, spelling as documented:

Part of Fernworthy 17, James Friend;

New Royal Oak 32, Great Close 168, Coombow 124, Beara 91, Part of Fernworthy 17, Cloke's Hill 3, Little Beara 6, Black Broom 240, Higher Black Broom 92, Little Crandford 24, Cocks Heath 2, Great Crandford 170, Heath 40, Part Great Close 3, Stannen 88, Burley Wood Quillets 5, Bridhays 4, Part of Coombow, Calmady Hamlyn;

South Ball or Ball Tenement 18, North Ball 4, North Ball Tenement 31, Ball Tenement 2, East Ball 79, Luxmore (Rector);

Way 424, Part of Elsworthy Town 52, Millaton 156, Stone 100, Old Houses 26, Long Ham 148, Battishill 283, Brambleham 255, Parish Ham 5, Raddon 125, Part of Brambleham 5, Shallowford 45, Great Yelland 37, Lower Stone 22, John Gubbins Newton;

Part of Fernworthy 78, John G Newton, Calmady Hamlyn, ? Robins;

Little Beara, Thomas Osbourne;

Smelland 37, William Palmer;

Furze Brake (Smelland) 10, ? Redcliffe;

White Hart Inn 2, Margaret White;

Great Bidlake 205, Little Bidlake 83, West Parks 15, Cross Lanes, Bidlake Mill 4, Major's Tenements 3, Woodfordham, Woodhead (7), Kersford 209, Fernworthy 38, Revd John Wollocombe;

Part of Kersford 111, Revd John Wollocombe, George Lethbridge;

Churndon 257, John Morth Wollocombe;

Elsworthy Town 465, John Morth Wollocombe, John Gubbins Newton;

Fernworthy Commons 160, Revd John Wollocombe, John Gubbins Newton, Calmady Hamlyn, ? Robins;

Pasture 7, Churchyard and Houses 1, Playground 1, John Gubbins Newton and Calmady Hamlyn;

Roads 64, Water 23, ? Robins and James Friend.

Protestation Returns for Bridestowe Parish 1641 (all in the same hand)

Austine, Roger gent.
Beckalake, Arthur
Beckalake, John
Bidlake, Henry gent.
Blachford, John
Blatchford, Walter
Brey, Richard
Burrough, Nicholas
Calmadie, Sir
  Shilstone Kt
Calmadie, Josias Esq.
Calmadie, Shilstone
  gent.
Colling, Walter
Coone, William
Crossman, Edward
Crossman, John
Crossman, William
Cruse, Walter
Dachcome, John
Dod, John
Dod, Richard
Doide, William
Doidge, William
Doidge, Philip
Doidge, Robert
Dowe, Roger
Ebsworthie, Alexander
Ebsworthie, Paul gent.
Ebsworthie, Peter senr
  gent.
Ebsworthie, Peter junr
  gent.
Esworthie, Peter of
  Ebsworthie Town
Esworthie, Richard
Freece, George

Frend, Richard
Gill, John
Gill, William
Gubbin, Leonard
Hawton, Walter
Hawton, John
Hockadaye, Thomas
Howell, Edmund
Jefferye, Michael
Johnes, Robert
Knight, Pancras
Lillicrapp, Robert
Lillicrapp, Walter
Macka La Hane, John
Marten, Daniel
Mayior, Daniel
Mill, William
Mungey, Hugh
Newcome, Andrew
Newton, James
Newton, Roger
Newton, Thomas
North, Peter
Parson, Hugh
Peckord, Humphrey
Pelly, William
Person, George
Poade, Samuel
Prust, Richard
Redstone, John senr
Redstone, John junr
Reed, Edward
Reed, Thomas
Roundle, Robert
Rowndell, John
Saunders, Edward
Saunders, Ezekiel

Saunders, James
Seilly, Ellis
Sheer, John
Sinkell, Walter
Smyth, John senr
Smyth, John junr
Smyth, William senr
Smyth, William junr
Soper, Edmund
Soper, John
Soper, Peter
Standon, Thomas
Stockman, Thomas
Tapplye, Richard
Taverner, John
Taverner, Thomas
Trebell, William
Treloder, William
Vine, Stephen
Walkey, Toby
Walter, Peter of
  Bidlake Mill
Walter, Peter of
  Verworthie
Walter, Peter junr
Walter, William
Weekes, John
White, John
White, John
Wilkey, John
Williams, Richard
  of Bremlham
Williams, Stephen
Williams, Thomas
Wonacott, Thomas
Yoldon, John
Yoldon, Richard

James Tooker Curate
William Ebsworthie Constable
Richard Tapson Constable
Walter Gill Overseer

Henry Horne Overseer
Richard Tickell Overseer
John Quint Churchwarden

Land Tax, Parish of Bridestowe 1781 (Proprietors, Occupiers and Property)

Warwick Calmady.

Edward Allen, Leawood; William Gubbins, John Newton, Coombow; William Gubbins, Great Close; John Collings, Royal Oak; John Northcot, Radon; George Newcombe, Fenworthy; Ann Keen, Higher Waterleats; Robert Allford, Higher Crandford; Robert Allford, Little Cranford; Henry Voyzey, Heath.

William Arendel Harris.

Ebsworthy Tapson, Lower Stone; Charles Friend, Brombleham; Charles Friend, Yeallands; Richard Friend, Yeallands; William Chewings, Longham; John Newton, Lower Waterleats; Henry Voyzey, West Beare; Tristram Conday, Shellaford; Thomas Daw, Little Beare; John Martyn, Sprighill; Asa Walter, Broomball; Henry Voyzey, Quints Tennements; Richard Friend, Oxpark; Asa Walter, Winkhill; Nicholas Tapson, Crospark; John Gills, Crospark; William Lee, Budlebrook; Asa Walter, Bromblebrook; Henry Voyzeys, Leazes; John Gothem, Water gates.

John Herrin, John Heron, Phillis Bidlake.

Peter Featherstone, Great Bidlake; William Friends, Condys Kersford; John Blatchford, Kersford; John Collings, Kersford; William Friends, Kersford; George Newcombe, Fenworthy; Thomas Roberts, Woodhead; Robert May, Jean Major, Woodfordham.

Arthur Tremain.

John Pellow, Way; William Williams, Batishill; Richard Maddaford, Ebsworthy Town.

Reverend Joseph Haberden.

John Newton junr, Rectory; John Brook, Standon; Walter Youldon, Northball; Henry Voyzeys, Tennement; John Tapson, Denbole Park; John Pellow, Crosmans Southball.

John Wolcombe.

Henry Blatchford, Churnon; John Martyn, Ebsworthy Town; Roger Tickel, Ebsworthy Town.

Mr Huish, Mary Harris.

John Newton, Old Houses; John Newton junr, Higher Stone; Joseph Newton, Fearnworthy; Thomas Daw, Kersford; William Kersla[ke], Kersford.

Ebsworthy Tapson.

John Brok, Ebsworthy Town; Ebsworthy Tapson junr, Little Bidlake.

John Newton.

John Newton, Millaton.

William Palmer.

William Palmer, Smelland.

Mary Luxmoore.

John Martyn, Sprighill.

Rebecca Hocking.

Edward Allen, Blackabroom.

George Passons.

Nicholas Tapson, Fearnworthy.

Walter Radicliffe.

Henry Voyzey, East Beare;

Thomas Daw, Little Beare.

John Brook and William Newton Assessors and Collectors 8 June 1781.

Tithes: Bidlake Family 1662

Costomary Tyethes of ye p'ishe of Bridistow
Tyethes to be p^d ye 29 September or within six days after
Hay Tyethes Great Bidlake £0.0s.6d
Strain of Kine Every [Milch] cow a penny
A [H]ewer Cow a half penny
4 Ewes a penny
For every Calf 6d.
Lower Stone Mills 2s.
Costomary to be pd at Easter for every Colt 1d.
For Every Communicant 1½d. but for ye first year ½
Garden 1d. heath 1d.
Costomes to be pd at ye time
Churching of woman 4d.
For every marraige 4d.
For every funeral sermon 6s.8d.
Cristininge & buryalls free
These costomes ware confermed by William
*   Knapman William Hutton & Edwd Drew*
*   Rectors of Bridistow*
Ye originall bears date August 16th 1662

Looking down Poole Hill, 1950s. (Doug Gale)

Royal Oak, 1920s. (Doug Gale)

West Bridge from the Launceston Road. *(Doug Gale)*

Right: *The Launceston Road, 1920s.* (Doug Gale)

Royal Oak Annex and South Ball at bottom of Rectory Road, 1920s. (Doug Gale)

LOCAL DIRECTORIES

With the publication of *White's Directory of Devonshire* in 1850 (Billings and Morris also published directories with Kelly being the most prolific) a wealth of information was provided to give an insight into the composition of each parish within the county. The directories provide details of the landowners as well as tradesmen, services for the public and the various religions.

A summarised entry from *White's Directory* tells us that Bridestowe at that time was a 'neat and improving' village in a pleasant valley near Dartmoor, six miles south-west of Okehampton. The parish had 1128 souls who occupied 5661 acres of land including Combebow, Watergate, Fernworthy, Bidlake and many scattered houses. A large tract of moorland hills contained lead and copper mines. The manors and owners were Cobham-Wick and Blatchford, J.G. Newton; Leawood, S.C. Hamlyn; with J.M. Wollocombe, the Revd J. Wollocombe and many smaller owners having estates in the parish. Millaton, the seat of J.G. Newton, is described in a little detail, as is Leawood. A brief account of the church and rectory is given, and we are informed that a field of three acres, the Parish Ham, was vested for the reparation of the church. We are also told that the Baptists and Bible Christians had small chapels. About 200 children attended the National School that had been established about ten years previous. Cattle fairs were held in the village. An extract from the *Directory* of 1851 reads as follows:

Brock Betsy, victualler, Royal Oak; Brownson John H., schoolmaster; Churchward Henry, auctioneer, land surveyor, etc. Stone; Gill and Rundle, lime burners; Gould James, butcher; Hamlyn Shilston Calmady, Esq., Leawood; Hockin William, cooper; Howell Revd Hinds, Rectory; Jackman Robert, victualler, Fox and Hounds; Linton James and John, masons; Newcombe William, currier etc; Newton John Gubbins, Esq., Millaton; Palmer James, brewer and maltster; Pike John, shoemaker; Youlden Samuel, millwright etc; Younge Richard, victualler, White Hart; Alford William, Bowden John, Coombe Edward, Sercombe Samuel, blacksmiths; Bevan John, Joyce James, saddlers; Peard John, Southcombe Thomas, tailors; Coombe John, Peard John, Rundle John, shopkeepers; Alford Walter, Chebb Robert, Shopland James, Weekes John, carpenters and wheelwrights; Post Office at J. Bowden's; Farmers: Bowden William, Baker Thomas, Ball George, Ball William, Batten Daniel, Bickle John, Bolt John, Brook John, Brook Philip, Dodge Arthur, Ellis William, Friend James, Hill William, Hortop Roger, Jackman Robert, Kennard John, Kennard Thomas, Lavis Edward, Lock William, Martin John, Mason John, Orchard Richard, Palmer John, Palmer William, Rule George, Stanbury William, Vodden William, Yelland David and Yelland William.

Bridestowe Cattle Fair on West Bridge. (Brian Maddaford)

In 1857 the number of people in Bridestowe eligible to vote for MPs was 24, Okehampton being the polling district. The Vivid Coach to Truro passed through the village on Mondays, Wednesdays and Fridays at 11am, returning to Exeter on Tuesdays, Thursdays and Saturdays at 4pm, from the Royal Oak Inn. Letters arrived in the village Post Office at 8am, being despatched at 5.30pm. The nearest Money Order Office was at Okehampton.

For 1866 Bridestowe was in the Southern Division of the County; Lifton Hundred; Okehampton Union and County Court District; Rural Deanery of Tavistock; Archdeaconry of Totnes and Diocese of Exeter. Mining operations still took place, but with limited success, although the extraction of lime and stone were stronger businesses.

Cattle fairs in 1870 took place on the first Wednesday in June and on 29 July if a Tuesday, Wednesday or Thursday. If the 29th fell on any other day of the week, the fair was held on the following Tuesday.

In 1873 the soil was shown as being clay, the subsoil shale. The chief crops were wheat, oats and barley; a great deal of the land was used as pasturage. The gross estimated rental of the parish was £4102, with its rateable value, £3565. Listed in the directory were five blacksmiths, one land agent, one butcher, two carpenters, two boot and shoemakers, two tailors, twenty farmers, one beer retailer, one painter and glazier, four shopkeepers, one saddler, three innkeepers, one wheelwright, three masons and one schoolmistress, Miss Mary Ann Peard, who ran a mixed school supported by J.G. Newton. (This is not to be confused with the National School in the village.)

The population in 1881 was 642. An average of 78 children attended the National School. Listed were nineteen farmers, one butcher, one shoemaker, two blacksmiths, one saddler, one painter and glazier, three carpenters, a cowkeeper, a farrier, a miller, a mason, an assistant overseer, two shopkeepers, a tailor, three innkeepers, a lime merchant, a station master and a firm of auctioneers and land agents, this being Ward and Chowen whose business is extant.

Bridestowe Post Office, 1920s. (Doug Gale)

A telegraph office at the railway station in 1893 transacted business on behalf of the village Post Office. Postal orders could be issued, but not exchanged for their cash value. Constable Richard Holwill represented the county police. A men's social club had been formed and a cab proprietor was now in business. An average of 132 children attended the school, run by three teachers.

Bridestowe Post Office. **Left to right: *?, Renie Barkell, Jim Barkell, Beat Turner, Dick Philpott, ?, Emily Howard (Sub Postmistress), Alf Ellis.* (George Lavis)

In 1851 Bridestowe had 205 houses, which were inhabited by 1049 occupants (524 males and 525 females) with an average of five people per household. At this time there were about 32 farmers. The use of limestone quarries was at its peak, whereas copper and lead mines were not as successful. All this meant employment for a large number of people, hence the high population. Around 100 agricultural labourers were living in the parish who were sometimes referred to as 'waggoner' or 'outside farm servant'. Some had their board with the farmer they worked for, others occupied their own home. People employed in the quarries and mines numbered approximately 67; there was a mine agent, quarry labourers, lime-burners, tin, lead and copper miners, searcher of mines, foreman of lime quarries and a mineral surveyor. Those providing services were painters and glaziers, masons, cordwainers, tailors, curriers, seamstresses, millwrights, dressmakers, land agents and auctioneers, huntsmen, farriers, blacksmiths, wheelwrights, carpenters, millers, gardeners, boot- and shoemakers, thatchers, a laundress, coopers, saddlers, glovers, milleners, maltsters and brewers, bread sellers, shopkeepers, hostlers, inn keepers and butchers. The variety of tradespeople ensured that the parishioners did not have to venture outside the parish boundary to seek the supplies and skills required for their everyday existence. Bridestowe at this juncture had reached the pinnacle of its prosperity.

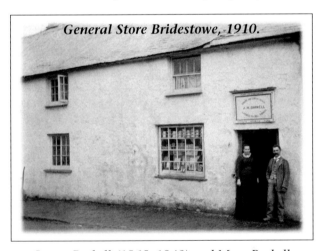

General Store Bridestowe, 1910.

James Barkell (1865–1940) and Mary Barkell (1869–1923). (Howard Barkell)

There were of course the gentry and annuitants. These people employed domestic staff, including a governess, ladies maids, cooks, nurses, house servants, housekeepers and coachman.

The population in 1866 dropped to 832 with a further fall to 762 in 1871. By 1891 the population fell dramatically to 586 with an even lower figure in 1901 of 452. This period also saw the gradual reduction in the number of craftsmen who served the village, combined with the decline of the mining and quarrying industries.

Bridestowe lost a part of its parish in March 1884. By Local Government Order No. 16,405 the detached land of Longham was officially amalgamated with Coryton in the Tavistock Union. Situated near the River Lyd about half a mile below the White Lady waterfall in Lydford Gorge, and a bridge known as 'Ox Clam', Longham was originally part of the manor of Cobham Week. In 1755 the property was conveyed to Arthur Tremayne of Sydenham, whilst in 1843 it was transferred to John Gubbins Newton of Millaton. It later passed on to Daniel Radford of Lydford who sold it in 1882 to Thomas Holdsworth Newman of Coryton for £2130. At one time a rhyme ran, 'Lamerton and Lew, Cut Bridestowe in two'.

However, in combination with its neighbour, Sourton, Bridestowe has also extended commons on Dartmoor Forest. In the whole of the commons encircling the forest this is the only instance where land is held jointly by two parishes.

SOURCES

Devon County Sites and Monuments Record.
CIN=5628; CIN=1612; CIN=1613; CIN=30123.
Devon and Cornwall Notes and Queries Vol. VI, Part 3.
Devon and Cornwall Record Society.
Feudal Aids, Nos. 355, 405 and 550.
Devon Record Office: Tithe Map and Schedule of Portionment.
Fulford, Williams H., MSS West Country Studies Library, Exeter.
Gover A., Stenton F.M., *English Place-Name Society, Vol. VIII*, 'The Place-Names of Devon'.
Higham, R., *Early Castles In Devon (1068–1201)*, Chateau-Gaillard IX-X.
Hoskins, W.G., *Devon* (1992 ed.).
Hoskins, W.G., *Fieldwork In Local History* (1982 ed.).
Howard, A.J. and Stoate, T.L. (eds), *The Devon Muster Roll For 1569.*
Howard, A.J. (ed), *The Devon Protestation Returns 1641.*
Kelly's Directory for Devonshire (1893).
Lipson, E., *The Economic History of England Vol. I* (12th ed.).
Morris, J., Editor Phillimore Edition of Domesday Book (Devon).
Newman T., *The History of Coryton.*
Ravenhill, W., and Shorter A., Gregory K., *Southwest England.*
Risdon, T., *Survey of the County of Devon* (1811 ed.).
Rowe, S., *A Perambulation of Dartmoor* (1985 ed.).
Sellman, R.R., *Illustrations of Devon History.*
Stoate, T.L. (ed), *The Devonshire Lay Subsidy of 1332, 1543–5.*
Stoate, T.L. (ed), *The Devon Hearth Tax, 1674.*
Transactions of the Devonshire Association, Exeter.
Trewman's *Exeter Flying Post*, Apr., Oct. 1841, May 1842.
Welldon, Finn R., *Domesday Studies: 'The Liber Exoniensis'.*

Chapter 2

BRIDESTOWE FAMILIES

Five ancient families of note have dwelt in the Parish of Bridestowe but only one has kept its lineage and still occupies its seat, albeit through the distaff members of the family. There is much to write about the Calmady-Hamlyn and Bidlake families, the Millitons and Ebsworthys can be treated to a lesser degree, whilst the Shilstons can be mentioned in passing.

THE BIDLAKES OF BIDLAKE

Like many families the Bidlakes took their very name from the dwelling where they lived. Besides their homelands, which they kept in hand and farmed for themselves for over 500 years, they possessed further property in parishes around Bidlake acquired through the centuries by purchase and marriage. The Bidlakes were quite well off in their day and lived a comfortable life. They trace their descent from Ralph of Combe whose original seat was Combe or Combebow in Bridestowe. Ralph appears to have come from a family known as le Riche as an undated deed shows that a William Talbot had granted a furlong of land from his manor of Sourton to Henry le Riche. Among the witnesses were Hugh le Riche and Ralph le Riche of Combe.

In 1268 Ralph purchased from Warren de Saccaville all his land in Bidlake along with its mill and wood. William of Combe who was Ralph's eventual heir had three sons, of whom John was heir to William.

John's son and heir, Geoffrey of Bidlake, also had a son called John who married firstly Matilda, daughter of Nicholas de Luffincott, whilst his second wife whom he married in 1408 was Alice, daughter and heir of Richard of Combe, Bradstone. Consequently the Bidlakes obtained property in that parish. The heir of John Bidlake was his son, also named John.

This John married Johanna, daughter and heir of John Wolcot. The Wolcot property, Wollacott, Blacklands and Gatecombe, thus came to the Bidlakes. It seems John became a widower as he took for his second wife in 1454 his cousin, Joan Combe, for which marriage he had a dispensation of the Popes Legate.

A great-grandson of John left a note that explained how Joan was John's cousin. The note recites:

It should seme that this William (son of Ralph of Combe) had another brother from whome Joane Combe the weif by dispensation of Jo. Bidlake ye 3 and her twoe sisters, married to Courtenay and Wether, came; and that they were daughters and heirs of one that came from him... for to him must that John and Joane come to be cousins equally of ye 4th degree.

The rental of John (husband to Joan) shows that he held in Bradstone 'Combe, Waytehyll, Spridell, Holond, Maggelond, Braston, Sandyparke, the waste "sub Baucomb", Stonyhame and Bemefordhame.' In Thrushelton 'Thrushelton (tenement) and Wollecot'. In Sourton 'Wyke, Rouadon and Chouysdon'. In Bridestowe 'Ferneworthy, Crasforda'. In Broadwood 'Wetherdon and Northeysdownys'. In Boyton (Cornwall) 'Southe Wescott'. John probably held Bidlake in demesne, as it does not appear in the rental.

Returning to the notes of the great-grandson once more we find that:

John Bidlake, sonne of John Bidlake, died Ano. 1484, as appeareth upon a tombe stone in the p'ishe churche of Brydestowe yn which p'ishe his ancestors before him and his heirs since have dwelled by the space of 346 years at least in their owne lands as appeareth by their ancient deeds.

An extract from a letter dated 26 August 1620 from John's grandson reads:

This is the printe of the seale wch I seale withall formed like the escuchion wch standeth in a windowe of Bridesto Churche whereunto ther is sett John Bidlake, being the name of my great Grandfather's father or his son whoe lie buried under a faire stone yet to be seen... I take it to be three white martletts in a red field.

Thomas Bidlake, son and heir of John, also married twice. His second wife Katherine was the daughter of Thomas Hadde of Kent. Thomas died in 1531 and an *inquisition post mortem* shows that he held land in Bidlake, Bridestow, Fernworthy, Sourton, Cowthysdon, Weke and Rowden, and tenements in Wolcote, Gatecombe, Blakelond and Thrushelton. He had six acres in Dunterton, 200 acres of land and six acres of meadow in Bradston, Holland and Combe held of Henry Clobery as of his manor of Bradston by knight and rent of a pair of spurs. Katherine, widow of Thomas, married 'with John Cooke of Thorn in St Mary Ottery Esq'er, and after his death with Willm Trente of Ottery aforesaid'. In turn, after this gentleman's death, she:

... long time lived a vertuous widdo and died in Alylesbere, where she lieth buried under a tombstone engraved with her name yn the chancell of the churche of Aylesbere.

James, son of Thomas, died between 14 February 1604, the date of his will, and 3 May 1604, the date at which his inventory was taken. James, like most people of his class, left money to the poor of the parishes in which family property lay. His will proved 17 January 1605 recites in part 'to the poor of Bradstone 3s. the poor of Bridestowe 5s. the poor of Bratton 5s'. The inventory taken 3 May 1605 shows that his apparel, purse, gurdle and money amounted to £20. His goods, which were shown in great detail, amounted to the sum of £248.5s.0d. The value of James' estate made him a very well-to-do farmer for this period in history.

James' brother, Henry Bidlake, heir to Thomas, was of a very tender age when his father died at which juncture he was made a ward for:

At four years of age or thereabout he was taken ward by George Rolle (grandfather unto Sir Henry Rolle, the elder knight), who most honestly brought him up amongst his sons at school and in his house fifteen years or thereabout, and then granted the wardship of him unto Roger Denys of Lodsworth, in ye county of Sussex, gent., whose daughter called Anne Denys, the same Henry Bidlake married and dwelt in Sussex 2 yers, immediately after wch time he came into Devonshire and dwelt in his land called Whetherdon (yn Brodwood Widger) untill Ano 1 and 2, Phillipp and Marie being Ano Dni 1555, at what time by the assent of the said Katherine (his mother) the said Henry dwelt at Bidlake.

Henry in 1565 purchased of Thomas Stoddon of Stoddon, in Bratton Clovelly, for the sum of £8, all his watercourse called Lywe (the river Lew) through all his land of Churndon in the parish of Bridestowe. This was in order to secure the water for Bidlake Mill, in this same year the 'leate was finished and the myll reedified'.

In 1575 it was recorded that in 'ye newe parlour and chamber over it' the 'windowes and chymney... were made of moore stones, as appeareth by the figures on ye chief stone of that parlour window.' Seemingly this work refers to the dwelling-house at Bidlake, which is of the Elizabethan style. In 1693 mention is made of the kitchen, the dairy, the brew-house, the new-house or wash-house, with chambers over. The hall, the great parlour, and chamber over the said great parlour, the malt-house, the larder and the little house at the higher end of the said malt-house, and chambers over the same.

Ralph of Combe	=	
William of Combe	=	
John of Bidlake	=	
Geoffrey of Bidlake	=	
John Bidlake	=	*Alice Da. of Richard of Combe in Bradstone*
John Bidlake	=	*Joan Combe of Bradstone 4th cousin*
Thomas Bidlake	=	*Katherine Da. of Thomas Hadde of Kent*
Henry Bidlake	=	*Anne Da. of Roger Denys of Lodsworth in Sussex*
John Bidlake	=	*Elizabeth Da. of Roger Lansford of Germansweek*
William Bidlake	=	*Agnes Da. of Roger Sture of Morley*
Henry Bidlake	=	*Philippa Da. of William Kelly of Kelly in Devon*
William Bidlake	=	*Elizabeth Da. of Anthony Furlong of Carbeel Cornwall*
Henry Bidlake	=	*Anne Da. of Thomas Seddon Rector of Throwley*
Elizabeth	=	*John Heirn of Great Torrington*
Mary	=	*Thomas Stafford Wollocombe Col. of the 2nd. Foot*

The lineal descent of the Bidlake family.

Bidlake House. **(Norman Gale)**

Amongst the Bidlake papers in Henry's handwriting is a copy of:

... the charge and payments of the p'ishe of Brydstowe by Henry Bydlake, John Adam and John Willyams of Bremleham and Leonard Ebsworthye, the iiij men therefrom chosen St Kathern's Daye 1596.

Payments were made among other things for 'goale rent', 'Chrystyde', 'Irland soldyers', 'clensyng of ye comon armor', 'shype money', and 'crests for the tower'.

Henry died 20 April 1604; his will dated 28 March 1604 reads in part:

To the moste poor people of Bridestowe 10s. Sourton 6s.8d. Lidforde 5s. Bradstone 3s.4d. and to the most poor prisoners of Launceston 5s. To every of my servants that shall be servants in any of my houses at time of my death 2s. To said Jane my wife all my grain and corn growing upon my farm of Combe in Bradstone except my mow made the last year. To said Jane 100 of my sheep pasturing upon my farm at Combe and also my horses, geldings and mares, pultrye and hogges being upon Combe at time of my death. To said Jane 8 oxen, 8 kyen, 6 weyning calves, 3 young steers and 4 heefars of such as most commonly do go and feed upon Combe or unto the moor [presumably Dartmoor]. To said Jane the standing and occupation of all the glasinge and glasse of all my glass windows in Combe so long as she shall dwell in Combe or hold Combe in her own hands the said glasinge and glass not to be removed but repaired by her from time to time and so left.

Henry's goods at 'Bridstow in the hawle and farm of Bidlake' was valued at '£338.13s.4d.' including his 'apparell with purse gurdle and money £80'. Goods in his house and farm of Combe in Bradston and on his land at Holland consisted of 'glass in the farmhouse at Combe £3.6s.8d. Sum of goods at Combe £127.16s.2d. Sum of goods at Holland £22. Total £593.9s.6d.'

John Bidlake, Henry's heir and the note writer mentioned earlier said 'I never dwelt at Bidlake, but at Week, seven miles from it'. He had married Elizabeth, daughter of Roger Lansford of Germansweek.

John's oldest son and heir, William, married in 1610 Agnes, daughter of Richard Sture of Morley. He lived at Bidlake. Life for William and Agnes was eventful to say the least. They got themselves into several disputes including one with Gilbert Germyn the parson of Bridestowe. William's father John in a letter wrote them to 'seek peace and ensue it', warning them: 'suits of law are as variable as the turnings of a woadercock'. John, however, was involved along with his son William in a lawsuit with the Ebsworthy family who occupied Stone. Letters show that John and his son William were also involved in a suit against Shilston Calmady of Leawood.

William died in the same year as his father – 1625 – leaving his widow living at Bidlake with their son and heir. William's inventory shows that the value of his estate had risen by £100 when compared to that of his grandfather Henry. His personal estate amounted to around £700, thus William was in the position of being a very rich farmer bearing in mind that the average yeoman left between £100 and £200. The inventory shows that he grew corn, rye, wheat, beans and peas, the value of which amounted to about £29.10s.0d. His livestock consisted of six oxen valued at £21, 14 pigs at £5.10s.0d., five keene and two calves at £14, yearlings at £4, ten calves at £5, young bullocks at £19, 50 yews and lambs at £17, 85 [?] and hogs at £[22].5s.0d., one mare at £3 and three little colts at £5. William, it seems, was also prepared to go to war, his armour being listed as one old [curashe] and headpiece, pike and sword.

William's heir, Henry Bidlake the Royalist, who was '13 years or more at his father's death', married Philippa, daughter of William Kelly of Kelly, on his coming of age in 1633. His mother, Agnes, lived on with him and his family at Bidlake until 1641, whereupon she retired to South Devon and seems to have indulged in more costly lawsuits before dying in 1651.

As a young man Henry joined the army of King Charles, he was made a Captain of Horse under Colonel Sir Thomas Hele, Baronet. It seems that the Roundheads took Henry prisoner on 6 December 1642 at Modbury. 'Sir Edmond Fortescue, High Sheriffe, Sir Edward Seimor, Baronet' and many other gentlemen, along with 'Captaine Bedlake' were marched to Dartmouth to be shipped to London. Another source tells that 'Hen. Bidlake', along with the other prisoners, was held in either Winchester House or Lambeth House in London, both of which were used as prisons. Henry was probably only held for a short period of time, eventually being exchanged for a Parliamentarian prisoner.

A few months later Hele gave:

... full power and authority unto Henry Bidlake of Bidlake Esq. to seize upon all such serviceable horse armour and furniture and to call before him those which formerly have found horses and armour for the Services of this County. Likewise to impose horses and armour on such persons as ye shall find. Dated second of July 1643.

In 1645, as one of the defenders of Pendennis Castle, Henry once again found himself on the losing side against the Roundheads. It seems that the articles for surrender by the Royalists were signed on 18 August, a copy being extant amongst the Bidlake papers.

From this time forward things did not go right for Henry. On 18 January 1645 the Standing Committee for Devon:

Ordered upon perusal of the inventory of the goods

of Mr Henry Bidlake amounting to Thirtie pounds that upon payment of fower and Twentie pounds unto the Treasurer or his Deputie by Mr William Kelly, the sequestration of the said goods shall be removed and taken off whilst the other Six pounds is to be allowed to Mrs Bidlake for her sixth part.

Following this Henry's estates were sequestrated. He made the usual humble petition to be allowed to compound for them and was eventually fined £300 in 1651, this being five years' value of his lands, which were thus computed by the Committee for Compounding to be worth £60 per annum. Papers reveal that he was 'seised of a reversion in fee tayle' after the death of his mother Agnes, of, and in certain messuages, lands and tenements called Bidlake, Bidlake Mills, Rowden, Broadpark, Combe and Holland in the parishes of Bridestowe, Bradstone and Sourton, of the clear yearly value 'before the troubles' of £60. Finally he was seised in fee of a number of farms in Bridestowe, Bradstone, Dunterton and Thrushelton, all of which were let for the usual Devonshire term of 99 years or three lives, yielding only £5 a year from the rents. The major income from these lands came of course from the heavy fines when the leases were first made, and of these we know nothing. The farms and land in question were Woodford, Kersford, Fernworthy, Broadstone Towne, Bremford Hams, Broadstone Wastes, Stony Hamms, Wrixall Wood, Thrushelton, Woolacott, Gattacombe and Blackland. Most farms and land mentioned appear in a fifteenth-century rental among the family papers. Others were either purchased or came into possession through marriage.

The fine of £300 imposed by the Committee was a substantial one and Henry was obliged to borrow from friends. His mother-in-law, Philippa Kelly, seems to have repaid, or paid the interest due to these friends, so, as security, Henry 'alienated, bargained and sold to her all his goods and chattels, only excepting his wearing apparel'. He was left with nothing but his clothes. Henry was to get his property back in 1654.

There are many tales of Henry the Royalist hiding from Cromwell's soldiers who had been sent to take him prisoner. One tale goes that he dressed himself in rags and some soldiers met him and asked if he had seen Squire Bidlake. 'Sure' he replied, 'he was standing on his own doorstep a short time ago.' The soldiers went to search Bidlake House whilst Henry went to a tenant named Veale who lived in Burley Wood. The soldiers eventually came to search the house in Burley Wood so Henry hid in a clock case. Hunting high and low the soldiers could not find him. One of them looking at the clock standing and seeing the hand at the hour asked, 'Why does it not strike?' Mrs Veale replied, 'It will'. Squire Bidlake suffered a chronic cough and just as he began the clock struck the hour and drowned the cough.

If Henry had been captured it would certainly have been recorded. In the *Mercurius Rusticus* of the year 1647 there is an account of a visit by a troop of horse sent to Bridestowe by the Earl of Stamford. There is not a word about the capture of Henry Bidlake although there is an account of a barbarous act committed in the cottage of a husbandman in Bridestowe, no name being mentioned. The man openly adhered to the King's party and a troop of horse was sent to apprehend him. He was not at home and his young son told the troop he was ignorant of his father's whereabouts. He was threatened with hanging but eventually was cut down after a while, as it was not intended to hang him to death. Eventually the troops left not knowing whether the boy was dead or recovered.

Henry Bidlake along with John Powell, as churchwardens of Bridestowe, made a rate for the repairing of the church on 20 December 1659. This must have been Henry's last act as he died before the year was out at the age of 48. William Bidlake, heir of Henry, was baptised on 29 September 1629 and buried on 22 November 1670. In 1661 he married Elizabeth, the daughter of Anthony Furlong of Carbeel in Cornwall. William was much straitened by his father's misfortunes. A letter, dated 20 December 1669 from William to his relative, Elizabeth Taverner, who lived at Combe, Bradstone, recites:

Kind Coz, I had provided a small parcell of money for some occasions which I had att Plymouth where I must ride tomorrowe, but I was yesterday att Tavistock... and there I was enforced to pay it away, and for my life I know not what to do if you cannot help me fifty shillings or three pounds.

William's wife outlived him, bearing him a son and heir, Henry. She married again in 1677 conveying her lands to her second husband, thereby barring her son by William Bidlake.

Henry Bidlake married twice. His first wife was Mary Ann, daughter of Edward Greenwood and widow of Edward Kneebone. They had two daughters, Mrs Beare of Sourton and Mrs Warne of Bridestowe, both of whom died childless. His second wife, Ann, daughter of Edward Seddon, Rector of Throwley, whom he married on 2 February 1710, had two daughters and one son by him. Henry's son and heir was buried at Bridestowe on 24 October 1718, being baptised on 17 April 1716. What was left of the Bidlake property went to the three daughters. Ann married John Herring in 1738, Elizabeth married

John Heirn of Great Torrington, Attorney, on 14 July 1741, at Bridestowe, whilst Philippa the third daughter never married.

The heir of the three sisters was Mrs Heirn's daughter Mary, who married Col. Thomas Wollocombe. The will of the last Henry Bidlake was proved in 1718.

Some years later a portion of Bidlake was leased. On 9 May 1771 a complex and lengthy contract was drawn up and agreed upon between John Herring of Langston, John Heirn of Great Torrington, Phillippa Bidlake of Bidlake and Peter Featherstone of South [Nounanton], in the County of Derby, to lease Bidlake. With the lease being agreed upon Peter Featherstone took up residence but by the year 1786, unable to make ends meet, he became bankrupt. He was in debt to his lessors to the amount of £287.12s.9½d. To secure this sum of money along with the interest due a bill of sale was instigated by the lessors.

Featherstone 'granted, bargained and sold' unto the lessors all and singular 'his cattle, horses, sheep, corn, goods and chattels' in order to attempt to clear his financial dilemma. All was to be sold and disposed of at the best possible prices, the money arising to be applied to discharge the sum of £287.12s.9½d. The sale was to include:

About six acres of wheat, five acres of barley now sown and growing on the farm, an acre of potatoes, thirteen acres of oats growing there, two steers, five milch cows, six calves, fifteen heifers of different ages, above two years, five ewes, one lamb, five yearling bullocks, [four] waggon or draft horses, two horses of three years of age, two colts, all the household goods and implements of household husbandry, one waggon, two carts, several quantities of hay and all other goods and chattels of whatsoever nature, kind or quality by the same are which the said Peter Featherstone now is or hereinafter shall be possessed of or entitled into save his wearing apparell.

Whether Featherstone knew that he was now in a similar position to the one in which Henry Bidlake had found himself is a matter of idle speculation. Unlike Henry though, Featherstone was unable to continue to farm the portion of Bidlake that had been leased to him. He 'transferred and assigned released and extinguished' all his term of years of, and in, the said Barton and Farm of Bidlake back to the original lessors on 26 June 1786.

Moving on a century we find the freehold estates known as Little Bidlake, Great Bidlake, and Bidlake Mills, together with a blacksmith's shop, cottages, gardens etc., along with the Kersford Barton Farms, in all about 674 acres, producing £1140 per annum all for sale at an auction to take place on 15 August 1890. The language used to describe the various lots bears some striking resemblances to modern-day estate-agent speak. An extract from the document of 1890 reads:

A sound, useful and superior grazing and dairy farm known as Little Bidlake and West Parks... this estate has the well-deserved reputation of being the choicest dairy farm of the neighbourhood. The shooting and fishing is estimated at £5 a year, the value of water power and necessary land for wheel etc., when the adjoining stone quarry and lime kilns are working at £10 a year bring the total rental to £15 a year.

All that exceedingly choice attractive freehold estate called Great Bidlake... a superior farm residence, being an excellent specimen of an Elizabethan Manor House suitable for a gentlemans occupation and of a pleasing manorial appearance ... the lands lie in a ring fence with important road and river frontages, extending to two hundred and seven acres or thereabouts, of superior, easy working and very fertile arable meadow, pasture, orchard and wood lands, well supplied with water and prettily timbered with oak, elm, ash, beech, fir and other trees, and (for mind) several eligible building sites, suitable for the erection of country villas or residences, which, owing to the bracing moorland air and picturesque surroundings, would offer

desirable summer retreats, or shooting boxes, the attractions and sporting opportunities being of a class rarely, if ever, to be obtained in Devonshire. As a sound, profitable stock and dairy farm also, this estate cannot be too highly commended.

A desirable and substantial water mill and premises called Bidlake Mills. Comprising Stone and Slated Grist Mill, with two pairs of stones and overshot water wheel with powerful supply.

Generally we are informed:

The shooting comprises hares, partridges, pheasants, woodcock, snipe, black game and rabbits etc. The rivers provide fine trout and other fishing. Numerous first class packs of foxhounds hunt the neighbourhoods, affording some of the best hunting possible. Otter hounds draw the rivers, and harriers and beagles are within easy reach. The neighbourhood is noted for its health giving powers. The picturesque country around supplies walks, drives and rides of surpassing beauty and there is good society.

Bidlake has passed into many hands since this auction took place, but the living history of such a place goes on for 'time out of mind'.

THE EBSWORTHYS OF EBSWORTHY

From the account of the Domesday Book we know that the seat of the Ebsworthy family was in being in 1086 and that it was held by a thane called Godwin. A charter dated 1317 mentions the earliest of the Ebsworthys traceable, but the family, no doubt, had been in existence for many decades prior. It is not possible to say with certainty that the first Ebsworthys observed are of a direct lineal descent, unlike the Bidlake family only scant traces of information have been procurable. For this reason the study of the Ebsworthy family has been minimal.

For our first Ebsworthy we will turn to the charter of 1317 which informs us that a William of Ebbellesworth was living at that time. The charter written in Latin recites in full:

Let those present and future know that I, William of Ebbellesworth, have given, conceded and confirmed in this present letter of mine, for myself and my heirs, and those assigned to Master John Milliton and Walter Milliton, the brother of the same John, to their heirs and assigned ones, all the land of mine in Easterlake etc., Given at Bridistow on the Sunday after the feast of the Birth of St John the Baptist (24th June) in the tenth year of the reign of King Edward, son of King Edward.

The charter of William mentions unnamed heirs. Whether Drew de Ebbollisworthie, a defendant in an action in 1327 over a 'dower' in Sourton concerning Anne Park (the wife of Edmund du Park) is of the same family can only be guessed at. The same may be said for Andrew of Eboldesworthi who appears in the Lay Subsidy of 1332. Although it has not proved possible to show any direct relationship of these early Ebsworthys, the dates given so far having only a minimal difference between them point surely to some family link.

A charter of Walter of Milliton shows that Walter of Ebbesworth had a son called John of Ebbellesworth, and that both of them were living in 1351. This charter also written in Latin recites:

Let those present and future know that I, Walter of Milliton have given, conceded and confirmed in this present letter of mine, to John of Ebbellesworth, son of Walter of Ebbesworth etc., Given at Milliton on the Tuesday before the feast of the Holy Lady [presumably 25 March] *in the twenty fourth year of the reign of King Edward III.*

In 1355 a John de Ebbelesworth was killed at Crediton by John Burstele who was acting as an aid to Baldwin (Polgru), the 'Keeper' of Crediton

Fair, who, apparently, had some reason to arrest John along with John de Holeway of Lydford. Burstele, it seems, must have been acting lawfully as he was pardoned for his actions.

Moving on we turn to a law court at Chagford where on 11 January 1432 a Thomas Ebbesworthy was 'at the mercy of the court for the detention of one brass pot, worth 11s.6d.' Some 14 years later yet another charter mentions a further John Ebsworthy:

Let those present and future know that I, John Ebbesworthy have given, conceded and confirmed in this present indented letter of mine, to Walter Hakeworthy of Okehampton all lands and tenements of mine, returns reversions with all things pertaining that I have in the town of Ebbesworthie on the Thursday (29 Sept) after the feast of St Michael Archangel in the twenty fourth year of the reign of King Henry VI.

This charter mentions John as living in 1446. More importantly it confirms his association with the place of Ebsworthy. For the next insight into the Ebsworthys the Lay Subsidy Roll of Devon for 1543–5 lists four Ebsworthys, Thomas, John, Richard and Robert. The two latter names in the Subsidy Roll are possibly the same Richard and Robert who are shown as brothers in the Heralds

Visitations of 1620. These brothers now give us a base around which to build a direct descent of the family. Before looking at the brothers, however, another Ebsworthy appears in an indenture made in the city of Exeter dated 24 November, 3 Eliz., (1560), which witnessed:

that the said Custos and Vicars Chorall... hath dimised... and letton... etc for 29 years to William Ebbisworthie, Clercke, all that their tenem'nt wth th' app'ten'ncesd sometime called the Little Callendarhaie, set, lyenge... etc., within the p'cincts of the Close of the sd. Cathedrall Church.

It is quite possible that this Ebsworthy who had taken up the position of 'Clerke' was a member of the Bridestowe family of that name, as we shall see later that other Bridestowe family members held positions in Exeter.

Peter Ebsworthy was a captain in the Devon Militia. He, along with other officers and men, was mustered during September 1572.

Returning to the aforesaid brothers, we discover that Richard was in all probability the 'Ebbesworthy' listed in the Devon Muster Roll of 1569 as an archer, and that their mother was called Jane (she being mentioned in an award dated 1594). The award, which is amongst the Bidlake papers, includes the following:

xvijth daie of January 1594 An Awarde made by Henry Bidlake esquire & William Wray esquire and John Bydlake esquire between Janne Ebsworthye of Brydistowe in the countie of Devon wyddowe of the one p'te and Richarde Ebsworthy of the same p'rish sonne of the saide Janne Ebsworthie of the other p'te/
Imprmus it is agreed and concluded upon that Richarde Ebsworthy shall yeld unto Janne Ebsworthie his mother in respect of hyr dower [in] Ebswo'thy [hall] one chamber rome at Ebsworthie hall... meat and drink/
Itm Robert Ebsworthy is to pay to Richarde Ebsworthy xxs yearlie viz vs a quartr the first quartr to be gyng at Lammas next & that if Janne Ebsworthy doe [?] of hyr meat and drink wth Richarde Ebsworthy her sonne then Richarde Ebsworthy shall pay unto Janne ebswr his mother xls by the year viz xs a quartr and then to hand all Ebsworthie hall to her sonnes use and behalf discharged of her dower retayning onlie her chamber rome during her life/
Itm it is agreed and concluded upon that Robert Ebsworthy shall have yearlie during his mothers life the three... llaks lease in Little Bydlak as Richarde Ebsworthie shall fence yt & occupy it wth cattle or sheep/
Itm Robert Ebsworthie is to have all the tillage in Litle Bydlak at [?] lande tyme for this p'sent lands lease/

William of Ebbellesworth =

Walter of Ebbesworth =

John of Ebbellesworth =

John de Ebboleworth =

Richard de Ebbolesworth =

... Ebsworthy = Jane

Robert of Ebbesworthie = Da. of ... Martin of Exeter

Peter Ebbesworthy = Alice Da. of ... Durant

Peter Ebbesworthy = Susan Da. Of John Alford

Peter Ebsworthy = Catherine Da. of Ebsworthy

Peter Ebsworthy

The lineal descent of the Ebsworthy family.
(The lines show a direct family connection)

Itm Robert Ebsworthie is to break yearly half [an] acre of land during Janne Ebsworthy her naturall life and for the tylling of the sd lande after wards for two yeares/

Item if Richarde Ebsworthy doe till [there] then Robert Ebsworthy shall till back the thyrde p'te only of sd landes as shall be broken and tilled by Richarde/

Itm Robert Ebsworthie is to repar all the hedges on

Litle Bydlak and to be contributor to the Repairing of the hedges and pay money for the first according to the full thirde p'te/

William Wray
Henry Bydlake
Thomas Williams
Georgio Moor
[John Bidlake]

Inventory of Peter Ebsworthy

An INVENTORYE of all and singular the goodes and chattells of Peter Ebsworthye Junr, late whiles hee lived, of Bridestowe in the Countye of Devon, Gent, deceased, taken, valued and appraised by Thomas Strut and Walter Blatchford, the Eighteenth daye of December Anno Domini 1645.

	£.	s.	d.
INPRIMIS his purse and apparrell	6	13	4
one labor horse and one Colte	2	5	0
six plowe Oxen	15	0	0
Twelve milch kine and twoe bulls	26	0	0
Twenty fower younge Cattle	20	0	0
Twoe hundred and fifty sheepe	26	13	4
his Swyne hogges	4	10	0
his Pultrye of all sortes	0	9	0
his Iron worke and plowe ymplements	3	5	0
his wooll	6	0	0
in the Parler of his dwellinge house two tableboards, stooles and other thinges	1	5	0
in the Hall two table boards with other utensiles	0	10	0
in the Kitchinge one table board and some Brasse worke there	2	10	0
in the Deerye provissions	1	0	0
in the Buttery Caske and other necessaries	2	10	0
in the parler chamber one hygh and trendle bedsteed with furniture	4	5	0
in the Hall chamber one high and one trendle beds with furniture	3	10	0
in the rest of the chambers bedsteedes with furniture and other household stuffe	7	0	0
his Linnynge	3	0	0
his bookes	1	10	0
his Corne thresht, unthresht, and Sowen	13	6	8
his weane and other his plowe ymplements	4	0	0
his silver plate	2	2	4
his Chattells	40	0	0
in things omitted	2	0	0
Summa	£204.14s.8d.		

Exhibitum erat vicesimo quinto die mensis May Anno Dni 1646.

Richard married a Shilston who was heir to her family and may have been from the Bridestowe branch of the Shilstons. Agnes, the daughter of Richard's great-grandson, Alexander Ebbesworthy, married Nicholas Tapson. The curious marriage settlement reads:

Between Alexander Ebbesworthie of Bridestowe and William Harris of Mellyon, Cornwall, John Tapson of Buckland Monachorum. In consideration of marriage between Nicholas Tapson, brother of John Tapson, and Agnes Ebbesworthie, eldest daughter of Alexander Ebbesworthie. Fifty pound to be paid by Nicholas Tapson to Alexander Ebbesworthie, and a further two hundred and twenty pound to be paid by and to the same, that is fifty pound 29 of October, 1639, seventy pound 29 October, 1640, and one hundred pound 29 October, 1641. Which two hundred and twenty pound to be paid to the said Alexander Ebbesworthie for the advancement in marriage of Katherine Ebbesworthie youngest daughter of Alexander Ebbesworthie, to be paid in the church porch of the Parish Church of Bridestowe. Grants to William Harris and John Tapson lands called Ebbsworthys Woode, East Bidlake, also that called Blatchford and Snatton alias Gnatton in Sourton in trust for Nicholas Tapson and Agnes his wife and their issue. In default to the right heirs of Alexander Ebbsworthie. Signed Alexander Ebbsworthie.

With this curious payment of money taking place in the church porch of Bridestowe we turn to Robert who married a daughter of Martin of Exeter. From this union came issue of a son and heir, Peter, who married Alice Durant. Peter and Alice had two sons. Paul married Catherine who was the sixth daughter of Vincent Calmady of Wembury. Peter, son and heir of Peter and Alice, married Susan, daughter and heir of John Alford, one time Town Clerk of Okehampton. They had four daughters and two sons.

Peter, son and heir of Peter and Susan married Catherine, the daughter of a namesake. Peter must have died between 8 December 1645, the date of his will, and 18 December 1645, on which day an inventory was taken of all his worldly goods. His will reads:

Peeter Ebsworthy of Bridestow, junr, Gent., sick of body. To my wife Catherine Ebsworthy all my goods and chattels. To my wife for life all my lands in Bridestowe, Okehampton, Lydford and elsewhere. Remainder to my son Peter Ebsworthy and his heirs forever. Remainder if my wife be with child or children to them and their heirs, and if not, to Sr Shilston Calmady Kt and his son Josias Calmady Esq., and likewise to Shilston Calmady, and Francis Calmady Gents., and their heirs. My wife to be my executor.

Overseers, the said Sr Shilston Calmady Kt, Josias Calmady Esq., Shilston Calmady and Francis Calmady Gents. sd Peeter Ebsworthy Junr. Witnesses Thomas Strut, William Collins, sign of Walter Blackford.

Peter's inventory includes mention of the rooms of the house in which his effects were found. We can see that Peter's house consisted of a hall with a chamber over, a parlour with a chamber over, a kitchen, dairy and buttery. The latter three rooms would have had, no doubt, the 'rest of the chambers of the house' over them. This house then, with its three downstairs living rooms, dairy and buttery, and presumably four or five bedrooms, thus made for quite comfortable and spacious living accommodation. The Devon Hearth Tax of 1674, for which a William Ebsworthy was responsible, shows the house at Ebsworthy as having five fireplaces.

Virtually half the wealth of Peter's estate was made up from the farm by way of the animals, corn and ploughing implements. Although the Ebsworthy family were far from being as wealthy as their distant Bidlake neighbours, nor their house as impressive, they were also quite well off in their time.

On 28 September 1653 administration of the estate of Peter Ebsworthy was granted to his daughters Agnes and Wilmot. No doubt this was presumably because Catherine his wife had died and Peter his son and heir was in foreign lands.

The administration of the estate of Peter Ebsworthy the son, late of Oporto in the kingdom of Portugal, bachelor, deceased, was granted on 21 January 1679 to John Francis and Thomasine, the wife of John Woolocombe. John and Thomasine were brother and sister on the mother's side of the deceased. In all probability Peter's death heralded the end of the male line of this Ebsworthy family.

Ebsworthy Wood which is shown on the 25-inch Ordnance Survey map situated east of Waddlestone Down and west of Lydford village is the wood referred to earlier in the marriage settlement of Agnes Ebsworthy. According to Newman in his *History of Coryton*, Thomas Holdsworth Newman of Coryton, late in the nineteenth century, purchased this wood from the Reverend J.B. Newcombe for the sum of £400 to add to his manor. Forestry Commission property now surrounds Ebsworthy Wood which is now shown on the 2½-inch Ordnance Survey map as Lydford Forest.

Newman further adds that tradition says that there was a terrible feud for several hundred years between the Bidlakes and the Ebsworthys, and that the last of the Ebsworthys was killed in a duel with a Bidlake. Tradition is right to say that the two families had their differences but whether the gruesome tale of the end of the last Ebsworthy is true we will probably never know.

THE MILLATONS OF MILLATON

White's Directory of Devonshire for the year 1850 describes Millaton House, the seat of the Millaton family, as a 'handsome mansion, with tasteful grounds' which had been 'rebuilt about the close of the seventeenth century, but was much enlarged and beautified some years ago.' It stood on the site of an old house that was the seat of the Millaton family of whom the earliest mention appears in an Assize Roll of 1238. As with the Ebsworthy family the Millatons can only be traced from various references by association until a limited entry appears in the *Visitations of Devon*, 1564.

The first Millaton of whom we have knowledge had false charges of assault made against him. An Assize Roll of 1238 informs us:

Wymarc, wife of John de Crandeforde, appeals John de Millentone of beating her so she miscarried, and that he did this evilly etc., she offers etc., as etc. John comes, denies all and puts himself on the country. The jurors testify that he is not guilty, so he is quit, let John de Crandeforde and Wymarc be taken into custody. Later John came and made fine for himself and his wife for 10s. pledges Adam le Brun and Richard le Clerk de Lidford.

It is probably safe to assume that this John Millaton lived at Bridestowe as he was described as being of Millaton, the person making the allegations against him being his near neighbour, she being of Crandford.

Moving on 50 years we meet the brothers John and Walter, both of whom we have previous knowledge from the account of the Ebsworthy family. A charter dated 1288 made by 'Robert de Brewelyshille', granted to 'John Millaton clerk and Walter his Brother, their heirs and assigns six shillings sterling of yearly rent' from the 'free tenement of Brewelyshill,' in Boasley in consideration of a 'fine of five marks'.

John is again mentioned in a grant dated 1310, it recites:

John Longus of West-wyk, merchant, grants to Master John de Millaton, clerk, for his homage and service all the meadow which he bought of Henry de Seccomb being that piece of meadow which lies between the land of La Toffe and the water which divided the land of Henry de Seccomb and the land of John de Cancell of Sutherdon to be held by Master John de Millaton his heirs and assigns of the chief lord of the fee, with free ingress and egress with all the liberties, uses and free customs belonging to the said meadow according to the charter which John Longus had of Henry de Seccomb paying to the lord of the fee the rent and services due.

With this grant of West Week in the parish of Lifton to John Millaton, we learn that he was a priest who had obtained a Master of Arts degree. The indications for this assumption are quite clear as he is shown as 'Master' and 'Clerk', both titles of which were used by men of the cloth.

From William Ebsworthy's charter of 1317 the brothers 'Master' John and Walter had been enfeoffed of land by William. John and Walter however had problems with a close neighbour over this land. From an undated memorandum we find that:

The said John and Walter Milleton had peaceful seisin from Thursday after the Feast of St Gregory the Pope to Thursday next after the Feast of Apostles Peter and Paul, on which day Nicholas de Combe and his servants, in the writ named, disseised them and by force of arms [allowed their cattle to eat their corn growing there] and violently prevented John and Walter from entering into the said land.

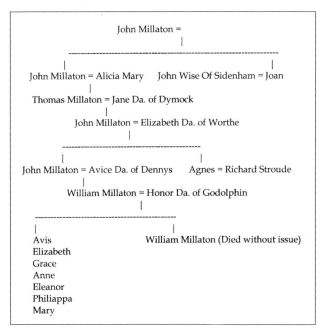

The lineal descent of the Millaton family.

A further charter dated 1331 which concerns land in Bridestowe gives Geoffrey de Millatone as 'parson of the Church of Lywtrenchard'. From a grant made in 1377 we find that another Millaton, named Geoffrey, had two sons, Richard and William, and four daughters, Joan, Matilda, Alice and Margary. Where this Geoffrey lies in relation to the other Millatons as seen so far, or indeed whether he is the Geoffrey mentioned earlier as the parson of Lewtrenchard is not clear. We also discover from this grant that the Millatons had a kinsman called Thomas de Mewey in the parish of Meavy, who, in

Millaton House. (Alan Pearn)

Millaton House (postcard date stamped 1938). (Alan Pearn)

the year 1378, appointed as his attorney Phillip de Combe. Phillip was to 'give seisin to Geoffrey de Mileton' of 'the land belonging to Thomas at Milaton'.

From Bishop Stafford's Register we find a Gilbert Mileton and Joan his wife being granted an oratory on 1 May 1396, there being no indication as to the location of their residence, where, no doubt, they had a room set aside as a private chapel.

Three years on details of a Richard Millaton appear; he was probably the son of Geoffrey de Millaton. From a release dated 1398 we have:

Richard Thorne, son of Thomas Thorn, releasing to Richard Mileton, of all right to a corn mill at Knolle, with the water course and 'moltura' to said mill belonging together with a cottage in Walkhampton all which premises said Thomas Thorne had by grant of Thomas Mewey.

The Register of Bishop Stafford informs us of the granting of a licence on 10 June 1411 for another oratory. Richard Mileton and Emmota his wife now had a chapel in their home at West Week.

Turning to Bishop Edmund Lacy's Register we see that a 'Licencia celebrandi' was granted to William Mylaton and to Joan his wife for 'Divine Service in their mansion of West Week, or, in any other place in Lifton, Dated 28 December 1438.'

The year of 1499 and Posloe Priory, Exeter, provides us with another Millaton, who not unexpectedly proves elusive when it comes to substantiating a family tie. Cecila Milliton held the position of Lady Superior at the priory.

A stage has now been reached whereby the 1564 *Visitations of Devon* can be drawn upon in order to obtain a definite descendancy of the Millaton family. The *Visitations*, which only allows for the descendancy of sons, shows only six generations. If we take 30 years per generation, we start the line off at around the beginning of the fifteenth century thus spanning about 200 years, the last of the Millaton sons dying in 1571. Prior to this we have been unable to establish whether

any of the Millatons were of direct lineal descent and we do not even know how many of the family mentioned so far resided at Millaton. The first member of the family shown in the *Visitations* is a John Millaton – the name of his wife does not appear. They had issue a daughter called Joan who married John Wise of Sidenham and a son called John who married Alicia Mary.

John and Alicia had a son called Thomas who married Jane, a daughter of Dymock. They had issue of a son who was also called John who married Elizabeth, a daughter of Worthe, at which time, according to some antiquarians, he seemingly gained land in Cornwall. From the Itinerary of John Leland (1534–43) we are informed:

Garsike alias Pengarsike was given by one of the Worthe's Wives with a Daughter of hers to one of the Milatuns of Devonshir. Milatun hath Milatun yn Devon.

According to Lysons the Millaton family acquired it by purchase. Carew says 'Pengueraz in Cornish importeth a head to help; from which some deduce the etymon of Pengersick, a fair house in an unfruitful soil.' A further source tells that the Millatons also 'became possessed of Pengerswick Castle in St Breock, Kirrier, by purchase temp Henry VIII.' Others, however, tell a different story.

One account of tradition relates that Mr Milliton in the reign of Henry VIII slew in the streets of London a man in a drunken brawl. He fled and went to sea. It is not known to which part of the world he went, but we are told that he became excessively rich; so rich that 'when he loaded his ass with his gold, the weight was so great as to break the poor animal's back.' Returning to his country and not daring to appear in any of the large towns, he bought the manor of Pengerswick and built this castle to defend himself in the event of his being approached by any of the officers of the law.

A miserable man, Milliton is said to have lived in a secret chamber in this tower and to have been visited only by his most trusted friends. Deeply deploring the crime that had condemned him to seclusion from the world he spent his dreary hours in ornamenting his dwelling. His own story is supposed to be told in the painting of an over-laden ass in one room, with a black-letter legend, importing that a miser is like an ass loaded with riches, who, without attending to his golden burden, feeds on thistles. There is also a carving of water wearing a hollow in a stone and under it the word 'Perseverance'. Of the death of Milliton we have no account.

Leaving aside the tales of tradition we find that John and Elizabeth had a son, John, their heir, and a daughter, Agnes. She married, according to the 1564 *Visitation*, William Strode, but other writers give more correctly Richard Strode, who as MP got himself locked up in Lydford castle over tinner's rights. Agnes and Richard had three sons, William their heir, Francis, Richard and two daughters, Cecily and Elizabeth.

John the husband of Elizabeth died on 10 March 1514. His inquisition was taken at Modbury on 16 October 1514 before:

John Ghylberd, Esq., escheator... by the oath of Francis Strechelegh, John Scos of Trewyn, William Crocker, Sen., and others (named), who say that John Milaton was seised of the manors of Mewy and Knoll, held of Mary lady of Hungerford of her manor of Southpole, worth by the year, clear, 10 pound also 1 messuage, 20 acres of land 4 acres of meadow and 30 acres of heath in Lydford, held of Robert Schilston, by fealty, worth ten shillings also 2 messuages, 100 acres of land, 10 acres of meadow, 2 acres of wood and 30 acres of heath in Smalcomb and Milaton, held of the said Lady Mary, of her manor of Cobham Wyke, worth 20 shillings also 3 messuages, 5 acres of meadow, 200 acres of land, 100 acres of heath in Lyfton, called Kerly, Lytylbeare and Wortham, held of the earl of Westmorland, worth 30 shillings.

In 1521 John Millaton, heir of John and Elizabeth, who married Avice Dennys, became captain of St Michael's Mount. In this post he was bound to find 'three priests'.

The Mount became a stronghold and in place of one of the priests a gunner who had been appointed there 'received the same wages'. For the years 1524 to 1527 John was appointed as a Commissioner and Collector of subsidies for the hundred of Penwith which position he was again to hold in the years 1543–45.

According to Polwhele, the Sheriff of Cornwall for 1548 was a 'Job Milaton de Pengersick'. Job in all probability was John Millaton who made his will two years later in November 1549. He bequeathed to his son and heir William Mylliton and Honor, his wife, a daughter of Godolphen, all his goods and lands making them his executors having died on 6 December 1549. John's inquisition was taken at 'Holdisworthie' 13 August 1550 before Thomas Tremyne, escheator. John was seised of the manors of Newye, Walkehampton and Knolle, land in Smallacombe, Myllaton and Sampforde Spyne. Smallacombe and Myllaton were held of the said earl's manor of Cobhamwyke, by fealty and 10d. rent, worth 20 shillings.

William, son and heir of John and Avice, was 35 years of age when he succeeded to the captaincy of St Michael's Mount upon his father's death. He had married Honor Godolphin. William died on 18 March 1571 leaving behind his wife and eight children. Amongst them was his only son, William, who was to die within a few weeks of his father, he being 'lost in his travels beyond the seas'. Thus he 'enriched six distaffs with his inheritance'.

The inquisition of William the father was taken at Exeter Castle on 4 October 1571 before Robert Carye and John Eveleigh. William Myllyton was seised of many lands in Cornwall but there is no mention of land in Bridestowe, which William must surely have held as Bridestowe residents appeared at the inquisition in the personages of William Harris, John Wray, William Battishill and Peter Ebsworthy. The answer regarding the omission may be quite simple but as yet it is elusive. As a widow Honor remarried shortly after the death of her husband.

William, the son of William and Honor, died on 31 May 1571 aged 17. He was the last of the

Millaton Lodge. (Doug Gale)

Len Harvey the boxer (holding child in arms) with the children at the Millaton Fête, 1954.
(Alan Pearn)

Millaton male line. Risdon perhaps concludes the story of the Millaton family for us; he says that Millaton was:

... the habitation of some that had that local name; one of which family was Captain of Mount St Michael, whose heritage was divided among Distaff's, in our remembrance.

Millaton eventually became the seat of the Newton family whose ancestors dwelt at Crabbton in Somerset. Returning to *White's Directory* of 1850 we find John Gubbins Newton in residence. At that time the house contained a fine museum of stuffed birds, etc., along with a richly-carved oak bedstead of the Elizabethan age. Some coins dating from the reign of Louis IX of France had been found on the site of an ancient domestic chapel.

It seems that in later years John Gubbins Newton was having financial problems for in September 1880 the Millaton estates were up for sale at an auction. The properties on offer were either freehold, long leasehold for terms up to 500 years, or copyhold, comprising four mansions and several farms in the parishes of Broadwoodwidger, Bratton Clovelly, Thrushelton, Bridestowe, Sourton, Lydford, Lewtrenchard, Inwardleigh and Okehampton, containing over 8000 acres.

Newton's property in Bridestowe was quite substantial as shown by the auctioneer's catalogue.

Millaton House is described as being a 'residence of ample accommodation' for a family of 'position' situated in a 'very picturesque district, the fishing and hunting being good'. Millaton estate consisted of 'hot houses, green houses, lawns and pleasure grounds, coach house, stables, farm buildings and extensive woods and plantations'.

Certain dwelling-houses, cottages and closes of accommodation land in the village of Bridestowe also formed part of the Millaton estates, as were several of the farms lying within the parish of Bridestowe. There was Longham and Brambleham, which were considered as having 'about the best woodcock shooting in the County', Great and Little Yellands, Shallowford, Raddon, Fernworthy, Battishill, Ebsworthy Town, Sprig Hill and Way, which had 'excellent beech timber, scotch and spruce fir'. Alongside Millaton was that entire 'capital farm' with very 'convenient farm house and excellent newly erected farm buildings', called Stone Farm. Newton, however, was still resident at Millaton in 1902 and he was followed shortly after by Frederick Woodgates. Lord Carrington became the next owner in 1924 or thereabouts. He did a great deal of work to modernise the property by installing bathrooms, central heating and greatly enlarging the gardens – eight gardeners were employed to keep them in immaculate order. A butler named Dewar, who, it appears, 'appropriately enough, drank a great deal

Medical Corp using the cricket pavilion during the Second World War. (Alan Pearn)

Cricket New Year's Party, Parish Hall, 1954/5.
(Alan Pearn)

folk who knew him, has held many important positions and it might well be thought appropriate to consider him a 'Bridestowe boy', albeit some time in the past.

He was born 6 June 1919 and educated at Eton and Sandhurst. In 1942 he married Iona, the daughter of Sir Francis McClean. During the Second World War he served in north-west Europe, became a Major in the Grenadier Guards winning a Military Cross in 1945. Positions held by him have been of a high office to say the least: Secretary General of Nato 1984; Parliamentary Sec. Ministry of Agriculture and Fisheries 1951–54; Parliamentary Sec. Ministry of Defence 1959; First Lord of the Admiralty 1959–63; Minister without Portfolio and Leader of the House of Lords 1963–64; Leader of the Opposition, House of Lords 1964–70; Sec. of State for Defence 1970–74; Sec. of State for Energy 1974; Sec. of State for Foreign and Commonwealth Affairs 1979–82; Chairman, Conservative Party 1972–74.

Beatie Lake as a young woman; she lived at Cross Lanes. (Brian Lavis)

of the whiskey named after him', occupied a lodge erected at the entrance to the drive.

Lord Carrington enlarged the cricket ground, erected a fine handsome pavilion and ran his own club called the MCC, the 'Millaton Cricket Club'. A follower of test-match commentaries will know that it was not uncommon to hear the Millaton ground mentioned by the now deceased Brian Johnston, he being a past visitor. Peter Walker, a fellow commentator, also appeared at the Millaton ground with a touring side.

An active role was to be played by Lord Carrington in village life; an entry in the Parish Council Minutes Book on 10 April 1931 mentions that he was elected as a member of that council. Two months later an entry reported that he had made a generous gift of six chestnut trees for the Sporting Green. At a special meeting of the Parish Council on 23 January 1938, before any business was carried out a moment's silence was observed in respect to the late Chairman, Lord Carrington.

His son, The Rt Hon. The Lord Carrington, affectionately called Peter by those village

Sir Giles Sebright bought Millaton from the Carringtons in 1946. Sadly, it was upon his death that the estate's demise began; a trend that continued as it fell into many hands. In the last 30 years of the twentieth century, the house and grounds have seen more change to the detriment of the estate than at any other time. The house was turned into a nursing home, the farm sold and the coach-house converted into a dwelling, as were other outhouses. The lodge, that stands at the ornamental gated entrance of the once colourful drive lined with rhododendrons and daffodils – now divided by a defunct village bypass – is no longer part of the estate.

There are still people about who can remember seeing Millaton much as it was when described in *White's Directory* for the year 1850. Thankfully, Mr and Mrs Watts, the owners at the time of writing, are doing some good work to restore Millaton to its past glory.

THE SHILSTONS OF LEAWOOD

The name Shilstone is of Old English origin derived from 'scylfe stone', meaning 'shelf stone', 'stone slab' or 'dolman', such a monument being preserved at Drewsteignton. Four Shilston families are traceable. One family lived at Modbury, one at Totnes, and two lived within the Okehampton area. The particular line of Shilstons concerning Bridestowe stems, not surprisingly, from one of the families who were associated with the Okehampton area. Four generations spanning a period of just over a century held the estate of Leawood which, through marriage, has been carried in succession up to the present day. Two Shilstons, William and Thomas, who were in all probability brothers, lie at the head of the family line which held Leawood. William, 1430–1503, held land at Drewsteignton and Throwley as well as elsewhere in Devon, his successors do not concern our exploration of Bridestowe. Thomas, born in the year 1435 died on 21 July 1499, leaving two sons, Robert his heir, and John.

The *inquisition post mortem* for Thomas held on 26 October 1499 tells us that Thomas held amongst other property a tenement in Hurdwyke held of John Tremayn as of his manor of South Lideham and a tenement in Cranford and Burdeswyll held of John Rondell as of his manor of Blakebrome. Two messuages and land in Lywode and Heth were held of the manor of Weke Cobham. From the *inquisition post mortem* we see that Thomas held Lywode, how this property had come into the possession of his ancestors and for what period of time they had held it has not been substantiated. Thomas Shilston's son and heir, Robert 1465–1516, was aged 32 or more when his father died. Robert died on 12 April 1516 leaving his widow Joan to care for their children Robert and Agnes.

The *inquisition post mortem* of Robert the father was held at Okehampton on 4 November 1516 before Thomas Bidlake, a juror. In part it reads:

Robert Shilston held no land of the King in Chief on the day of his death. He held five messuages and a mill (corn) and three hundred acres of land, twenty acres of meadow, one hundred acres of furze heath in Leywooder, Combe, Craneford, Heth and Farneworthy, held of Mary Hungerford as of her manor of Cobham Wyke. He held a messuage and sixty acres in Hyll held of John Wyse as of his manor of Willysworthy.

Robert enfeoffed his brother Sir John Shilston, Roger Elford and Walter Wrey as trustees to see that his will was performed and to see that Agnes his daughter wed.

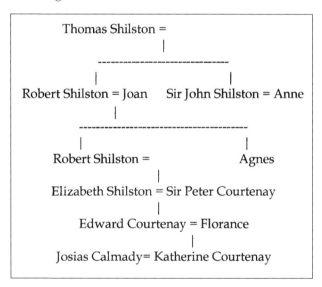

Thomas Shilston =
|
Robert Shilston = Joan   Sir John Shilston = Anne
|
Robert Shilston =   Agnes
|
Elizabeth Shilston = Sir Peter Courtenay
|
Edward Courtenay = Florance
|
Josias Calmady = Katherine Courtenay

Lineal descent of the Shilston family.

The second son of Thomas, Sir John Shilston 1470–1530, married Anne the sister of Charles Brandon, Duke of Suffolk. Sir John was Sheriff of Devon from November 1515 to November 1516. He died without issue in or about January 1530, his *inquisition post mortem* being held at Exeter on 28 April 1530. His heir was Elizabeth, the daughter of his nephew Robert. Sir John's will dated 10 December 1529 was proved on 22 April 1531; in part it reads 'to the wardens of the parishes of Bridstow, Sourton and Lydford, twenty shillings that the curates may pray for my soul every Sunday'.

Robert Shilston (1494–1525), son and heir of the first mentioned Robert and nephew of Sir John, having married, had issue of a daughter Elizabeth

(1520–1605) who was nine years old or more when she became heir to her uncle, Sir John. She married Sir Peter Courtenay of Ugbrook in Chudleigh. Elizabeth survived her husband by 53 years and was buried at Chudleigh on 11 November 1605.

Edward, the eldest son of Elizabeth and Peter, was executed for treason as a popish recusant. He married Florance the daughter of Thomas Moore of Taunton. They had a daughter, Katherine, who married Josias Calmady, thus carrying the Leawood estate into that family. With Leawood in the hands of Elizabeth upon the death of her father the Shilston family ends as far as our interests go. It is worth pointing out however that Shilston daughters married into the Wrey families who lived in Northrussel in the parish of Thrushelton. Bridget, daughter of a Robert Shilston, married Walter Wrey whilst his father John married a Constance Shilston, daughter of John Shilston. Neither Robert nor John is identified with the Shilstons of Leawood but no doubt a family link exists. The monument in Bridestowe's church to John Wrey shows a Shilston impalement. This John Wrey, however, is the grandson of John and Constance.

THE CALMADY-HAMLYNS OF LEAWOOD

In the Calmady-Hamlyns we have the most important of all the Bridestowe families. Although the Calmadys, the predominate members within the Calmady-Hamlyn family, can claim a direct line of ancestors going back to the period of the Norman Conquest, they are unable to show that they were as ancient a family as the Bidlakes. Whereas the Bidlakes originated locally the Calmadys did not; indeed they were not even natives of Devon. The mere fact that the Calmady family does not claim to be of Devonian stock does not preclude them from being linked with those who contributed to the history of Devon. On perusal of their direct lineal descent we find that 'blue blood' lies at the foot of their family. Elizabeth Courtenay bought this distinction to them upon her marriage to Josias Calmady. In later years the family name was to become extinct because of the lack of male heirs, but the resurrection of the family appellation came about with the assumption of the name Calmady by female descendants who instigated proceedings by royal licence and deed poll.

Upon investigation we find that the Calmady-Hamlyn 'blue blood' connection evolves from members of royal families from various countries, relatives of William the Conqueror and the Courtenays, all of whom were united by marriage. Initially we have Henry I, King of France, married to Agnes, daughter of Jaroslop, the First Duke of Russia. Their great-granddaughter, Adama, married Henry, Prince of Scotland, his father and grandfather being respectively David I and Malcolm III, Kings of Scotland. Passing on down this line eventually we find Humphry de Bohun, Earl of Hereford and Essex, married to Elizabeth daughter of Edward I, King of England, whose wife was the daughter of Ferdinand III, King of Castille. Humphry de Bohun and Elizabeth had a daughter, Margaret, who on her father's death received Powderham as a marriage portion. She married

Hugh de Courtenay, the Second Earl of Devon. Thus Powderham came into the hands of the Courtenays.

The original seat of the Calmady family from the year 1304 appears to have been Calmady in the parish of Poundstock in Cornwall. The first six descents of the Calmady pedigree as shown in the *Visitations of Devon* for 1620 tell us of the sons who inherited the family seat from their father, plus the names of their respective wives.

The first Calmady, as shown in the *Visitations,* who was living in 1337 married Florence, daughter and coheir of the Strodes of Strode in Ermington. Their son, living in 1339, married the daughter and coheir of a Morton. John Calmady, their son, married the daughter and coheir of the Gayer family of Trenbrace in Cornwall. Another John, the son of the last mentioned John, in the time of Henry VI married Prudence, daughter and coheir of Vivian Penwarne. The next son, William, married Mariote, the daughter of Stephen Gifford 1458/9. Their son, Stephen, in the time of Henry VII married Loveday, the daughter and coheir of Humphry Cavell of Treharrick in Cornwall.

Stephen Calmady, it appears, like many of his fellow West-Country men, was not a supporter of

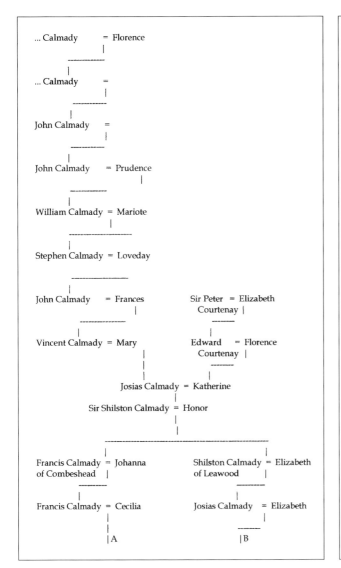

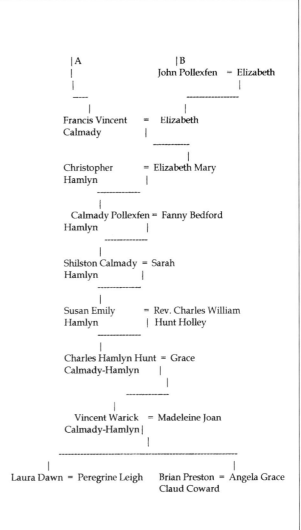

Lineal descent of the Calmady-Hamlyn family.

Richard III. During the rebellion against Richard, Stephen allowed the Salisbury rebels John Cheyne and Giles Daubeney to make their escape to Brittany with the Exeter rebel John Halwell, on a boat which he owned. Stephen suffered for his defiant opposition towards the King. His boat was seized. A further rebellion by West-Country men against another of their kings, Henry VII, was overcome in 1497. As a result of this attempted insurrection Henry imposed fines against his disobedient subjects. Stephen Calmady was amongst those persons who were to 'take several parishes under their charge', drawing up the roll for the fines and making themselves responsible as 'mainpernor for the rest, raising the fines and paying over to the royal officials.'

John Calmady, the son and heir of Stephen and his wife Loveday, married Frances, the daughter of Francis Vincent 1520/21. Upon this marriage we get a much fuller descendancy of the Calmady family who were now beginning to take up residence in Devon as a whole. For reasons of space only the heirs in succession will be treated unless importance dictates otherwise until we reach the occupation of Leawood. At this point we also see family surnames which future generations took for Christian names.

John and Frances had five sons, their eldest, John, living in 1560, married a daughter of Stephen Gayer of Trenbrace in Cornwall by whom he had five children. Their only grandchild, Barbara, born to their heir, became the last of the direct line from the eldest son of the Calmadys of Calmady. The Calmady estate came into the hands of her great-uncle, Vincent Calmady of Wembury, the third son of John and Frances. The second son of John and Frances, Richard Calmady of Farwood in Colyton, became Member of Parliament for Plympton. Vincent Calmady, the third son and eventual heir, was of Wembury and an attorney at law. He purchased from the Crown in 1555 the estate of Langdon. It seems that Vincent may never have lived at Langdon but it appears that he perhaps used stones from

Plympton Priory for the rebuilding of the house, having been granted permission to do so by Queen Elizabeth I. The Lysons brothers further qualify the fact that Vincent lived other than at Langdon as they wrote that he had 'purchased several estates in Devonshire in the reign of Queen Elizabeth and settled at Brixton.' The Calmady family was to occupy Langdon for 320 years before selling the property in 1875.

Being a very productive father Vincent's offspring became scattered, forming junior lines of the Calmady family over a large area of Devon. No less than 13 children were born to him and his two wives. Mary Hicks was the first whilst Wilmot Alford became his second.

Vincent's first son and heir, Josias Calmady, born on 9 June 1565 was only 14 years of age at the time of his father's death in 1579. Perhaps of most importance to us is that this Josias was the first Calmady to establish a line of his family in the parish of Bridestowe, with the acquisition of the Leawood estate upon his marriage in 1584 to Katherine Courtenay.

Amongst the Calmady papers are charters which give earlier mentions of Leawood. One, dated 1352 between Ralph son of William de Combe and Master Henry de Pyk, clerk, mentions a messuage and lands at 'Lymdrie' in the parish of Bridestowe, which, it has been suggested, may be Leawood. Another undated charter between Henry son of William de Capella and William de Millatonne, alias Bredlby, gives the 'town of Lewode' in Bridestowe. Lastly, another undated charter mentioning Leawood between Nicola, daughter of Petrille, Lord of Berdeswalle and William, son of Richard of Berdeswalle, shows that the moiety of her lands of Berdeswalle was a 'parcel of the Barton of Lewoode'.

To continue with Josias, we find that he entered Hart Hall, Oxford, on 20 May 1580 aged 15. He was admitted to the Middle Temple in 1584.

Before Josias died on 12 December 1611, aged 46, his wife Katherine gave birth to a daughter and three sons. Son and heir of Josias and Katherine was Sir Shilston Calmady, knight, who was aged 26 at the time of his father's death and who was knighted at Theobalds in 1618, supported the Parliamentarians for whose cause he was slain near Ford Abbey and was buried at Membury on 4 February 1645. It would be easy to sum up Sir Shilston's life in this manner but this would not do him justice as he was an important figure. We can deduce that he was born in about the year 1585 and that he was about 60 at the time of his tragic death. Sir Shilston, like both of his brothers, also married twice. His wives were from well-to-do Devon families who, like himself, were on the side of Cromwell. His first wife, who he married at about the turn of the second decade of the

seventeenth century, was Elizabeth, the daughter of John Coplestone of Warleigh. A report in a local newspaper tells that Miss Calmady-Hamlyn was of the opinion that Sir Shilston's 'first wife planted the lime trees in Bridestowe churchyard'.

After producing three children over four years she died, being buried at Wembury on 28 October 1617. The first child died in infancy and was buried at Bratton Clovelly in 1613. A year later their second child, John, was baptised at Bratton Clovelly. John married Anne Arscott whose family upheld Sir Shilston's views of politics. Their third child, a daughter, Elizabeth, baptised in 1616, was buried at Wembury a year later.

Less than a year after the death of his first wife Sir Shilston married Honor, the daughter of Edmund Fortescue of Fallopit and widow of Humphry Prideaux of Soldon, Holsworthy, the marriage licence being dated 17 September 1618. This union produced four sons and four daughters.

Leawood House, 1860s. (Joan Calmady-Hamlyn)

Amongst the sons were Josias of Langdon, eventual heir, Shilston of Leawood and Francis of Combeshead. Of the daughters, Gertrude, the eldest, who died without issue in 1699 at the age of 77, had married John Arscott of Tetcott whose family supported the Parliamentarian cause. A memorial to Gertrude and her husband lies in the church at Tetcott.

Sara was buried at Bratton Clovelly in 1624 whilst Frances was baptised at Bratton Clovelly on 1 February 1628. Elizabeth, the last daughter, married Sir William Martyn of Oxton. She was buried in the church at Kenton in 1695 where a monument was erected to her memory. The remaining son, Vincent, was baptised on 2 May

1624 at Bratton Clovelly. He became First Captain of Cavalry in Cromwell's army.

On returning to Sir Shilston we find that he was prominent amongst the members of the gentry of Devon. In the name of Charles I, the Commission of the Peace in 1630 named Sir Shilston as being amongst 64 other knights and esquires who were to carry out duties as Justices of the Peace. It must have been from this period onwards that Sir Shilston formed his Parliamentarian views, more of which later. Sir Shilston's position as a Justice of the Peace was to place him in a foremost position with the Parliamentarians, he being numbered amongst such powerful men as the 'Earl of Bedford, the Rolles, the Bamfyldes, the Drakes of Ashe and of Buckland, the Strodes and Northcotes.' Sir Shilston's daughters married prominent Parliamentarians, namely the Fortescues, albeit they were a divided family with some members supporting the King, and the Martyns of Oxton.

Sir Shilston, it appears, attempted to become a Member of Parliament, seeking election for the borough of Okehampton on 27 January 1641. Lawrence Whittaker and Edward Thomas were elected:

... whereupon Sir Shilston Calmady came hither shortly after and endeavoured a new election, and required Mr Mayor to have the Town Seal to seal another indenture which Mr Mayor and the burgesses denyed him, whereupon Sir Shilston delivered some petition to parliament but this was without effect.

Despite his rebuke by the townspeople of Okehampton in 1643 Sir Shilston was appointed a Commissioner for the assessment of Devonshire by Parliament. This office, according to Cotton, was inevitably held by 'political leaders on the parliamentary side'. Sir Shilston Calmady also held other stong Parliamentarian positions. He was Second in Command of the Parliamentary Forces in the West of England; Commissioner to obtain supplies for Devon for the Parliamentarian army; and a member of the Committee of Sequestrators for Devon to carry out an Ordinance passed 1 April 1643. Sir Shilston was not just a committee man, he also took the part of a fighting soldier. Indeed, evidence of his participation on the battlefield is far easier to come by than that of his administrative roles.

Whilst Sir Shilston performed his active role for the Parliamentarian cause, Leawood was, according to Snell, used as a garrison. Despite no strong evidence of this, it seems a likely supposition. What is not so acceptable however is Snell's claim that Leawood was 'the scene of determined fighting during the Civil Wars'.

Our first insight into Sir Shilston's fighting role is portrayed at the Battle of Braddock Down on Bodmin Moor on 19 January 1643. Sir Shilston was with Colonel Ruthin's army when it suffered defeat at the hands of the Royalists. One of the opposing foe, the Royalist, Sir Bevill Grenville, who took part in the battle, wrote to his wife to tell her of the victory and related: 'we have taken 600 prisoners, among them Sir Shilston Calmady is one.' One source tells that amongst the Royalists who crossed Parliamentarian lines to take horses, sheep and oxen, was a 'master Blight the chiefe among the theeves' who, on one occasion whilst partaking in such activities, was captured. The Royalist, on offering 'Sir Shilston Colemady' in exchange for Blight were met with a refusal by the Parliamentarians; to them the arrangement was unacceptable. Whether Sir Shilston would have wished to be exchanged for such a man is a matter of conjecture, nevertheless, he eventually gained his freedom for we once again find him taking part in an action against his enemy, just three months after his capture.

Miss Calmady-Hamlyn gave the following account of Sir Shilston's part in this action which took place at Sourton Down:

At this battle at Sourton Down, Sir Shilston is said to have vanquished one thousand Royalists with his one hundred and eight men. Fog helped and the Royalists fearing vast numbers against them fled to Bridestowe. 'See they run they run' are the words that history puts into Sir Shilston's mouth.

Whether or not Sir Shilston was actually present on Sourton Down or commanded from a distance is not known.

A year later he was apparently in action again for we find that, amongst others, he was party to a letter dated September 1644 to William [?] certifying to the 'gallant conduct' of the Plymouth Regiment 'at the late disaster at Foy'. This letter no doubt refers to an event of 31 August, when the Parliamentarian horse under orders from Essex broke out of the Fowey peninsular after finding themselves penned in by the Royalists. Some five months after his escape from Fowey Sir Shilston was to find himself once again in the thick of an encounter with the opposing foe, but on this occasion his previous good luck was to abandon him. An entry in the register of Membury Parish Church under burials records '1645/6 Sur Shilston Cadlade was buried the IIII day of this instant February'. He had fought his last battle having died in a skirmish at Membury of which 'nothing is known, excepting for the fact that he was killed at the gateway of what is now Ford Farm.'

He was buried in the chancel of the church at Membury where a monument was placed upon the north wall. A shield with the Calmady Arms was placed above the monument. When the vestry was built in 1893 the Calmady monument

Picnic on the moors. Included are: 'Tailor' Cook, Mrs Cook, Hannah Maddaford, Joyce Maddaford; the children are: Marion Maddaford, Ivy Maddaford, ? Towl. (Brian Maddaford)

was moved from the chancel to the Yarty aisle. The inscription has now perished; James Davidson copied it but he apparently mistook the date of death. The inscription reads:

In Memory of Shilston Calmady Knight who dyed
the 13 day of Feby Ano Dom 1645.
This toomb's sublimed to a shrine, and doth containe
An holier saint than could all legends faine
Whose virtues supersede our spice and baulme
Whose name perfumes ye breath yt sounds the same
As when a fly's involved in amber t'were
Less gaine to live than find such sepulchre
So lif's not worth such honor as to have
Fame write his epitaph, hearts afford his grave.

Like many a soldier Sir Shilston lies buried near to the place where he gave his life.

Turning now to Honor his wife we will find that she was baptised on 11 May 1584, being one of eight children born to Edmund Fortescue of Fallopit and his wife Marie, the eldest daughter of Henry Champernon of Motherie. On 30 March 1600 at East Allington Honor – about 16 years old – had taken Humphrey Prideaux of Soldon near Holsworthy, as her husband. He died of smallpox shortly after his fortieth birthday in 1617 and Honor's young offspring were raised by their grandfather, Roger Prideaux of Soldon.

A widow in her early thirties, Honor married Sir Shilston during the year in which he was knighted. We have seen that fate had made her a widow for a second time on his demise. Their children were baptised at Bratton Clovelly, as indeed had the children from Sir Shilston's first marriage. The reason for this may be quite simply that the Calmadys were occupying their seat called Eastlake, which, at that time, lay in Bratton Clovelly but which now lies in the civil parish of Broadwood Widger.

Little is known of Honor other than that she made a gift of plate to the churches of Bratton

Clovelly and Bridestowe. She also seems to have contributed to the church plate of Wembury where a flagon weighing two and a half pounds bears the inscription 'ex dono dominae Honoris Calmady, Ecclesiæ de Wemburge'. Dame Honor Calmady died in her eightieth year on 17 December 1663 and was buried at Bridestowe. The inscription on her memorial to some may appear curious if not bewildering:

To the memory of the Lady Honor Calmady
who departed this life the 17th day of Dec. 1663.
Eight fruitful branches still are springing sound,
Though here the roote lies dead within the ground,
Two husbands in their toombes divided lye
Who both in the bed of Honor dye.
But here the King of Terrors (O unjust!)
At last has lay'd this Honor in the dust,
Till that which here is in dishonour sown
Be rays'd in Honor to a glorious throne.

In her will Honor left 40s. to the poor of Bridestowe and Okehampton, and 20s. to the poor of Sourton and Lydford. To her servants both 'men and maides' she left 10s. apiece.

We return to the three sons of Sir Shilston and Honor, Josias, Francis and Shilston. Josias Calmady of Langdon as the third son was the eventual heir to his father. He was baptised on 10 October 1619 at Bratton Clovelly, matriculated to Exeter College, Oxford, and was admitted to the Middle Temple in 1640. His first wife was Thomasine, the daughter of Sir Richard Buller. Josias married a second time – presumably he had divorced his first wife as he took as his second wife, Elizabeth, daughter of Richard Coffin of Portledge. This second marriage produced four children; tragically they were all doomed to short lives with the longest survivor dying in her very early twenties.

Josias was named as a Justice in the Commission of Peace for 1647. He was thought worthy to be appointed Sheriff of Devon in 1675 but, living 40 miles from Exeter where the assizes were held – and also citing his own corpulance as a hindrance – he chose not to take the post. Further accounts of the ailments that made him unsuitable for Sheriff were presented again in 1676. Strangely, during the year 1660 he was elected as Member of Parliament for Okehampton along with Edmund Wise – and to this position he made no objection. Josias was buried on 15 March 1683 shortly after making his will 7 March 1683.

Francis Calmady of Combeshead, sixth son of Sir Shilston, was baptised on 1 February 1628 at Bratton Clovelly and was buried at Stoke Climsland on 12 October 1704. He married Johanna, the eldest daughter and coheir of Walter Fursland of Bickington. They had seven children. Their eldest son and heir, Francis, married Cecilia,

John Turner, the gardener at Leawood, 1901.
(Joan Calmady-Hamlyn)

the daughter of Warick Pollexfen. The first son and heir to Francis and Cecilia was Francis Vincent Calmady. He was baptised at Stoke Climsland on 20 August 1705. For now we leave this particular line of the Calmadys to whom we will revert later and turn to the remaining son of Sir Shilston and his wife Honor.

Shilston Calmady of Leawood, fourth son to Sir Shilston and Honor, appears to be the first of the Calmadys to have become fully established at the family residence in Bridestowe. Like his brothers and sisters Shilston was baptised at Bratton Clovelly, his baptismal date being 29 April 1621. He went to Exeter College, Oxford, at the age of 16 in 1639 and was admitted to the Middle Temple in 1641.

He married Elizabeth, the eldest daughter of Humphry Gayer seemingly about the year 1654 as in this year he 'gave a fat bullock to the poore people of Okehampton at the time of his marriage'. Shilston followed his family and supported the Parliamentarians, he was listed in the Commission of Peace for the County of Devon in 1653. Shilston was apparently ousted from the 1653 commission but this does not mean that he remained in the background of events during the Civil War; a royal pardon tells us that Shilston, not

unlike his father but perhaps not to the same intensity, must have been at the forefront of Parliamentary matters, political and military.

With the restoration of the monarchy in 1660 Shilston was to find himself in a similar position to that of Henry Bidlake who had been made to pay for supporting the losing side in a war by having his estates sequestrated. His pardon, dated 23 January 1661, tells us that he had been cited for 'involvement in insurrection, conspiracy, criminal malice and robbery during the reign of Charles I' and that the 'restoration of lands, goods and rights' had been granted to him. Shilston died in 1688, his wife having survived him. His will included a request for a meagre burial:

Testator desires his bodye to be laid by his dear wife without any pompe or unnecessarie expences, sadly lamenting the many lamentable irregularies and brutish disorders that most usually attend great funerals, therefore do appointe and order mine to be private and only some bottles of wine and sweete Bisket to be expended in solemnising thereof.

Josias Calmady of Leawood and Langdon, the third son of Shilston and his wife Elizabeth, became the family heir. Josias also went to Oxford but he matriculated to Trinity College at the age of 16 and went on to the Inner Temple in 1676 becoming a barrister. He married twice, his first wife was Elizabeth the eldest daughter of Edward Waldo, knight, of Cheapside and Pinner, Middlesex. Before she died in 1694 Elizabeth presented her husband Josias with four sons and three daughters of whom the third son, Waldo Calmady of Langdon, was baptised 23 February 1690. He too went to Oxford in 1708 attending Christ Church and was admitted to the Inner Temple in 1711. He married Elizabeth the daughter of Richard Doidge of Elfordsleigh on 29 January 1732 at Plympton. Waldo was Sheriff of Devon in 1735. He became the eventual heir to his father and it is apparent from his will that he lived at Leawood, which had been put in trust to Shilston Calmady, kinsman to Waldo the seventh son of Francis and Cecilia. He was buried on 4 December 1755 leaving his wife a widow, she being buried in 1785. The marriage was childless. His will in part reads:

In the Name of God Amen. I Waldo Calmady of Langdon in the County of Devon Esquire being of sound and disposing mind and memory for which I return thanks to Almighty God and seriously considering the uncertainty of death Doe make and publish this my last Will and Testament in manner and form following.

First I give and bequeath to the Parish of Bridestowe twenty pounds for the binding out two poor boys to trades that shall be nominated by him whoever shall be my Heir. Also I give to twenty poor families in the parish... peck Loaf of Wheaten Bread to each family to be nominated by my heir within ten days after my death.

To every other man servant and maidservant living with me at Leawood a guinea to each (Apprentices excepted).

And it is my will and desire that my funeral may be very private and that I may be buried in my brothers grave if conveniently can be.

Josias took as his second wife in 1699 Jane, the daughter of Sir Thomas Rolt of Milton in Bedfordshire. Jane was to outlive her husband Josias; she died aged 92 and was buried at St Mary le Bow, London, in 1756.

Josias held many offices during his lifetime. In 1676 he stood for a successful election as Member of Parliament for Okehampton coming second to Henry Norleigh who had '102 voyces' whilst Josias had 48. It seems Josias lost a vote due to a dispute between the church and borough of Okehampton.

Mr Hussey [the son of the last incumbent] *gave his voyce for Mr Calmady, his voyce was refused because he could not prove his Vicaridge to be within the Borough.*

Josias remained in this office until 1681. He was also a Deputy Lieutenant for the County of Devon; a Commissioner of Shore Inquiry in 1690; a Freeman of Plymouth in 1696; a Deputy Lieutenant of Plymouth in 1701 and was Sheriff of Devon in 1695. From the Devon Militia Officers List for 1697 we find that Josias held the rank of Lt Colonel. The date of Josias's death is unclear although we find that his will was proved 20 November 1714.

Elizabeth, the first daughter and eventual heiress of Josias and Elizabeth, was baptised in 1687. She married John Pollexfen of Mothecombe in 1705, his family surname replaced that of Calmady of Leawood and Langdon. There was an only child from this union, a daughter, Elizabeth, of whom more presently.

Before proceeding any further with the Calmady descent we will return to a great-grandson of Sir Shilston Calmady, namely Shilston, who had had Leawood placed in trust to him by Waldo Calmady. Little is revealed of Shilston until his death when details can be gleaned from his will dated September 1766, which was proved in September 1770. Shilston rewarded 'Leonard and William Gubbins of Bridestowe Gentlemen the sum of Five Guineas each', they, no doubt, being faithful servants to the Calmadys at Leawood. At this point I would wish to argue that the Gubbins family that lie under the gravestones in Bridestowe churchyard are of the stock of these 'gentleman' and not, as some writers would have us believe, of the rogue Gubbins family who lived in the woods of Lydford.

From the will we can probably safely assume that no marriage had taken place. For confirmation of this we turn to Vivian and find that he makes no mention of Shilston having taken a wife. But what of issue? The main body of text

East Bridge cottages and blacksmith's shop, part of the Leawood Estate. (Doug Gale)

Right: *Royal Oak Inn, part of the Leawood Estate.* (Doug Gale)

Below: *Leawood House.* (Doug Gale)

within the will leads us to a Miss Honor Hocking, the daughter of Rebecca Hocking, once of Callington but by this time a shopkeeper in Bridestowe. What, we ask, was the interest in Miss Honor Hocking that particularly led Shilston to leave her benefits which would not in all likeliness have otherwise come her way? Perhaps she was an illegitimate child who took the surname of her mother Rebecca. Was Rebecca a married woman, widowed or single? We can only speculate.

Shilstone's inventory shows that on the farm at Eastlake most of the manual labour was carried out using eight working oxen, each worth around £5. The number of varying cattle amounted to 29, there were 4 horses, 62 sheep and 11 pigs. Grain consisted of oats and wheat whilst hay was stored in three ricks and the hayloft. Deadstock consisted primarily of items for use with the oxen. On the farm at Combebow there was only a pair of oxen but 18 horses. These were all in varying states of health which, sadly, inclined to be of wretchedness with old age. The horses were mainly used in the transport of lime at the quarry in Combebow. Sheep totalled 142 whilst there was one ass.

The part of the inventory concerning Leawood lists the rooms in the house with their contents. We have a dining room, parlour, hall, kitchen, pantry, passage, 'best chamber', closet, middle chamber, lodging room, maid's chamber, 'garrot', staircase, little room and 'apothecaries shop'. Each room had its contents listed along with an estimated value of the same. Whilst deadstock was listed at Leawood no farm animals were shown. The total sum of the goods and chattels valued amounted to just under £540. Taking into account the value of various properties held by Shilston his estate was worth over £2200. A lease dated 1738 names Shilston as an apothecary so

it would seem from his inventory that he was actively engaged in this line of work at Leawood.

Just prior to his death Shilston let part of Leawood. The lease includes a good description of the house:

... the Hall with cellar, the Great Parlour, the Little Parlour, the shop with the two rooms behind it the stair case, Gallery adjoining the hall, one chamber called the Garden Chamber with the Chamber or Garrott over the same, the Dineing Room, the Middle Room or Chamber and the chamber wherein Shilston Calmady usually lyeth.

The lease also includes mention of some of the crops grown and farming methods of the day. Conditions were set within the lease that allowed the inhabitants of Leawood to cope better with everyday life. Water was to be at hand along with provision for wood and furze ricks as well as dung heaps. The brew-house along with the bottle- and wash-houses was to be accessible to the Calmady family. We have mention of a carpenter's shop, a walled garden, a chaise house and a stable. At this time there were quarries and mines on the Leawood property whilst at Combebow there were lime kilns from which the tenant was to draw all the lime for use on the land at Leawood. Hawking, hunting and fishing all took place locally. All in all, the will provides a relatively agreeable and comfortable picture of life for the Calmady family at the end of the seventeenth century. At the time of writing, Leawood house is described as:

... set in an eighteenth-century Park. Plain fronted with a range of one-two-one bays, concealing an older house with two storey wings flanking a courtyard. At the back, very pretty Georgian Gothic windows, Doric porch, and a sixteenth century or earlier doorway. Stables dated 1711 with the Calmady arms and well-preserved interior. A lodge with Gothic glazing.

Donkey and carriage, Leawood House.
(Joan Calmady-Hamlyn)

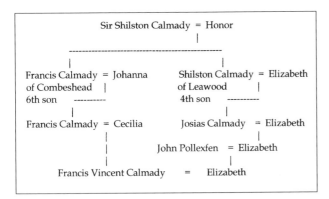

*Lineal descent showing the uniting
of two lines of the Calmady-Hamlyn family.*

To continue the Calmady descent we return to Francis Vincent Calmady of Combeshead, who, upon marriage, united two lines of the Calmady family.

From the section of the family tree shown above (the genealogy that appears on page 45) we can see that Francis Vincent Calmady married Elizabeth, the grand-daughter of Josias and heiress of the elder line of Calmady. The name Calmady now replaced Pollexfen at Leawood. Elizabeth and

Francis had four daughters and an only son, Francis, who died aged 21 childless. Elizabeth was buried at Stoke Climsland in October 1764 whilst Francis died just three months later. He was likewise buried at Stoke Climsland on 23 January 1765. On the death of Francis once again the family name of Calmady associated with Leawood is lost due to the lack of a male heir. Unlike the first occasion when the line continued through a daughter the singular family name of Calmady at Leawood was not to be retained. It did however live on through its use as a Christian name for sons born to the distaffs of the Calmady family.

Elizabeth Mary, the first daughter of Francis and Elizabeth, was baptised on 18 September 1749 at Stoke Climsland. She married Christopher Hamlyn of Paschoe in Bow and it was to him that she carried the Leawood Estate as heiress of the Calmadys. Of the Hamlyns, the Lysons brothers claim that the ancestors of this family who had resided in Exeter as early as the middle of the fifteenth century settled in Paschoe in 1611.

From the marriage of Elizabeth and Christopher came an only son, Calmady Pollexfen Hamlyn, who was born on 18 January 1775. Elizabeth would not see her son grow out of infancy as she died just two years after his birth and was was buried at Colebrook on 12 January

Lodge to Leawood House. (Doug Gale)

King George V rides Arabian Night in London. This horse had been bred at Bidlake Vean by Sylvia Calmady-Hamlyn and was accepted by the King in 1931. (Joan Calmady-Hamlyn)

Sylvia Mary Calmady-Hamlyn aged 11 months, 1882. (Joan Calmady-Hamlyn)

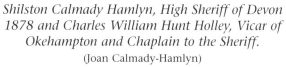

Shilston Calmady Hamlyn, High Sheriff of Devon 1878 and Charles William Hunt Holley, Vicar of Okehampton and Chaplain to the Sheriff. (Joan Calmady-Hamlyn)

1777. Christopher remarried, but his second wife, Frances Marshall, produced no children.

As an attorney Christopher acted for 'Old Uncle Tom Cobley' of the Widecombe Fair folk-song fame. Uncle Tom, who lived at Spreyton to a very old age, went to Christopher at Paschoe to have his will redrawn in January 1787. As Uncle Tom was hard of hearing and his eyesight was failing, Thomas Piercy, clerk to Christopher, wrote the will in rather large writing so that Uncle Tom could read its content himself.

Calmady Pollexfen Hamlyn, son and heir of Christopher Hamlyn, was a Justice of the Peace and a Deputy Lieutenant. He married Fanny Bedford the only daughter of Richard Cross of Duryards near Exeter on 27 June 1805. Calmady died in July 1846, his wife following him to the grave in 1855. They left a surviving son, Shilston Calmady Hamlyn, who was born on 7 November 1811, and two daughters.

Shilston was lord of the manor of Willsworthy, Justice of the Peace, Deputy Lieutenant and was High Sheriff of Devon in 1878. He married Sarah the daughter of Richard Carter of Neston, Cheshire, on 25 March 1841, and the couple had three sons and five daughters. Upon Sarah's death he married Mary the eldest daughter of Commander Charles Hensley in 1859. Shilston died on 7 October 1885.

The third son of Shilston and Sarah, Vincent Waldo Calmady Hamlyn, was born on 6 August 1854. He was educated at Balliol College, Oxford, and gained a Master of Arts degree. Vincent became lord of the manor of Willsworthy, a Justice of the Peace, Barrister at Law (at Lincoln's Inn) and a Captain in the Royal North Devon Yeomanry. In November 1880 he married Emma Josephine the daughter of Sir Joseph Whitwell Pease 1st Bart. of Hutton Lawcross, York. Vincent died on 2 September 1897. From the *Exeter Gazette* of 3 September 1897 we learn the circumstances of his death:

The deceased left his residence (this being Leawood) at about 11 o'clock yesterday morning on horse back, and was riding over a portion of a farm known as Crandford. Hearing some shots fired he dismounted, tied his horse to a gate near the railway, and ran across some rough ground. Before he had gone very far he seems to have fallen, and was found at about 12.30pm lying on his arm dead. Mr Lavis, one of the deceased gentleman's tenants, with his two sons, who were working in an adjoining field, saw the fall, and went immediately to give assistance, but they found him dead. Mr Calmady Hamlyn had of late complained of pains in the region of the heart, and Dr Young, of Okehampton, had been in attendance on him. He was very highly respected by his regiment, in which he proved

himself an excellent officer, and he had the regard of his brother Magistrates, his trained judgement and knowledge of the law being of much value to him on the Bench. He was most popular with his tenantry, and all that knew him held him in great regard. Much of his life was spent in London. But some time since he took up his residence at Leawood with his stepmother, and took a quiet but active part in the affairs in the parishes in which he was interested. In connection with the Diamond Jubilee, he gave to the parish of Sourton a house and land in addition to a handsome donation towards providing a Parish Room and Schools.

Vincent's daughter, Mary Sylvia Calmady-Hamlyn, a Justice of the Peace, assumed the additional name and arms of Calmady by Royal Licence in 1898. She was born on 9 August 1881 and was educated at Wycombe Abbey. Breeding Dartmoor and polo ponies was her life's aim. In 1931 King George V accepted Arabian Night, a skewbald gelding which had been bred at Bridestowe by Sylvia. At the outbreak of war she became one of the initial organisers of the Land Girls. She died unmarried on 10 June 1962 at her home in Buckfastleigh having previously lived at Bidlake Vean, Bridestowe.

Susan Emily, the eventual heiress of the Leawood Hamlyns, married the Revd Charles William Hunt Holley, Vicar of Okehampton, on 12 January 1876. He was the youngest son of James Hunt Holley of Norfolk and Horatia, daughter of

Sylvia Calmady-Hamlyn meets Princess Elizabeth, Newton Abbot, 1952. (Howard Barkell)

Vice Admiral Windham, also of Norfolk. He was educated at Uffculme and Oriel College, Oxford, was ordained Deacon in 1870 and Priest in 1871 becoming the Vicar of Okehampton in 1872. Upon his death in May 1891 the Reverend Holley was buried at Okehampton. His widow assumed by Royal Licence the surname and arms of Hamlyn in 1902 and later assumed the additional surname of Calmady by deed poll.

The couple had three sons and two daughters. The first son Francis Calmady was born in February 1877 but died just prior to his first birthday. The third son Lancelot Pollexfen was born in June 1887 and died in September of that year. The first daughter Gertrude Mary died in 1928, whilst the second, Honora Cecilia, married in 1909 Major John Colquhoun Walford. He died on 5 May 1953 and his wife died shortly after on 15 June of the same year. The remaining son, Charles Hamlyn Hunt Calmady-Hamlyn, became heir to the family on the death of his mother in 1936.

Major Charles Hamlyn Hunt Calmady-Hamlyn TD, of Leawood and Paschoe, the second son, was born on 25 November 1880. He was educated at Exeter School followed by Trinity College, Oxford, gaining his Bachelor of Arts in 1903 and a Master of Arts in 1910. He was a Justice of the Peace in 1912; served with the EEF, in the First World War; enlisted in the North Devon Hussars; was Joint Master of the Tetcott Foxhounds; lord of the manor of Willsworthy; Patron, with his mother, of the living of Okehampton; Deputy Ruling Councillor of the Primrose League, Okehampton Habitation; Vice President of the Tariff Reform League, Exeter Branch; Clubs: New Oxford and Cambridge, Pall Mall, London.

He married Grace, the youngest daughter of the Reverend Sabine Baring-Gould of Lewtrenchard, on 16 July 1913. The Revd Baring-Gould, so Hoskins informs us 'was one of the last of the "squarsons," a hymn writer, theologian, antiquary, novelist, and musician, who published over a hundred volumes.' The hymn 'Onward Christian Soldiers' is perhaps a lasting epitaph in which Baring-Gould is remembered, but to Devonians he should be renowned for his great interest in Dartmoor and all matters relating to the West Country. In between his various activities, however, he found the time to father a large family.

Whilst serving as a Lieutenant in the North Devon Hussars we find that Major Calmady-Hamlyn was a man of poetic bent. From an extract quoted by Freeman from the Royal North

The Lavis clan (Leawood tenants) at a wedding party at Crandford. (Brian Lavis)

Devon Hussars Fine Book we learn that Second Lt. Calmady-Hamlyn was fined £1 for wearing his spurs upside down. He wrote:

Halt, stranger! Ere you pass me by
And o'er these pages cast your eye!
Can I stand by and see you sink
While yet you're trembling on the brink?

No! I'll extend a helping hand
And draw you safely to the strand!

But, first of all, observe with care
The precepts that I've set down here.

Take your life easy while you may!
(This training is a holiday!)
Don't get up till you feel inclined.
Your squadron leader will not mind!!

Shirk all the drill that you well can!
(The Major is a kindly man.)

When out on squadron drill you find
That somehow you've been left behind,
Don't with others try to keep,
But light your pipe and go to sleep.
Cast care aside! Away with fear!
(The Adjutant is nowhere near!!)

Again. When R-b-rts comes to view
If you all earn your weekly screw
Don't slave like some benighted Turk
Doing your own (and others') work,
But chat with-Daphne-in the shade
(Until you see that lunch is laid).

Others will dub you rude and rough,
Your language coarse, your manner gruff,
By all you'll be condemned as low,
Even your friends will quickly go.
But still this course should be pursued
Conscious of moral rectitude!

No matter if the vulgar crowd
Proclaim their thoughts in accents loud.
This will be pardoned, this condoned
And-'for that fault he has atoned.'
In peace at night you'll always sleep
If you one single rule will keep!

In short, break every sacred rule!
In every known way play the fool!
With careless aim the marker shoot
At harmless yeoman fling your boot!
BUT-when you breakfast, dine or sup
BE SURE your spurs are right side up.

Grace presented her husband with one son and one daughter before she died 23 July 1948. Major Calmady-Hamlyn died on 26 October 1963. Their daughter, Cecily Christine, was born in June 1914 and married Paul Furnivall Lambert. Lieutenant Colonel Vincent Warwick Calmady-Hamlyn, heir of Charles and Grace, was born on 5 December 1915. He was educated at Cheltenham and at the Royal Military College, Sandhurst. He was later commissioned into the Royal Sussex Regiment and served in Palestine between the years 1936 and 1939. He also saw service in the Middle East, during which time he was mentioned in despatches, and finally in India where he received the Independence Medal. His main interest was in horses, as had been the case with his father. He took up steeple chasing and played polo, his club was Delhi Gymkhana. He was also a Master of the Delhi and Meerut Hunts.

He retired from the Army in 1951 whereupon he returned to Leawood and followed with family tradition by taking a role in local administration. He was Chairman of the Bridestowe Parish Council; a member of the Rural Council for the Okehampton District representing Bridestowe; a Governor of the Okehampton Schools; a Parochial Church Councillor for Bridestowe; the Patron of the living of Okehampton Parish Church; and District Commissioner of the Lamerton Hunt Pony Club.

He married first, on 25 January 1945, Marguerite Kilmeny Sarah, only daughter of Lieutenant Colonel Percy Calvert Lord Bey, OBE, Royal Engineers and Chief Engineer of the Sudan Government Railways. This marriage, from which there were no children, was dissolved by divorce in 1957. Vincent Warwick married Madeleine Joan, the only daughter of Henry Albert Moulden of New Malden Surrey, on 20 November 1958.

There were two daughters from this second marriage. The eldest, Laura Dawn, born in April 1960, married Peregrine Leigh in June 1992. The second, Angela Grace, born July 1961, married Brian Preston Claud Coward in June 1992.

Vincent Warwick Calmady-Hamlyn died on 6 November 1993. His funeral took place on 11 November at the Parish Church where many of his ancestors were laid to rest. Bridestowe church became once more of service to a member of a family associated with it for over 400 years. With this epitaph not only do we lament the personal end of a life but perhaps also the demise of a long-standing name.

It must be true to say that there cannot be many families living today within a radius of several miles of Leawood who can claim such a coeval history as we have seen with the Calmady-Hamlyns, with whom blue blood arrived in the village of Bridestowe.

Above: *The Delhi Hunt at one of its last hunts before disbandment, 1948. The Master, Major V.W. Calmady-Hamlyn is on the light horse to the right of the pack of hounds.* (Joan Calmady-Hamlyn)

Below: *Charles Calmady-Hamlyn.* (Joan Calmady-Hamlyn)

Right: *Charles Hamlyn Hunt Holly (note his dress) aged 22 months, 1882.* (Joan Calmady-Hamlyn)

Top Right: *Calmady-Hamlyn family graves, Bridestowe churchyard, c.1990.* (Susan Cann)

Right: *Captain Vincent Warwick Calmady-Hamlyn.* (Joan Calmady-Hamlyn)

SURNAMES LINKED WITH BRIDESTOWE

Exeter's receiver for the year 1357/8 was one Nicholas de Bridestowe. Receivers often became mayors and Nicholas de Bridestowe was to wait only six years before his appointment to that very position, in which he remained for the period 1364–7. Martin Battishull became receiver for the year 1365/6 and the Mayor in 1369/70. The receiver of Exeter was a steward who had financial responsibility for the civic funds whilst the Mayor had authority for making decisions as chief citizen of the city.

Both men were connected with Bridestowe but we need to look at family surnames to see how the connection is verified. It was in the eleventh century that surnames first began to be used in this country, particularly amongst the upper class. The middle and lower classes, however, adopted this method of family recognition a few centuries later. Surnames generally fall into four categories:

1. Ancestral, derived from a parent or ancestor.
2. Locative, indicating place of birth or family residence.
3. Occupative, indicating office or employment.
4. Descriptive, including nicknames.

From a document dated 11 October 1358 Michael atte Mede, the son and heir of John atte Mede, granted to Nicholas Brittestouwe called Taverner of Exeter and Agnes his wife, a tenement in 'Smythen Streete in the back of la Heyscheffolde next to the entry to the Heschfold'. The Mayor's Court Roll of 1364 describes Nicholas de Bridestowe as 'Nicholas Tavener' whilst the receivers Roll gives him as 'Nicholas de Brittestowe'. From this we have an innkeeper at Exeter who was a member of a Bridestowe family.

During his period of mayorship Nicholas took an active role in a dispute between the citizens of Exeter and the Dean and Chapter of the Cathedral over the right of the latter to 'hold a view of frankpledge in St Sidwell's fee'. Upon being granted a hearing over the dispute the Dean and Chapter made allegations that upon the justices coming to hold the assizes:

Nicholas de Britstowe, mayor of Exeter, caused proclamation to be made throughout the town (sic) commanding all and singular the inhabitants thereof to shut their doors, furnish themselves with arms and armour, and come with power before the said justices to hinder the execution of the said writ, that great numbers of them so arrayed and furnished assembled, ran by the streets and repaired into the presence of the said justices, so grievously threatening the said dean and chapter and the jurors of the said inquisition that they dared not come before the justices the dean and chapter to sue and the jurors to acknowledge the truth, and so the business remained undone.

Nicholas however was cleared of this allegation. He is mentioned in the Receiver's Accounts of Exeter where in the year 1351/2, under allowances, 40s.0d. had been paid for the 'amercement of Nicholas Brittestouwe'. The entry however had been crossed through.

As for Martin Battishull (Battishill in Bridestowe) he filled a position in the Exeter administration as a clerical assistant in the law department. Some records describe him as 'Martin Clericus' (or le Clerc) while in others he is listed as Martin de Battishulle. It seems that Martin may have been a man of means as the following extracts from the Exeter City archives show.

On 19 October 1367 Joan (who was the wife of Richard Braylegh) granted in perpetuity to Martin Batteshull and Meralda his wife, a tenement in the High Street (of Exeter) between the tenement of Clarice Plente on the east and the said Martin's tenement on the west. From a grant dated 29 January 1371 we learn of a tenement belonging to Martin situated in North Street whilst in the same year we find a shop in the High Street being leased to Martin and his wife Meralda. In 1392 Alice, who was the wife of John Nymet of Exeter, leased to Meralda Batteshulle two shops in the High Street situated between the entrance to the messuage of the said Meralda on the west, the tenement of John Talbot on the east, the High Street on the south and a cellar of Meralda on the north for the term of a life and the rent of a red rose. Martin is also mentioned in the Exeter Receiver's Accounts where he received various amounts of money going about his duties.

Other people living in Exeter described as 'of Bridestowe' were Matthew de Bryttestowe, a skinner mentioned in a release of 7s.0d. of rent arising from a piece of land near the road to Polleslo, dated January 1273/4. Matthew de Brittestowe, who was probably the same Matthew as above, is mentioned in a grant for a tenement called La Crofte without the Eastgate dated 1307. Jordan de Brittistowe was mentioned in a memoranda dated 1302–4(?) whereby Stephen de London had given Jordan a tenement. Isobel Brydestowe appears in 1327 as wife of Jordan de Brydestowe, Clerk.

SOURCES

Baring-Gould, S. Revd, *Devonshire Characters. Book of the West.*

Devon and Cornwall Notes and Queries, Vol. VIII, IX Part 2, XI., XVII., XX., XXI.

Devon and Cornwall Record Society.

Receivers Accounts of Exeter 1304–53.

Crown Pleas of The Devon Eyre 1238, No. 632.

Feet Of Fines, County of Devon 1311, No. 987.

Devon Notes and Queries Vol. III.

Devon Record Office:

Calendar of Deeds and Documents in Exeter City Library. (A number of documents were used from this source).

189M. The Wollocombes of Bridestowe.

1292M. The Calmady-Hamlyns of Bridestowe.

Freeman, B., *The Yoemanry of Devon.*

Horrox, R., *Richard III, A New Study.*

Lysons, D. and S., *Magna Britannia Vol. VI,* Devonshire.

Notes and Gleanings Vol. V.

Reynolds, H., *The Diocese of Exeter.*

Rowse, R.L., *Tudor Cornwall* (1969 Edition).

Transaction of the Devonshire Association. (Numerous volumes have been consulted).

Vivian, Col., *The Visitations of the County of Devon.*

Walrond, H., *Historical Records of the 1st Devon Militia.*

Westcote, T., *A View of Devon in 1630* (1845 Edition).

West Devon Record Office.

Acc. 372 (The Calmady Manuscripts).

West Country Studies Library Exeter.

Burnett Morris Index.

White's Directory of Devonshire, 1850.

Williams, B.H., *Ancient Westcountry Families, Vol. 1.*

Chapter 3

INFRASTRUCTURE

HOUSING

Upon taking up the living of Bridestowe the Reverend Coryndon Luxmore built at his own expense houses in the village of Bridestowe for the 'occupation of the labouring poor who most frequently apprentice out their children at eight or nine years of age.' An undated letter of his explains why he did this:

I had no conception of the real situation and distress of the poor, till I settled here with Mrs Luxmore in 1792. I soon perceived that in consequence of several houses belonging to small farms being suffered to become ruinous, the poor were distressed for habitations, and were obliged to herd together in a manner both destructive to morality and delicacy; and determining to obviate this defect, as far as my small ability would allow of immediately began the work and where two dwellings originally stood, I have erected twelve cottages, taken down two others (not habitable), to the ground, and entirely rebuilt them, and am now preparing to take down three others, to rebuild them all this season. Nine of the cottages form a row on the right hand side of the turnpike road leading to Falmouth, and were built previous to the building of the row on the opposite side.

As my idea was to accommodate those only who depended on their daily labour for support, and whose children are generally apprenticed by the overseers of the poor, and sent from their parents care at ten years of age or under, I conceived that no evil could arise from each house being accommodated with one bed room, and the children sleeping in the same with their parents; but, in so much request were these cottages, that they became tenanted by

The New Bridestowe Cottages.

those whose industry kept them from the necessity of apprenticing their children; and I soon perceived that the want of a second bed room was a great evil. This, in the last erected cottages I have corrected, and, instead of a lean to, have made a double roof, by which means the back upper room is a comfortable bed room. Each of the cottages is let for one shilling per week, and I adopt this mode, that I may instantly remove a disorderly tenant. My agreement is, that as long as they frequent the church, and behave themselves soberly, and carefully, and as good neighbours to each other, I will not remove anyone from the dwelling.

Coryndon Luxmore makes the situation perfectly clear as to the condition of housing in Bridestowe but what is not clear is the year in which the cottages were constructed. Taking into account that he settled in the village in 1792 and Vancouver's report on Devon to the Board of Agriculture – this contained conditions of housing – was published in 1808, we have a span of 16 years in which to place the building of the new homes for the poor. It is thought that they may have been built in Fore Street close to Church Gate but of this we cannot be sure.

The construction of the cottages was fully detailed by Luxmore:

... the first range of these buildings were constructed uniform, and nearly in the following manner: room below, sixteen feet square, one door and one window in front; fireplace with an oven opening into it with a flue; door opening back into a shed or lean-to, for covering fuel, labourer's tools, shelter for a pig, &c.;

Right: *The Retreat.* (Doug Gale)

Left: *Granny Kent at the 'stable door' of Poole Hill Cottages.* (Doug Gale)

Mrs Allen and children at Great Crandford Cottages. (Brian Lavis)

Mrs Bessie Ball at the Poole Hill Tea Rooms. (Sam Ball)

another door from this lean-to opens into a small back yard, fenced off from a small garden attached to each tenement; under the stairs in the front room, leading to a bed room, is a pantry fitted up with shelves; opposite to the fireplace, over which there is a mantle piece, a sort of dresser is fastened to the wall with shelves, and these constitute the fixtures in the room below. The bedroom above is the same size as the room below. The walls of the first eight feet of these cottages are built with stone, the super-structure with cob, covered with a slate roof, and cost, upon an average, when finished in a plain and useful manner, from 38s.0d. to 40s.0d. each. The slate costs 10s. per thousand; a quantity fully suffi-cient for the making of a square of ten feet; the slate is bought rough at the quarry, and fashioned after-wards: one cartload, or ten horse loads, of stones, will build a perch and a half of wall, 20 inches thick; three cart loads of clay are required for an equal portion of cob wall; eight bundles, or one horse load of straw, is mixed and tempered with nine cart loads of clay, and consequently equal to the building of 4½ perch of cob of nearly the same thickness as the wall below. When the wall is 16 feet high, of stone only, the mason's demand is 2s. per perch of 16½ feet; if stone, 8 feet, and cob 8 feet, 1s.10d. per perch; if cob only, 1s.6d. per perch. In all cases, it is supposed that the materials are laid down in the rough, for the masons to dress and temper, and serve themselves. Four Winchester bushels of lime are used for every perch of stone wall: the lime ash floor below costs 6d. in the square yard, tempering and laying down; and the floor above is made of rack deal, or any soft wood plank most convenient to be procured. As I make but very little use of my carriage, I employ my horses in drawing clay and stone at their leisure, by which means the expense becomes more moderate and I keep a mason and carpenter regularly employed throughout the year.

As the rent for each cottage was one shilling per week and if we divide that into the cost of the building of the cottages, we can conclude that the Reverend Coryndon Luxmore had a quick return on his outlay. Leaving the finances to one side his parishioners, it might be said, were lucky, for Vancouver described a typical house within an area around Bridestowe as consisting of 'three mud walls and a hedge-bank' which formed 'the habitation of many of the peasantry'.

The new houses built by Coryndon Luxmore, along with existing properties, made up a total of 91 houses in the village, of which 7 were vacant and the other 84 occupied by 98 families. These fami-lies in all totalled 289 males, 292 females (including children), of which 111 were in agriculture, 16 in manufacture and 454 in various forms of employ-ment. The population of Bridestowe at this time, being the year 1801, was 581. There were just under seven people per household.

Barley, bread and potatoes composed a large part of the diet of the general population. Wheat broth seasoned with a small piece of meat and pot herbs, formed – along with pies made of bacon and potatoes – the mainstay of the local diet.

At this time 'the country bordering upon Dartmoor' was to be 'found to carry the human frame to greater longevity and health of age, than [was] the case in some other parts of the county.' During the year 1805 with the population of Bridestowe still standing at about 580, there were 'ten deaths of which three were infants whilst the remainder were respectively 63, 64, 69, 73, 75, 78, 84 and 89 years of age.' (This would indicate 11 deaths but I have followed Vancouver here.) Even though the people of Bridestowe at this time lived a very hard and distressing life, particularly if poor, they did, in the main, achieve a remarkably good lifespan.

Another form of housing was 'squatting' but unlike his modern day counterpart, who takes over living accommodation already in existence, the squatter of the early-nineteenth century was industrious. He built his own home on land that appeared to him to have been of no use to the owner. Squatter's cottages were built using traditional methods and they were generally placed beside a road in a narrow enclosure taken in from the roadside verge.

Such a cottage was built possibly in the mid-1850s during the population explosion at Bridestowe at the height of the mining and lime-quarry industries. Just down from the Okehampton side of the Fox and Hounds on the Tavistock Road the ruins of this cottage lies in vast undergrowth, no longer noticeable from the road.

The cottage, being very small and simple, was only 15ft 6in by 15ft 3in externally, there being one room up and one room down. There was a fireplace but no decorative features. The west wall was of stone only to the first floor level with stud and plaster above the sidewalls that were carried on slightly. It was in occupation up to the 1960s and was known as the 'salt box'. It is said that if built in a night with the roof on and a fire in the hearth, the builder had a right to remain where he was (see also *The Book of Widecombe in the Moor: Uncle Tom Cobley and All*). At first a simple hut may have been put up perhaps consisting of sticks and turf and, once accepted, replaced with a stone-and-cob structure.

Sam, Hubert and Bessie Ball at the Poole Hill Tea Rooms. (Sam Ball)

Bridhayes Water Supply. (Susan Cann)

Left: *Water Supply to right of Royal Oak Annex.* (Susan Cann)

Bottom Left: *Poole Hill standpipe (to the left of tea rooms)* (Susan Cann)

Below: *School standpipe.* (Alan Pearn)

BRIDESTOWE WATER WORKS

At a meeting of the Parish Council held on 22 July 1895 it was proposed to break through the rocks at Bridhayes to provide a new water supply to the village, its existing supply presumably being only rudimentary. During the meeting it was also decided to form a committee to preside over the new water supply with the undertaking to request a sum of £10 from the District Council to be put towards the cost of the work involved.

A month later it was decided that the water supply at Bridhayes would be sufficient for the village needs and it was proposed to bring water from the Bridhayes well to the village. The Calmady-Hamlyn family was to be approached for permission to lay iron pipes from the new water source to a reservoir at the back of the well. To help fund the water works the parish was canvassed for subscriptions and the commoners were asked to make a grant from the commons fund.

Mr Samuel Weeks was instructed to prepare plans and specifications along with an estimate for laying drains and other necessary work to carry water through the village for a fee of £2. Tenders to be submitted by 31 October 1895 were invited to carry out the work as specified in Mr Weeks's plans. Frederick Dawe's tender of £98.15s. was to be accepted provided that he agreed to employ as far as possible Bridestowe workmen. Mr Dawe duly signed a contract and Mr Weeks was appointed as clerk of works at a salary of seven and a half per cent of the tender. The Chairman of the Parish Council was empowered to act as the treasurer of the water works.

Initially, standpipes were erected in the village, but on 23 December 1895 private householders were permitted to tap into the mains water supply. Along with this luxury came certain conditions which had to be met. The user could tap into the water main provided that: it was at his own cost; the water was to be used as a source for drinking water only; a stopcock was placed between the water mains and the exterior of a dwelling and Parish Council officials to have control of the stopcock; the user was to be responsible for any repairs, which became necessary to their pipes and taps; the pipe connected to the water mains was to be laid not less than two feet below the surface of the ground.

Further work was carried out to develop the new water supply in Bridhayes Field. At this time a tap, sink and drain were installed in the schoolyard whilst beneath the eastern standpipe a stone was laid across the gutter and pavement.

With defects in workmanship corrected the Parish Council then took over the water supply during May 1896. Mr Weeks became superintendent of the works at a salary of £1.5s. per annum. A man was to be employed to work on the drain running through the village.

From the time at which the Parish Council took control of the water works ongoing entries in their minute-books relating to the water supply appear. Notices were issued in June 1897 offering a reward of £1 for such information that would lead to the conviction of the person who had removed the tap from the standpipe in the Okehampton Road.

In May 1899 Mr Weeks continued in the post of superintendent at a salary of £1.5s. He stayed in this position for a number of years but it seems he lost interest in his work because a committee was set up in August 1901 to ensure that any necessary work in connection with the water supply 'was properly carried out by Mr Weeks'. A year later he was asked to see to the repair of the leakage in the school water pipes at the first opportunity.

During June 1906 the Bible Christian Chapel was granted permission to tap into the mains water supply in Station Road. They were bound to the terms as mentioned for private householders.

Commencing January 1907 all households with private taps were to pay 2s.6d. a year for the privilege of having the use of running water in their homes. It seems further improvements in the water supply to the village were going to take place that year as Mr Weeks was asked to prepare an estimate to bring water from the chapel pipe to the Launceston Road.

Bridestowe Water Works appears to have been a successful operation, as testified by a letter dated 14 January 1923 regarding a sewerage scheme. In part we learn that the general health of the village was good and that there had been no outbreak of epidemic disease since the water supply was installed in 1894. The existing system had the advantage of being flushed by a never-failing supply of water. The Council had received no complaints about the system.

At a Council meeting in June 1936 the Chairman and Clerk of the Rural District Council discussed with the sanitary inspector a new water and sewerage system that was later installed. It seems the new system was not enjoyed by all as 'some houses were still not connected to the water supply by 1940.' The RDC was asked how long it would be 'before a householder would be compelled to do so?'

An outbreak of poliomyelitis began in Bridestowe on 12 June 1949. There were 13 notified cases of which one died, two were classed as handicapped and six retained muscular weakness. Following the outbreak 18 houses not connected to the sewer had closets with water supplies installed.

TWO BRIDGES

The Calmady-Hamlyn family papers reveal a legal case concerning the construction of bridges, dated December 1829:

In the County of Devon and between Okehampton and Launceston is situated a village called Bridestowe thro' which runs the Great Western or Mail Coach Turnpike Road from Exeter to Falmouth. At the two extreme ends of this village run two small streams or Rivulets across this Turnpike Road, over which no sort of Bridge whatever was ever erected, except a small one at one end for the accommodation of foot passengers only, and which in this County is commonly distinguished by the name of Clapper and consists of two flat pieces of Granite wide enough for foot passengers only which is shown in the annexed plan. These streams are in general very shallow, seldom more than four or six inches in depth at any part of it, but when of course a flood does take place, this depth is increased but never to such a degree to render the passage through them of any difficulty. The only case where any difficulty of passing can arise is in the event of a severe frost, when if these Rivulets become frozen, there must exist particularly with carriages, great difficulty of passage until the ice is broken and removed, and some inconvenience may also arise to Horses in frost, from the frozen state of the edges of these streams which have been covered by the water in its current. This road has run through the Village of Bridestowe for a great number of years and the Mail Coach has passed over it for these forty years past, and consequently

Above:
Clapper Bridge behind Sporting Green, 1920s.
(Doug Gale)

Right:
West Bridge.
(Author)

East Bridge. (Susan Cann)

What's this then? A horse-less carriage outside the Royal Oak. (Alan Pearn)

the road in question has become one of consequence, but during which all time these two streams or Rivulets have always been in their present state, and if any change had taken place in them, it has been for the better. No complaint has ever been made respecting these Rivulets until very lately, although the mail and other coaches have been running over the road, and through these streams for forty years past or before as stated. The turnpike Road which runs through the Village of Bridestowe and which I have denominated the Great Western Road belongs exclusively to the Trustees of the Okehampton Trust, and who exercise over it an exclusive jurisdiction by collecting the Tolls upon it, letting the same to contractors to repair etc, and the Parish of Bridestowe do not now pay even a composition towards the maintenance of this part of the road which runs through the Parish in consequence of the income arising from the Tolls having been found equal to the expenditure. The part of this road which is within the Jurisdiction of and belongs to the Okehampton Trust commences several miles before it reaches Bridestowe, and terminates about a mile and a half below it. Below the Village of Bridestowe, but within the parish, there also runs another small stream of water called Stone Buddle, across that part of the road which is within the Jurisdiction of the

Okehampton Trust, and over which the Okehampton Trust at their sole expense some few years since erected a small bridge or Culvert. The stream previous to the erection of the Bridge or Culvert in question was in every respect similar to those now running thro' the Village of Bridestowe, except that it was not quite so wide or deep, though certainly as easy of passage through it, and equally as liable to inconvenience to Horses and Carriages in case of severe frost.

The outcome of the situation was that bridges were erected over the two rivers in question. Details such as when and whether the parish or the Trust built the bridges and at what cost are not readily available, the Okehampton Turnpike Trust papers having been destroyed shortly after that body expired. It seems that they were stored in Okehampton Church when it was destroyed by fire in 1842. Neither has anything been discovered from the records of Quarter Sessions. The two bridges are clearly marked on the Tithe Map of 1844 leaving a gap of 14 years during which time they must have been built. Turning to the attached 'annexed plan' of Bridestowe Village as mentioned, we find that the clapper or footbridges were on the same side of the road as the Royal Oak and White Hart Inn.

ROADS

The Romans were perhaps the first people to improve lines of communication by constructing a road from Exeter that went around to the north of Dartmoor by way of North Tawton, Okehampton and Sourton Down, leading westwards into Cornwall. As mentioned previously the site of a Roman road was found at Bridestowe. Once the Romans left Britain no attempts were made to make solid roads for wheeled traffic. Any repair of the roads was apparently left to chance with the Monasteries doing most of the repairs. There was no general authority requiring repairs to be made or for raising the necessary money to carry out repairs. Lords of the manor were ordered

to keep roads open by King Stephen between 1135 and 1154.

In 1239 the Statute of Winchester was passed. It provided that all highways leading from one market town to another should be enlarged where bushes, wood, or dykes stood in the way, to prevent there being 'dyke nor bush, wherein a man may lurk to do hurt, within 200 feet on the one side and 200 feet on the other side of the way.' This Statute was passed to protect travellers against highwaymen.

The responsibility for the maintenance of roads was placed upon the parish as a whole and every inhabitant thereof by a Statute of Philip and Mary

Above: *Snow-clearing gang below Blackabroom after the 1927 blizzard. At rear: Arnold Cole;*
left to right: Dick King, John Pellow, Margaret Soper, Mr Wickett, Mr Coleman, Charlie Brendon,
Bill Shaddick, Bill Hellier, John Orchard. (Howard Barkell)

Below: *Ern Barkell sitting proudly in his Model T Ford, one of the first cars in Bridestowe, c.1920.*
This car and those that followed were used in a busy taxi service.
(Howard Barkell)

passed in 1555. Every year a parish surveyor was to be elected, but was not paid a salary. The parishioners were called upon for personal services and not for any monetary payment, this being later referred to as Statute Labour. The elected parish surveyors appear to have been the first local government officers appointed under Statute.

An Order of Sessions dated 1637 concerning the roads in Okehampton – and it is assumed that Bridestowe suffered many of the same problems – provides a valuable insight into the conditions of roads at that time as well as the problems experienced in connection with their upkeep:

An outing to Exmouth by charabanc. (George Lavis)

By reason of sundry greate showers of rayne fallinge on the hilly wayes and rayne water standinge in divers partes of the said parish the said highwayes often neede repayre, and the repaires thereof are within short time after frett and washt away; and that many places of the said highwayes of late have been and now are pitched by workeman of skill, and raine water turned and to be often turned, and other pitchinge and pavements to be made to prevent the frettinge and washinge away by reason of the suddaine raynes that fall on the hilly wayes.

In another Order of Sessions we find that bridges were also to be kept in good repair; we have, among others, Sir Shilston Calmady JP being ordered to inspect Hayne bridge in the hundred of Lifton and also 'to enquire who was responsible for its statutory repair.' Once identified, the liable persons were 'then to take speedy course for repairing the bridge.'

In 1663 the first Turnpike Act in England came into force, although turnpikes did not become commonplace until the early part of the eighteenth century. Groups of landowners and businessmen cooperated to maintain and improve roads in their own localities. They put their own money into the roads and recouped their investment by levying tolls at tollgates or turnpikes. In 1871 nearly all turnpikes were abolished. The main highway through Bridestowe came under the Okehampton Turnpike Trust. An Act in 1760 authorised the repair of:

... the roads leading from Crockerton Well in the Parish of Cheriton Bishop... thence through the Parishes of Okehampton, Sourton and Bridestowe to Coombe Bowbridge in the parish of Bridestowe aforesaid, and from a place called Haleys House (Sourton

Cross) in the road aforesaid in the said Parish of Sourton, through the Parishes of Sourton, Bridestowe, and Lydford [which] are very ruinous and cannot be amended by the Ordinary Course of Law.

This Act provided for the appointment of trustees to carry out the necessary work, the raising of money, the levying of tolls, the erection of toll-gates, the power to take materials, the making of causeways, the erection of bridges, the measuring of roads, as well as the erection of mile-posts. The work began in Okehampton and gradually progressed further afield.

The next Act to concern any traveller on his way to Bridestowe was the cost of travelling on turnpike roads, which was to go up. An Act of 1829 decreed:

That all his Majesty's Justices of the peace acting for the County of Devon for the time being, together with [at this juncture many names are mentioned, those familiar to Bridestowe being Calmady Pollexfen Hamlyn, John Gubbins Newton and the Reverend Coryndon Luxmore] being duely qualified to act as Trustees of Turnpike roads, should be Trustees for amending, altering, and improving the said roads, and for otherwise putting the Act into execution.

The trustees were well chosen as the Okehampton Turnpike Trust was one of comparatively few that paid off all its debts and improved the roads. Section 29 of the Act of 1829 concerned various tolls:

For any horse, or any other beast drawing a coach, stagecoach, berlin, landau, barouch, chariot, chaise, chaise-marine, chair, curricle, phaeton, calash, sociable, car, gig, caravan, van, hearse, or litter, the sum of sixpence.

For every horse, or any beast, drawing any wagon or other such four-wheeled carriage, or any cart or other such two-wheeled carriage, the sum of sixpence.

For any horse, mule, ass, laden or unladen, the sum of one penny halfpenny.

For any ox, cow, or head of neat cattle, the sum of one halfpenny.

For every calf, sheep, swine, or lamb, the sum of one farthing.

Due to the vein of limestone, which ran almost parallel to the roads from Drewsteignston to

Top left: *At the filling station. Are you sure that you have filled the tank? Hubert Ball with nozzle in hand, c.1935.* (Sam Ball)

Top right: *Dr Barbara Moore being cheered on by the school children on her way from John O' Groats to Lands End. Late 1950s.* (Alan Pearn)

Above: *Some more distance walkers.* (Alan Pearn)

Above left: *Do we need mounting steps to get in to the car?* (Doug Gale)

Left: *Bridestowe Railway Station, 1920s.* (Alan Pearn)

Combebow Bridge and beyond, a large quantity of lime was being carried on the Trust's roads at the time of the 1829 Act. Section 11 of the Act stated:

that no toll shall be taken for or in respect of any horses, beasts, or cattle drawing any wagon, cart, or other carriage, employed in carrying or conveying, or going empty to fetch, carry, or convey, or returning from carrying or conveying on the same day any lime to be used for manure.

To enlarge on the first Act of 1760 we find that the Tavistock road left Okehampton by way of Shobhill, past the present turning to Holsworthy then direct to Meldon and on to Sourton Down. The road proceeded through Sourton to Pigsleg Corner (where the road to Bridestowe which was possibly authorised by the Turnpike Act of 1829 turns off to the right) past the Fox and Hounds Hotel, over Veal Down to the 'End of Okehampton Trust' stone at Down Town Cross Lanes.

The Launceston road was effected by the Local Turnpike Act of 1832, which authorised the mending, altering, turning, widening, improving, and keeping in repair, the road from Okehampton to the 'End of Okehampton Trust' stone at Combebow Bridge in the parish of Bridestowe.

The 'King Way', a very early trackway found within the Bridestowe and Sourton Common Lands on the edge of Dartmoor, at one time linked Okehampton to Tavistock. According to Hemery 'it is so named because the King's Mail was always taken that way (between the two towns) before the regular postal service began.'

Probably being of medieval origins the King Way appears to have left the line of the old A30

A 1926 Bullnose Morris known as a 'Doctor's Coupe'. The first car belonging to the Lavis family at Great Crandford. (George Lavis)

road south-west of Okehampton leading up to Meldon Hamlets. The track proceeded to the open moor between Corn Ridge and Sourton Tors. It then passed to the west of Great Nodden and continued to Nodden Gate where it went on to cross the River Lyd. Beyond this point the old route seems to be traced by the modern road to Tavistock. The King Way was probably in use until 1817, at which time the new road between Okehampton and Tavistock was constructed.

The name 'King Way' appears on the Sourton Tithe Map of 1844. Looking at a modern-day Ordnance Survey map the name 'King's Wall' is used to describe an 'ancient wall of orthostats and boulders backed by an earthen bank' that 'marks the eastern boundary of Bridestowe Parish', which 'obviously owes its name to the proximity of the King Way.'

From Nodden Gate a track leads off the 'King Way' towards the Fox and Hounds Hotel from which place it undoubtedly continued to Bridestowe village. Later tracks from Bridestowe went up to peat on the moor near Rattlebrook Head and Kitty Tor.

The old lines of communication are mixed with the new in the parish. Many of the farms in the area still retain their old trackways whilst the bypass which was built in the 1970s gave the parish its newest stretch of roadway. Prior to the construction of the bypass the granite bridges that spanned the Crandford Brook and River Lew respectively were replaced by wider concrete affairs. Now that the village bypass has itself been bypassed, the needless removal of the two bridges which lent some charm to 'this dirty village' seems all the more destructive; well-intentioned improvements that may be welcomed at the time do not always turn out to be improvements.

Frank Maddaford's lorry with its load, 1930s.
Left to right, at back: *Blanch Maddaford, Hannah Maddaford;* girls sitting on truck: *Joyce Maddaford, Marion Maddaford;* front: *Ivy Maddaford, Tricy Towl, Greta Towl, Pam Towl;* driver: *Bill Gale.*
(Brian Maddaford)

Horse and cart at the West Bridge end of the village.
(Alan Pearn)

A heavy load by Wynns being pumped up to get over West Bridge, 1950s. (Alan Pearn)

THE RAILWAY

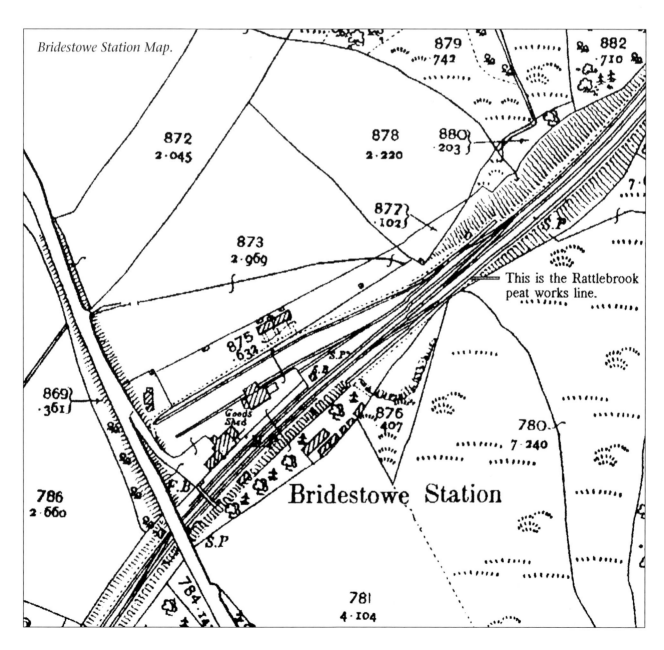

Bridestowe Station Map.

Camping Coaches Bridestowe Station. (Alan Pearn)

The alternative means of communication to the highways, the railway, came late to the fringes of Dartmoor. The London and South Western Railway route to Plymouth around the northern and western side of Dartmoor reached Okehampton only in 1871.

It was another three years before the construction of the line reached Lydford. This stretch of line involved a climb of 950 feet above sea level, the highest point in the system of the London and South-Western Railway. Bridestowe Station, nearly at the highest point on the line, was situated one and a half miles away from the village. Roche informs us that:

Train approaching Bridestowe, 1961. (Doug Gale)

Bridestowe station was built on a curve, the down platform, behind the diminutive shelter, thick with rhododendrons. The up side sported the substantial station house, a typical London South Western structure similar to that at Lydford, and beyond it there was a small goods yard with a cream-painted line of railway cottages, conspicuous in the view from the high moor. Waiting for a down train was quite exciting, because you could hear it a long time before it got there, roaring out of the cutting by Sourton, round under the slope of Corn Ridge over Southerly Viaduct, then blanketed by the final cutting till it appeared under the main road bridge, rocking and swaying as the driver reduced speed. In the reverse direction a steep wooded hillside hid an up train until it was almost in the platform.

Roche also tells that 'a statistician once worked out that Bridestowe sent away annually more rabbits than passengers'.

The line from Okehampton to Bere Alston closed to passengers in May 1968 as a result of the Beeching Report.

Bridestowe Station, 1960s. (Sam Ball)

SOURCES

Devon Record Office: 2750A/PX1; 1292M
Gill, C., *Dartmoor – A New Study*.
Hemery, E., *Walking Dartmoor's Ancient Tracks, A Guide to 28 Routes*.
Hoskins, W.G., *Devon* (1992 Edition).
Roche, T.W.E., *The Withered Arm–Reminiscences of The Southern Lines West of Exeter*.
Transactions of the Devonshire Association, 1936, 1938, 1969.
Vancouver, C., *General View of the Agriculture of the County of Devon* (1969 Edition).
Cockburn, J.S. (ed), *Western Circuit Assize Orders 1629–1648*.

Beech Avenue from the Fox and Hounds to Bridestowe Railway Station. 1920s. (Doug Gale)

Beating the bounds, 1960. (Alan Pearn)

Chapter 4

FOLKLORE

Bridestowe is a rich source of folklore, a parish abounding with popular traditional beliefs and customs. Fortunately, an avid collector, Miss L.M. Francis, daughter of the Reverend Francis, the rector of Bridestowe, recorded many examples of folklore from personal knowledge. Gleaning local folklore was also of interest to a cleric, the Reverend W.H. Mitchell, who was resident in Bridestowe prior to emigrating to New Zealand.

One traditional practice is the calendar custom of Shrovetide – the cooking and eating of pancakes on Shrove Tuesday. On the Monday before Shrove Tuesday, the young people of Bridestowe customarily sang for their crock (cake) (Note hence Lent-crocking). Small groups of Bridestowe children went around the parish to extract offerings of eggs, flour, butter or a halfpenny from the inhabitants to provide for the Tuesday feast. As they went about the task they sang:

> *Lent crock, give a pancake,*
> *Or a fritter, for my labour,*
> *Or a dish of flour, or a piece of bread,*
> *Or what you please to render,*
> *I see, by the latch,*
> *There's something to catch;*
> *I see, by the string,*
> *There's a good dame within.*
> *Trap, trapping throw,*
> *Give me my mumps, and I'll be go.*

This ditty is reputedly indigenous to the village whilst another version of the song apparently introduced by a schoolmistress from another part of the county at about the middle of the nineteenth century went:

> *Shrove-tide is nigh at hand,*
> *And we are come a-shroving;*
> *Pray, Dame, give something,*
> *An apple, or a dumpling,*
> *Or a piece of crumple cheese,*
> *Of your own making;*
> *Or a piece of pancake.*
> *Trip, trapping throw;*
> *Give me mumps, and I'll be go.*

A boy who lived in Bridestowe wrote another version of the song in prose for the Revd Mitchell in 1884. This particular song, rearranged by the Revd himself, ran:

> *Lean crock a pancake,*
> *Flitter for your labour;*
> *Dish a meal, piece of bread,*
> *What you please to give me.*
> *I see by the string,*
> *There's a good dame within.*
> *I see by the latch,*
> *There's something to catch.*
> *Trepy, Trepy, Tro.*
> *Please give me mumps and*
> *I'll be go;*
> *Nine times, ten times,*
> *I am come a-shroving;*
> *Pray, dame, something-*
> *Apple or a dumpling,*
> *Or a piece of truckle cheese of your own making,*
> *Or a piece of pancake of your own baking.*

The custom of Lent-crocking was being carried on by schoolchildren as late as the 1950s. Indeed, some of the parents of those particular children remember calling on the Parsonage where Miss Francis lived; at that time she had difficulty hearing and used an ear trumpet to listen to the children singing.

Another calendar custom was for Bridestowe children to go around the parish on Maundy Thursday chanting for the Maundy occasion in the hope of being given a penny. At one time, it was even thought that adults went along too. The song on this day ran:

> *Hot cross buns, hot cross buns,*
> *One a penny, two a penny, hot cross buns.*
> *Give them to your daughters,*
> *And, if you have no daughters,*
> *Give them to your sons.*
> *If you have no sons,*
> *Remember we have many,*
> *So if you have no buns,*
> *Please give me a penny.*

Whit-Monday is the day when the 'beating the bounds' of the parish is carried out. It is supposed to take place every three years in all parishes on the confines of Dartmoor when the parishioners electing to beat the bounds follow the parish boundary line, examining and verifying each landmark. At certain points 'bound beaters' from adjoining parishes sometimes met. Along the way stops are made for refreshments consisting of sandwiches, bread, cheese, drinks and buns. In former days it was the custom to take along the boys of the parish and beat them at every landmark impressing the boundary on their memories. Miss Francis considered that by her day times had become too easy-going; the boys were being stuffed with buns and the minds of the children had become confused as to the terms. Their name for the custom was 'beating the buns' or the 'bun-beating'. Bridestowe parishioners meet with their fellow parishioners of Sourton for the occasion of beating the bounds, as both parishes share common ground on the moor.

At one time a strange custom took place whereby people went to the church gate on Midsummer's Eve. At midnight they went into the church and supposedly saw the 'doubles' of those who were about to marry, or those who were to die within the year. Those who were to marry were seen to come out again; the others were not. In connection with this superstition the companions of a young farm labourer told him that they had seen his spirit go into the church and not come out again. Whether they thought that they had seen his spirit, or had told him just to frighten him is not known, but it upset him very much. Shortly after the event he caught a slight chill in the harvest field and, believing that he was going to die, took to his bed. The doctor, however, could detect nothing seriously wrong but nonetheless the young man died. The doctor declared that it was from the 'sheer want of will to live', the young man had simply known that his 'time had come'.

On the same evening of the year it was said that a love charm placed under one's pillow consisting of a bit of bridecake which had passed through a wedding ring would bring the sleeper a dream of the person he or she was destined to marry. A girl can, according to another charm, go into a spare bedroom after dark with a candle on New Year's Eve, look into a mirror and see, looking over her shoulder, the face of her future husband.

Certain times of the year were to be avoided by those wishing to marry. May was considered a very unlucky month for a wedding. The thirteenth of any month, or a Friday, were unlucky days, but New Year's Day was considered to be particularly lucky. Rules that a bride had to observe stated that she must never put on her full wedding dress before she was actually dressed for the wedding, nor must she look into the glass when fully dressed before she went to church. It was unlucky for her to wear any kind of jewellery, especially pearls, unless given by the bridegroom; but she must wear, 'something old, and something new, something borrowed, and something blue.'

The bride was not to see the wedding ring, much less put it on, before the ceremony. If upon the conclusion of the wedding service when the married couple left the church the woman was to put her foot out of the door before the man she was to be master.

If the bride were to look back at the church door after the wedding, she would lose her husband within the year and if a man were to address her by her maiden name upon that day, she would have ill luck all her married life.

Once in her new home, the bride, on sweeping the floor for the first time, had to sweep inwards and not back towards the door, or she would sweep out all her luck.

To serenade a newly-wedded couple an odd custom of 'beating the kettle-drums' was performed by the youths of Bridestowe on the evening after a wedding ceremony. Old tin pots and pans or anything else that was capable of producing a resounding noise and clatter were used. The custom, so Miss Francis proclaimed, was said to have 'fallen into disuse because even those it was intended to felicitate did not appreciate the hideous din.'

Witchcraft seems never to have been far from the minds of the residents of Bridestowe. At one time folk visited a white witch in a neighbouring parish in order to have their needs 'attended to'. A white witch could be a man or a woman, usually being the seventh child of a seventh child.

Above: *Ern Barkell with Maundy money presented by HM the Queen at Exeter Cathedral, 31 March 1983.*
(Howard Barkell)

Beating the bounds, having a meal at
Iron Catch Gate. (Brian Lavis)

Their living depended on the gullibility and stupidity of the people who paid them for advice and 'blessings' during times of strife and difficulty. According to the witches they did nothing but good, believing in their own occult powers as firmly as did their clients so their 'blessings' worked and their council bore good fruit. One, a man visited by Bridestowe people, would 'bless' for them 'lucky stones' and other talismens for their benefit, at a price of course. Another neighbouring white witch 'blessed' handkerchiefs or bandages which were to be used to bind a wound or the seat of a disorder, without the patient coming to see him and cure him thereby.

Then there were 'ill-wishers', people who glorified in their malevolence in the most shocking way. They held their neighbours in thrall by the firm belief of their evil powers. A woman told the Revd Francis of her firm belief that a malevolent neighbour had 'done for one of her pigs'. She said that Mary (naming a neighbour) had 'killed 'en, she ill-wished 'en'. Mary was a terror; when she ill-wished it came to pass, her neighbours all declared. After a time she left the village to the relief of everyone, for even those who did not credit her powers could but shrink from her maliciousness.

Two other persons in the parish were with 'evil eye'. In some mysterious and awful way they did obtain their ill wishes, those they cursed being blighted with misfortune or even tragic death. It is impossible to say whether they possessed some sort of prophetic instinct or second sight which enabled them to foresee the future, a power which they worked for their own ends, or whether they really did use the aid of the evil one, as one woman boasted she could. Miss Francis tells of how she could vouch for the truth, and could give names and details of ill wishers and of those whom they cursed, but that this was at all costs to be avoided. Her father was often called in to reason with the ill wishers because it was thought that their curses could not harm the parson. Some also believed that the parson could 'turn the curse' with a prayer or exorcism if this was pronounced as soon as the curse had been uttered and before it had begun to work. Others believed that the 'curse takes hold' at once, as it is

Bridestowe and Sourton parishioners beating the
bounds, 1935. (Sam Ball)

spoken, so exorcism would be of no avail.

A rich source of charms for medical ailments emanated from a Mr Blatchford, one-time sexton of the church. The sexton's wife was a talkative old lady who was especially garrulous about her husband's gifts of healing. On the Revd Mitchell visiting her she declared that a little girl was expected that evening or early next morning to be healed for a wen (a cystic tumour forming a permanent swelling beneath the skin). Anyone who wished to be healed had to be 'strook' by Blatchford an odd number of times over the diseased part and this had to take place on a Tuesday, his birthday. It was also thought that this should take place on an odd number of Tuesdays, as it was often deemed necessary to do it seven or nine Tuesdays following, as the cure was not always rapid. Blatchford first discovered that he possessed this healing power when very young, just after birth 'before he had been washed or dressed' when he happened to strike some afflicted person and heal them. If he had not done this, then his gift would never have been revealed. If it had not been revealed then, he maintained, he would never have been able to make use of it afterwards. Blatchford was the eldest son of the family, but it was not thought that there was any bar to the second, third, or any other son having the same gift.

It was not necessary for Blatchford to say any words for wens, but it does appear that faith in the possibility of cure was necessary for healing to take place. Blatchford was not always successful; but when he was, the gratitude of those who were cured showed itself in presents of scarves, silk handkerchiefs and waistcoats.

Blatchford did not have the gift for healing any other kind of sickness or disease but he had charms for various things. Mrs Blatchford said she could give them to a man but not to a woman and that Revd Mitchell could give them to a woman but not to a man, or their efficacy would be destroyed. The charms ran:

For Burngout: Three or four maidens coming from divers lands crying for burngout; aching, smarting, burning, and all kinds of burngout. They went to the burrow town, there they had brethren; they went to the Salt Seas; and they never more returned again. He or she shall have their full health again. In the name of the father, and of the Son, and of the Holy Ghost. Amen. So be it.

For a Sprain: Our Lord Jesus Christ rode over a bridge. His horse lighted, and He lighted; He said, 'Marrow to marrow, and bone to bone, and sinew to sinew, and blood to blood, and skin to skin,' and to the others in the name of the Father, and of the Son, and of the Holy Ghost, I cast this sprain away. Amen. So be it.

For Inflammation: Our Lord Jesus Christ came from the mount's foot, saw Abraham asleep on the cold ground. Our Lord spoke and said, 'What best show her for?' Abraham spoke and said, 'It is good to know what I be here for taken with an out blow, aching, burning that I know not what to do.' Our Lord Jesus Christ said, 'Rise up, Abraham, from the cold, cold ground. I will make thee safe in the name of the Father, and of the Son, and of the Holy Ghost. Amen.'

For the sting of a serpent: As Gabriel and his man went in the wood the vermin stung Gabriel's man by the hand, Gabriel said unto the serpent, 'Why stingest thou my man?' The serpent said, 'I know not thy man.' Gabriel said, 'What shall I give in exchange for the spear?' The serpent said, 'Three hog's lard, and thy man shall be restored to thee again in the name of God the Father, God the Son, and God the Holy Ghost. Amen.'

Anyone could use these charms and no striking or preternatural gifts of any kind were needed but the full name (Christian and surnames every one) of the person to be cured was to be said before repeating the charm, otherwise all efforts would be of no avail. It would not hinder a cure were the sufferer to be absent.

A cure for thrush was made from honey and borax with the use of 'the words'. A young mother living in Bridestowe was in some anxiety because her first-born baby was suffering with 'white mouth' (thrush). On being told to use honey and borax an old grandmother living with the family said she had forgotten the words that her man, long since dead, used. They were taken from the Book of Psalms in the Bible and mentioned something about the mouth of babes and sucklings. Psalm Eight, Verse II, was suggested, and the family Bible was promptly produced and the daughter read out the text. About a week later the baby's mouth was cured. Another cure for thrush, or white mouth, was to take the afflicted child to a running stream and, according to an old woman, there 'draay dree rishes droo' the mouth of him (for the uninitiated, draw three rushes through). In order to be successful, both cures had to be performed for three days running. Parents who searched the neighbourhood of Bridestowe until they found a donkey of the female sex effected another cure for thrush. Their child was passed three times under the belly of the animal.

An old dame of Bridestowe recounted that when a son of hers, as a lad, had very bad boils on his neck, a gipsy woman gave her a cure. The boy was to go into a field where daisies were growing, go down on his hands and knees and eat the flowers off the ground, but he was not to touch them with his hands. On the first day he had to eat three, on the next five, and then two more each day until the boils had gone. In a week or two the boils had healed. The old dame concluded that she did not know if it was a charm or some herbal virtue in the daisies, but the lad never had any further boils.

An old farmer who was on his deathbed passed on a cure for a viper's sting in the form of a curious charm to the Revd Francis. It was written on a slip of paper, in old-fashioned characters, the ink browned with age, and read:

Our Blessed Virgin Mary Sot & Soad
her Blessed babe Sot & Plead their-
Came a Ting worm out of Eldern wood he
Ting our Blessed Saviour by the foot his
Blader Blew and never thin Shall
(Name)
Break – N – B – Tong Ting Or Ring Ting in
the Name of the Father and of the Son and
of the Holy Ghost Amen Pray God
Expel the Ting

There were several cures for whooping cough such as taking a child into a field where there were sheep for three days in succession, sitting it on a spot from which a sheep had just risen. The patient could be given a piece of Good Friday bun, three days in succession. A child could be taken to a four-cross road, into three parishes or be carried around the parish, all of which were to be performed for three days in succession of course!

Not forgetting the animals we find that a cure for inflammation in cattle was to make a bolus of sow-pigs (wood lice) mixed with lard, or drench the insects with hot water, to obtain 'sow-pig tea.'

A charm for finding lost property was told by a maid of the Francis household and runs:

St Anthony Rich in wonders
seeketh things when asked.
Lost goods are found again.
He helps in every need.

The charm was to be repeated three times with a promise of something for charity, otherwise the missing article would not turn up. Perhaps it could be used by the owner of a 'crock of gold' buried somewhere in Burley Wood Camp. A word of warning to other people, however, for it is said that anyone attempting to dig for the gold would be scared from his purpose by terrible thunder and lightening. Not only that, according to one old farmer who lived close to the Camp, the area was also 'haunted by the ghost of Squire Bidlake'. He was obviously a feared figure for the village mothers threatened troublesome children that 'his ghost would come after them.'

Another ghost story is that of the procession of the 'Death Coach and Black Hound'. Bridestowe is honoured by the 'spook' of Lady Howard. In expiation of her crimes (tradition has it that she murdered her husbands, but this is doubtful) she is condemned to travel every night in a coach made of bones, drawn by headless horses, preceded by a black hound with one eye in his forehead. Lady Howard must leave her residence, Fitzford House in Tavistock (of which only the gateway now survives) to journey to Okehampton Castle. The hound must pluck one blade of grass from the castle mound and then all must return to Fitzford where the blade of grass is to be laid at the threshold of the gate. The penance must continue till the last blade of grass has been plucked from the castle mound.

The route taken by Lady Howard, according to some Bridestowe folk, passes Lydford Castle, across a down between that and Bridestowe, and along a narrow lane which intersects the road to Bridestowe from the Fox and Hounds pub. An ancient and blasted oak tree stands at this junction and is called by some the 'ghost tree'. A woodsman, employed by Shilston Calmady Hamlyn, a former owner of the property where the tree stands, wanted to cut the tree down. Shilston would not comply with his woodsman's wish and by way of compliment to him for his sparing of the tree it was renamed Shilston's Oak.

The Shilston Oak or the ghost tree (in the centre leaning to the left). (Susan Cann)

Another tale relates a different reason behind the naming of the tree. Apparently Shilston Calmady Hamlyn was riding along the road between his home and the Fox and Hounds when, on arrival at the old oak tree, he was accosted by a highwayman who made a demand for money. Shilston produced his drinking flask, pointed the neck at the offending highwayman who mistakenly thought he was facing a pistol and took off with great dispatch. From henceforth the tree came to be known as the 'Shilston Oak'.

From ghosts we turn to a song that was continually sung in Bridestowe for weeks after the Battle of Waterloo. An old dowager who was a girl at the time of the battle had no recollection of the tune to which the song was sung, but according to her memory it went:

At twelve o'clock on Sunday the bloody affray begun:
From that very minute till the setting of the sun,
Both Horse and Foot we did advance,
The bugles we did blow,
The men of France, we made them prance,
That day in Waterloo.

Another battle song sung by Eliza Walters of Bridestowe under the heading 'An Armada Catch' ran:

The bug and the flea, they went to sea,
Along of the Spanish Armada;
The bug was drowned, but his breeches were found
In the midst of the Spanish Armada.

She also knew another ditty:

When shall we get married, dear Nic'las Wood?
Why, next Sunday morning, be sure, cheel;
'Tis better that we should.
What shall we have for breakfast, dear Nic'las Wood?
Why, titties and bacon, be sure, cheel;
'Tis better that we should.

In all probability this stems from the writings on Nicholas Wood by John Taylor, the 'Water Poet', c.1660.

A local omen states that if you hit a tumbler so that it resounds someone is killed. Apparently Devonshire sailors have a similar superstition: every time a glass is made to ring a sailor is drowned. How many times have tumblers been made to ring in ignorance of this omen?

According to another omen a picture falling from the wall foretells of misfortune. Should it be a portrait of which the original is still alive, it portends his death. Miss Francis remembered that whilst staying with a friend in the parish a portrait of the master of the house fell down. He became depressed and unwell for days on account of the incident but lived for some years after.

Situated near the Rectory is a field known as the 'Sanctuary Field'. When the Revd Francis came to Bridestowe some old wiseacre informed him that 'he could not be arrested for debt if he went to the Sanctuary Field.' He was also told that 'he might hang whoever he was minded to' in the same field. Sanctuary fields are to be found in several parishes and the right of gallows (infangenethef and utfangenethef) was sometimes granted to small manors. As past rectors of Bridestowe have held the position of lord of the manor and the fact that a field known as the 'Sanctuary Field' was on their glebe land, we might consider that the wiseacres were not after all just the village know-alls.

The Revd Mitchell recalled a Mrs Matthews, a labourer's wife, aged 74 of Bridestowe, who thought she had 'canins' coming over her eyes, and had the 'canin stone' put to them, but in vain. The 'canin stone' exists at Millaton and Lake, but its exact location is not known. The Revd Mitchell believed 'canins' to be the same as 'catricks' (cataracts).

Apparently you should see the first lamb of the year before you hear it and it should be looking at you or it is unlucky.

You must pick apples when the moon is waxing, for if gathered when the moon is waning they will shrivel and not keep. In fact, this is not idle hearsay but true, and is probably due to the fact that the moon influences all liquids, the sap goes back from the apples as the moon wanes, and they lose some of their firmness. It is also said that bacon must be cured when the moon is waxing or it will not keep.

As for babies we find that it is unlucky to cut their nails before they are a year old; should they grow too long mother or nurse must carefully bite them down. Until it is a year old a baby should likewise never see itself in a mirror or be photographed.

'A tear in one eye, like a Jerusalem rat' is a proverbial saying that is said to have been used by an old nurse whose name is unknown but who was born in Bridestowe. The saying is rather odd as no mention of a rat is made in the Bible. It was thought that perhaps the mole rat, which has its eyes completely buried in its skin, might possibly be the animal to which the old nurse was referring.

SOURCES
Risdon T., *Survey of the County of Devon* (1811 Edition).
Transactions of the Devonshire Association.
Wreford H., *Secret Westcountry.*

Chapter 5

THE VILLAGE SCHOOL

The earliest mention of education within the bounds of Bridestowe Parish that was found by the author comes from the Act of Uniformity which for the year 1662 gives one William Smith, a schoolmaster, as a subscriber. This is all that we know of him.

Those people who wished to pursue their individual skills petitioned the Church for a licence, which was issued either by a bishop or the chancellor. A petition, from c.1665, recites the following:

To the Right worpll Edward Masters Dr of the [Divine] [Lawes] and Chancellor to the Right Reverend Father in god Seth Lord Bishopp of Exon.

Wee the Inhabitants of the parish of Bridestow within the Countie of Devon doe hereby humbly Signifie unto yor worshipp That Richard Yoldon of our sayd parrish hath for [this] Thirtye years and upwards kept a Schooll for the educating of youth By

which means he hath been an instrument of doing much good amongst us and (as we humbly concedin) is the fittest person for such an undertaking of any on[e] that is now resident in this parrish.

Will Bidlake	***The marks of***
Shilston Calmady	Nicholas Burrow
Fran Calmady	Walter Hawton
Phillip Bidlake	Nicholas Tapson
Edward Fortescue	James Pengelly
William Nicholl	Richard Tickell
Walter Nicholl	
John Blatchford	
Roger Maddaford	
Robert Tapson	
John Tickell	

Apart from the fact that the petition dated the presence of a school and master in the parish just prior to the outbreak of the Civil War, no other clues lie within it. At this time Bridestowe may have had the luxury of two schoolmasters in Smith and Yoldon but it may well be that Smith had taken over the position of schoolmaster from Yoldon and that Yolden was now petitioning the bishop to regain his old position, Smith having left Bridestowe for some reason or another.

Some set questions for a bishop's visitation to a village such as Bridestowe included:

1/ Is any schoolmaster of good religion, sound teaching and licensed?
2/ Does the schoolmaster receive communion and cause his pupils to do so?
3/ Does the schoolmaster teach catechism?
4/ Does the schoolmaster privately instruct in superstition, disobedience, etc?
5/ Are there any papists, and do they keep any schoolmasters?
6/ Does any schoolmaster teach grammar other than the 'King's Grammar'?

From the time of Richard Yoldon's petition an entire century passes before the next mention of schooling in the parish. This is gleaned from Bishop Frederick's visitation where we find that although there was not a 'publick School' there was a 'private School' at Bridestowe.

Bridestowe School, 1920s. Mr Westcott the master with his dogs. (Doug Gale)

Bridestowe schoolchildren. (Doug Gale)

Return of Voluntary Schools – Bridestowe 1902, School No. 6404

Bridestowe Church of England. Premises situated in Bridestowe Village known as the Bridestowe School. Comprises one main room, one class room, one infants room and one teachers house. The area of the site is rather less than one acre, the following trustees hold them in trust: The Rector and Churchwardens of the parish of Bridestowe for the time being.

Teachers
Tom Sly. Mixed Principal Appointed Jan 1887. £115.7s.6d. with House & Garden.
Laura Sly. Mixed Assistant Appointed Jan 1887. Joint Salary with husband.
T & L Sly's salary includes grant of £60 plus ½ Government grant except fee grant.
Lucy Tickell. Infants Assistant Appointed Oct 1888 £40 Salary.

Moniteresses
Beatrice Turner. Infants Appointed Sep 1901 £7.
Helena Pike. Mixed Appointed Sep 1901 £7.

		Year ending			
Income	1901			1902	
	£.	s.	d.	£.	s.	d.
Balance	6	16	0			
Annual grant from Board of Education	110	16	3	111	14	0
Fee grant from Board of Education	57	0	0	52	0	0
Aid grant	12	5	0	10	5	0
Voluntary contributions	28	11	6	25	11	6
Other receipts	2	10	0	1	14	0
Balance if overdrawn	0	0	9			
Total	£211	02	9	£208	1	3
Expenditure						
Balance if overdrawn	3	3	9			
Salaries of teachers	165	10	0	168	5	4
Books & Stationery	10	18	6	10	4	3
Apparatus & Furniture	13	18	3	19	13	0
Fuel & Light & Cleaning	8	14	0	8	9	4
Rates Taxes & Insurances	0	16	8	0	19	0
Other expenses	1	5	0	0	9	6
Balance if in hand	6	16	0			
Total	£211	2	9	£208	1	3

Treasurer's Account at National Provincial Bank Okehampton Branch.
Particulars of Government Grants received year ending Dec 31, 1902.

Bridestowe schoolchildren, 1890. Headmaster Tom Sly is standing to the right at the back with the cap. Others include: Effie Hooper, Annie Mills, Bert Mills.
(Bridestowe School)

Two years later we have record of the village blacksmith relating that 'one Mr Mavin, a schoolmaster, sat in one of the seats.' Andrew Hockaday, in December 1766, was offering this statement to a Consistory Court hearing at Exeter, concerning a dispute over seating in Bridestowe's church. Hockaday did not explicitly state that Mavin resided in Bridestowe but as he was attending divine service in the Parish Church it seems likely that Mavin was providing some form of educational service for the local children.

Our next mention of education appears 40 years later. Turning to the Reverend Coryndon Luxmore's answers to Bishop Cary's visitation of 1821, we learn that there was at this time one school for boys and another for girls, each with up to 50 pupils. Coryndon Luxmore supported the schools to such a level as his personal means allowed. It is not clear, however, whether he was alluding to Sunday schools or otherwise.

In 1833 the Abstract of Education Returns mentions a day school attended by 18 boys and 22 girls. Subscriptions and fees to the sum of £12.10s. supported the school.

The next source of interest is the Vestry Minutes Book which contains an entry dated June 1835 which records that parishioners had agreed to pay 'nine pounds nine shillings per annum' to Mrs Mary Chapman to 'keep a girls school'. She was to 'keep nine schoaler provided there is so many required'. A second entry dated July 1837 shows that Mary Chapman was about to receive an increment to her salary as she was to be 'paid ten pounds fifteen shillings' from the church rate. Mrs Chapman no doubt taught the girls in a room within her own home.

But what of the village school we know today? There is no direct evidence of a specific opening date for the school. *White's Directory* for 1850 does provide a clue, for in the entry for Bridestowe we find that 'The National School established about ten years ago [was] attended by about two hundred children.'

The benefactor who contributed the site upon which the school stands was none other than the parish rector, the location being part of his manor of Bridestowe Sanctuary. Before the school could be constructed some existing buildings had to be razed to the ground, although a small cottage was left intact and put to good use to house the schoolmaster. The frontage outline of the original school building was from the present entrance porch to the right-hand end of the present building, a room some 35ft by 16ft.

From the Diocesan Training School in 1848 arrived Mary Emilie Rafael who had been appointed as the mistress with an initial salary of ten guineas per annum. Very soon after her arrival the salary was increased to £14, and she was also in receipt of board and lodging. Her position at Bridestowe School terminated in 1850 when she left for Cornwall. John H. Brownson, who accomplished 'improvement' in the school according to the 1853 Diocesan Report, filled her place. Whilst Brownson was performing the duties of master at Bridestowe it seems the rector was trying to enlarge the school. The 1856 *Directory of Devonshire* reports that he was 'endeavouring to establish a mixed National School on the plan of that at King's Somborne.'

Bridestowe C.E. School – the gardening class, 1920.
(Doug Gale)

William McCreery was master in 1857 and during his time it seems that an idea was mooted to convert the Poor House into a Parochial School. From a minute in the Vestry Book for November 1860 we find that a conversion was to be carried out 'as soon as funds could be procured'. This scheme was seemingly abandoned, however, in favour of the rector's endeavours as represented by the 1856 *Directory*. From various ongoing correspondence we find that the rector had to contend with opposition in order to reach his goal. A letter dated July 1861 from the Education Department at the Privy Council Office, Downing

Bridestowe schoolchildren, 1921. (Bridestowe School)

Street, to the Reverend C.W. Clarke, gives a direct insight into the problems he faced. We find that a Mr Vowler had written to the Education Department expressing his disapproval of the school site. His letter, headed 'Bridestowe Schools', reads:

I am given to understand that application is being made by the Reverend C.W. Clarke for a grant for school etc. As a resident in Bridestowe and one who takes a lively interest in the welfare of the inhabitants I beg to tender my protest most respectfully to my Lords against the appropriation of any money at their disposal towards the erection of the schools in question until my Lords have had satisfactory proof afforded them that the site selected for the buildings and proposed for their sanction is free from objection... The proposed site is well nigh surrounded with Buildings and consequently shut off from a pure circulation of air with the additional drawback and in my view an insuperable one of having nauseous drains, manure heaps with their exhalations and pig styes in close propinquity. As other sites exist equally if not more convenient as far as the population of the village and neighbourhood are concerned and from the grave objections I have above noticed I venture to pray my Lords hesitate to make the grant sought for until a proper site is submitted to them for their approval.

J. Nicholson Vowler.

Another objector to the school site was J.G. Newton of Millaton. He too wrote to the Education Department requesting them to refrain from granting a sum of money from their funds until 'another suitable site had been found for the school'. His letter in part reads:

I think if my Lords would be pleased to order an inspection it would be found that the walls of the proposed schools are bounded by a farmyard with other houses, Pig styes Privies and open foul drains, and added to this a great difficulty of obtaining any good outlet for sewerage. I feel assured my Lords would not lend their aid in the erection of these schools on the proposed site if proper evidence of the existing evils were lain before them.

Of the two objectors Vowler is the least known. He was a magistrate who sat on the bench for the Petty Sessions at Lifton taking his accommodation at Leawood. His name as far as Bridestowe goes has not been mentioned in any context other than in his capacity as a magistrate listed in the Devon County Prison receiving books as sending someone to that institution. The suggestion that he took a 'lively interest in the welfare' of Bridestowe parishioners seems to be an overstatement. That he claims to be 'a resident in Bridestowe' rather than 'a resident of Bridestowe' perhaps suggests that his stay at Leawood was only temporary, and no other evidence being found to suggest otherwise. Vowler however may have been acting objectively upon what he saw and felt about the practicalities of the school site rather than through selfish motives.

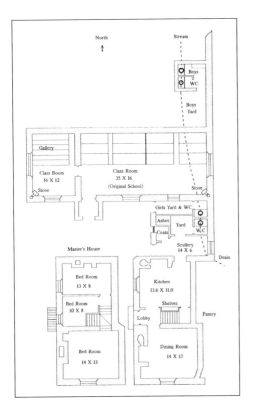

Left: *A plan of Bridestowe School after rebuilding, 1862.*

Below: *Bridestowe C.E. School. Class 1. Mr Westcott, the headmaster, is standing to the left on the back row.* (Brian Lavis)

John Gubbins Newton was a resident of Bridestowe and from the Tithe Commutation Schedule we can see that he was a tenant holding South and North Ball. Both of Newton's holdings lay next to the site that was under consideration for the building of the school. Newton may have thought that he was in danger of losing some of the land available to him as it was owned by the rector, on top of which a great inconvenience was surely to be found in the invasion of schoolchildren, particularly from the unruly elements amongst them, upon his property.

However, it would seem fair to say that the observations of the two men were correct. The site was close to a farm with all the distractions normally associated with such an environment. On occasions it would have exuded unpalatable conditions totally unsuitable for study to say the least. At the time perhaps it was thought better to go ahead with enlarging the school, rather than miss an opportunity afforded to have an establishment which would provide basic education for all.

Whatever the true intentions of Vowler and Newton may have been, they were not as forthcoming with their money as might be expected of two concerned parishioners with nothing but the welfare of children on their minds. Neither, according to a list of subscribers, contributed towards the enlargement of the school building, unless of course they donated money to the 'collections in church'.

Returning to the letter from the Education Department dated July 1861, we find that it also contained a request for a medical certificate. As a result of this request William Prater, MB, inspected the school on 2 August and certified that:

I think the same well adapted for the purpose and having been in constant attendance in the parish of Bridestowe for several years I can state that I have known no case of disease (reparable) to the locality.

The Reverend Clarke forwarded the certificate to the Education Department along with observations as to the suitability of the site. A swift favourable reply dated 7 August 1861 was received whereby the Reverend Clarke was informed that the site was acceptable, as long as a slight revision of the building plan be submitted. It was observed that:

There should be separate accesses from within the school room to the privies of the boys and girls; respectively at present there is only one door common to both sexes.

Upon the plan being revised the school was rebuilt mainly with the aid of public subscriptions. A grant was obtained from the Education Department upon the rector carrying out a paper

Bridestowe C.E. School, Class 3, c.1925.
Left to right, back row: *Miss Tickell, ?, ?, Cyril Lugg, John Guscott, Lew Dawe, Sam Ball, ?, Arthur Meadows;* middle row: *Jackie Westcott, Trissie Towl, Greta Towl, ? Shaddick, Iris Worden, Jessie Porter, Edna Walters, Phyllis Phillips, ? Bolt, Bill Hearn, ?,* sitting: *?, ?, ?, Francis Ellis, Parsy Kitt, Edie Heathman, James Hutchings, Lional Watts.*
(Alan Pearn)

exercise whereby he conveyed the school site and its buildings, valued at £150, free of cost to, ironically, the 'Minister and Churchwardens of the parish'. Along with the transfer of the site and buildings came a condition that the school was to be subjected to Government inspection and was to be conducted along the lines of the National Society principles. Added to this, a committee was to be formed consisting of the Minister and five other people who contributed not less than 20 shillings a year towards the school's upkeep.

William McCreery, having seen some of the obstacles facing the rebuilding of the school settled, left before the final stages of the work was completed. James Wakem was appointed to the school in January 1862 from St Lukes; his salary was £45 per annum plus lodging. During his first year as master he saw the school rebuilding pale into insignificance when compared with the impediments which had to be surmounted in order to execute the wish of Revd Clarke; the amount of floor space gained was not of much consequence.

The masons Samuel and James Lintern signed a contract dated 4 (month illegible) 1862, to carry out the alterations and additions to the school premises which they almost rebuilt in order to add a small infants' classroom to the east end of the old building. Sections of the original walls of the old schoolroom were merged into the new building, which was completed with a porch bearing the date 1862. The schoolhouse was enlarged at this time.

A *Directory* of 1866 shows that Wakem had left the school, James Loveday was by this time the

Bridestowe schoolchildren, 1927 (?). Left to right, back row: *Hearn, Rattenbury, Murrin, Philpott, Porter, Worden, Guest;* middle row: *?, Rattenbury, Phare , ?, Ball, Maddaford, Cox, Shaddick, ?, ?, Mr Westcott;* front row: *Daniels, Brayley, Lee, Heathman, Murrin, Worden, Ellis, Dawe and Dawe.*
(Bridestowe School)

Bridestowe schoolchildren. (Brian Lavis)

master and Miss Harriet Maddaford, who was the schoolmistress, supported him. The *Directory* also shows that Miss Mary Ann Peard was conducting a school. From the map in the auction catalogue of the Millaton Estates seen earlier, it is fairly certain that the school run by Mary Peard was located in the boundaries of the area of the village commonly known as the Tanyard. Further evidence to support this can be found in the 1873 *Directory* where Mary Peard was listed as Postmistress, as well as running the school (again the auction map referred to above indicates the Post Office as being in the Tanyard). Much like Mary Chapman it seems, Mary Peard seems to have run a school from her own home. The *Directory* also tells us that the school was mixed and that it was supported by no less a personage than John Gubbins Newton. Whether he was supporting this school in opposition to the school which he had objected to some 12 years previously we do not know. It should not be forgotten that the Tanyard was in his tenancy so he may have supported Mary Peard's venture for that very reason. Such schools were known as dame schools, but they disappeared after the 1870 Education Act. Mary ran her classes for a few years after the 1870 Act, but is not listed from 1878 onwards.

January 1869 saw Francis John Salter in the post of master during which time he received his Parchment. Salter had a pupil teacher, a girl. This seems to have been rather controversial with Her Majesty's Inspector, who asked:

... whether the Managers [were] willing to take the responsibility of the arrangement by which a Pupil Teacher of eighteen and a Master of twenty four years of age [were] to be employed together?

It is not known whether the Inspector was privy to some unpleasant circumstances surrounding Salter's dismissal from his position at Petrockstowe prior to his arrival at Bridestowe. The Managers, who must have been aware of Salter's dismissal, were of the opinion that the arrangement could continue as Salter was married; their decision was not in vain for nothing untoward occurred. It seems the Managers must have found favour with their guardian angels, as Salter was to receive at least two further dismissals later on in his career for reasons with overtones.

Salter, like one of his predecessors, was to see plans being put into operation for further enlargement of the school but he left his post before construction work was to be implemented. A drawing by John Rundle of Bridestowe, dated December 1870, shows that yet again, another room was to be built onto the back of the existing school accommodation. A letter dated 12 July 1871 denotes that the plans allowed for a schoolroom to hold 96 children at their desks; a schoolroom for 40 infants at eight square feet per child; and a third schoolroom available for either group of children which could accommodate 20 pupils. 'The Plans', the letter goes on to say, were satisfactory 'subject to there being only three rows of desks and benches in each group and a gallery being provided for the infants school.'

The Education Department approved of amended plans that complied with their request and made a grant of £75.17s.6d. on 30 September 1871 towards the costs of 'erecting and furnishing the new schoolroom'.

Charles Geen of Okehampton contracted to do the work for which he was allowed the sum of £125. He had to complete the task by 1 December 1872 and was authorised to take stones from 'part of the poor house' as well as from the quarry 'in the corner field' or 'other places belonging to the Rector'. Free access was allowed through the yard of the farm occupied by Mr Bickle near the schoolhouse, through a gate leading to the garden upon which the new schoolroom was to be built. The work was carried out in a similar style to the earlier rebuilding, the rust-coloured stone used blending in with the existing walls.

The replacement for Francis Salter arrived in June 1872. John Carpenter was destined to stay for a year only. Like the list of parish rectors, that of village schoolmaster by this time contained a fair number of individuals, many of whom stayed but a short while.

Carpenter had to use his own house as well as another to teach 164 children because of the building work being carried out to enlarge the school. In July 1873, shortly after the completion of the new room, Carpenter left Bridestowe.

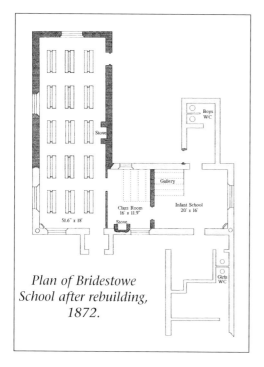

Plan of Bridestowe School after rebuilding, 1872.

His departure heralded an interval of nearly 12 months before the next certificated teacher was to appear on the scene. It was a difficult period in which the school system nearly collapsed – a local dispute over the question of establishing a school board being ongoing at this time. This probably stemmed from Foster's Education Act of 1870, which provided that England should be divided into districts that were to be managed by school boards. The schools were to be secular and undenominational, thus laying a probable root cause behind Bridestowe's problem, for after all, the person behind the major development of the school was a man of the cloth. A later amendment to the Act was to permit school boards to incorporate religious instruction if they so wished.

June 1874 saw the arrival of Joshua W.A. Hooper in residence as the master, and some semblance of normality began to reimpose itself upon the ailing school. Hooper's first week in the post saw an attendance on average of 22 children.

Prior to the arrival of the teacher many children were attending classes at Lydford, or, as in some instances, none at all. Five months into his time at the school Hooper recorded an attendance figure of 82 children; they were returning to the fold. Hooper was attempting to salvage some order to get the school running along the lines of improvement, but it seems he was not having a great deal of luck. In his second report there was a note of improvement but he proclaimed the school was 'still very far from being efficient'. His third and last report was to be much the same.

Hooper referred to a case of indecent assault at the school, and he passed the discriminating remark that 'the majority of Bridestowe boys are decidedly animal'.

Bridestowe schoolchildren. Mrs Westcott is wearing the hat. (Alan Pearn)

In January 1877 a new master, James Henry Arbory from St Luke's, arrived, but he was to have an unfortunate career. From his first report we see that the school was 'still very low in attainments', even lower than the previous year. 'The Master for his own credit,' wrote Arbory, 'ought to have done something towards providing more satisfactory results.' Arbory received his Parchment during his second year at the school when the Managers introduced a new scale fee. The scale per week was to be 1d. for infants whilst standards were split into two classes; farmers were to pay 4d. whilst labourers were to pay 2d. for each child.

The parishioners did not accept the new fees until changes had been made. People were indignant over the increased charges and in turn became antagonistic. The solution was to charge the full rate only for the first two children in each family, with the remainder paying 1d.

In 1882 at a Vestry meeting a voluntary rate of 1d. in the pound was voted towards the school funds. The following year saw an average attendance of 78 children at the school. Arbory seems to have achieved little success and departed in August 1885. He departed 'after due notice to the

Managers', but this seems misleading on his part as the real reasons for his leaving possibly revolve around his mismanagement and poor superintendence of the children. Prior to his departure an inferior report on the school had been forthcoming and, perhaps more importantly, an inquest was held over his alleged ill treatment of one of the pupils. Arbory did not record the finding and it is probable that he lost his Certificate as a consequence of his actions.

James French took up the post as master of Bridestowe School in September 1885, a month after Arbory left. His wife, who, like her husband, was a certificated teacher, accompanied him. Their stay was to be of short duration, their one report reading 'changes in staff have not of yet effected any marked improvement in the character of the school'.

They, as teachers in other village schools, were finding that regular attendances by the children in their charge were much less than desirable. French had his own views about the attendance system and passed caustic remarks on the occurring dilemma he was facing. In 1885 he remarked: 'It is impossible to make very much progress with such irregularity. The Education Act seems quite a dead letter in this district'. A year later he passed a further comment on the same subject, noting:

It seems only a farce to send in a list of absentees to the Attendance Officer, as they are not taking the slightest notice of, the same names being continually forwarded month after month.

During a Vestry meeting in September 1886 it was proposed that:

... the ratepayers who contributed to the support of the school, by paying a voluntary rate shall hereinafter be considered the qualified electors (as virtual subscribers) of members of the Board of Managers.

Shortly after this decision, in December 1886, there having been no inroads made into raising standards at the school, the Frenches left.

Thomas Sly, on filling the vacant post of master at Bridestowe School in January 1887, instigated an era of some considerable improvement. He was born in 1864, his training, spanning a period of two years took place at St Luke's and he took his Certificate in 1886. On his arrival at Bridestowe he noticed that the:

... children with a few exceptions [were] in a most backward condition – there seem[ing] to be no life or little activity among them, and a great lack of intelligence throughout.

Bridestowe Salvage Soldiers, 1943. (George Lavis)

Prior to his arrival the record of accomplishment at the school had fallen far below an acceptable level, it should be noted that conditions were not always conducive. The school had been subjected to major building programmes, disputes and a succession of short-term teachers, who, it appears, had decided to accept that it was better to throw in the towel rather than attempt to solidify their positions in order to raise the standards of the school. Thankfully, the situation was to change.

Thomas Sly must have worked efficiently because his pupils began to make a concerted effort. His first report relates that 'good order' and 'very substantial improvement in work' were now being produced. This may have been partially achieved by Sly's repudiation of the apparent accepted level of attendance at the school, which made a mockery of bylaws.

He did not rest until he had motivated the official who was charged with the unenviable task of ensuring that parents sent their children to school to receive their unequivocal right to education. The Attendance Officer at last began to take proceedings against those parents who spurned not only the law, but, more sadly, the opportunity open to their children, which allowed them to benefit from a system that was now beginning to receive the proper recognition due to it. Magistrates, in turn, from their benches commenced to apply the rigor of the sentencing powers available to them. Fines were at last imposed on the parents as 'this [seemed] the only plan [they could] adopt with effect, as notices, advice or persuasions [were] utterly useless.'

Prior to the now positive views on school attendance that the authorities were adopting, one mother, who, because she had evaded a punitive monetary penalty on appearing before the Magistrates, took a complacent self-satisfying view of the outcome. She thought she had obtained the position whereby 'having been before the Magistrates twice without being fined, she [could] send or keep away her children at her own pleasure.' The continuation of such beliefs on her part was not allowed to go unimpeded, and on being summoned for a third time to appear before the Magistrates she was fined five shillings.

Bridestowe Salvage Soldiers, c.1945. Left to right, back row: *Iris Trewin, Michael Screech, Marion Heathman, Norman Gale, Hazel Burnham, Miss Spicer, Mr Westcott, Mrs Milnes, June Lee, Dennis Allott, June Waymouth, Cecil Allen, Millicent Phare, (?);* 2nd row: *Bill Seymour, Symoan Cockwill, Ken Trewin, Joyce Lake, John Hockridge, Alan Bateman, John Horn, May Pellow, Martin Pellow, Joan Evans, Clifton Towl;* 3rd row: *Jack Crocker, Margaret Pellow, Betty Allen, Margaret Barker, Michael Gale, Michael Lavis, Roy Heathman, (?), Jean Chapman, ? Trewin, Elizabeth Trewin;* front sitting: *Peter Milnes, Rose Leach, Tony Johnston, Pauline Worden, Howard Barkell, Valerie Maddaford, Norman Woodman, Rosemary Trewin, Cycil Mudge, Ann Jewell, Jean Barker, (?), Josephine Short, Michael Seamna, ? Smith, Brian Maddaford, Ruth Crocker, Jimmy Kidd, June Lee, ? Smith.* (Brian Maddaford)

The authorities' actions soon took effect and the number of children attending the school began to rise with a weekly average of 132 being recorded in Sly's first year as master. His continued presence at the school was to have a marked effect upon the children; no more for them a constant flow of indifferent masters, here at last was someone who had a genuine heartfelt approach to his work.

The success that was achieved by Sly at the school caused the Vestry Meeting to take stock of their responsibilities in order to give him the support he deserved. In September 1889 it was thought desirable to place the Committee of Managers of the 'Bridestowe and Sourton National School' into a position of legality. A meeting was convened to elect six members to be associated with the Committee of Managers for a three-year term, from those people who contributed to the maintenance and funding of the school in the manner as specified in the school's deed. A further step was taken in April 1892 whereby a

committee of not less than three people was to be appointed from the Bridestowe and Sourton School district. They were to cooperate with the Okehampton School Attendance Committee; it seems the attendance system was at last being taken seriously.

Bridestowe schoolchildren, 1953/4. Left to right, back row: *R. Soul, V. Head, P. Lake, S. Meadows, C. Dennis;* middle row: *V. Pidgeon, J. Howard, T. Roach, R. Romain, M. Hawkins, M. Jewell, B. Pope;* front row: *B. Lavis, C. Dawe, E. Amhoff, author, P. Turner, V. Voysey.* (Brian Lavis)

A *Directory* at the end of the nineteenth century mentions that the school was enlarged in 1895, but no other source has so far offered any more details on this. It may simply be that the *Directory* is referring to internal alterations which had taken place along with structural changes to the porch, which have not been dated. Internally the layout of the school was changed to make three classrooms of more equal proportions. This came about with the division of the big classroom by installing a wooden partition. Additionally, the wall separating the infants' classroom from the one adjacent to it was removed. The porch was enlarged and eventually converted into a cloakroom.

In 1903 Sly and his wife received a joint salary of £130, with accommodation being provided at the schoolhouse. He continued to serve the school well but a somewhat unexpected early death ended his well-chosen profession. He had become an individual of profound standing and was recognised as having served the parish well. A brass plaque was placed in his memory in the church.

After Sly's death, John R. Westcott then became master and Miss Lucy Tickell remained at the school as the infants' mistress. From the log during Westcott's time at the school an entry of 3 August 1917 included the suggestion that:

... in future the holiday had better be so arranged as to coincide with whortle-berry gathering rather than the agricultural harvests as has been done this year.

Admiration for the walker travelling from Lands End to John O' Groats, early 1970s.
(Alan Pearn)

A Brief Outline of Schooling in England

British Schools, formed in 1808, were based on the monitorial system where the older children taught groups of younger ones under the supervision of paid staff.

Cathedral and Monastic Schools were attached to cathedrals and monasteries; at the Reformation many went out of existence or were refounded as grammar schools.

Common Day Schools were run by women as elementary schools, the fees being 3d. or 4d. per week.

Junior Schools were established after the 1918 Education Act. They taught seven- to eleven-year-olds whereas the earlier elementary schools taught seven- to fourteen-year-olds.

National Schools were formed in 1811.

Forster's Education Act was passed in 1870. From this point onwards, England was to be divided into districts with Boards being set up to manage each district. Board schools were the first local-authority-run schools. They could be secular and undenominational but an amendment called Cowper-Temple Conscience Clause allowed schools to have religious instruction if they wished.

Legislation of 1876 made elementary education compulsory for all children. School attendance committees were set up when no school board existed.

The Education Act 1880 made school attendance compulsory to the age of ten at which time a child could leave on obtaining a certificate; if his record of attendance did not meet a required standard he had to stay at school for a longer period.

Education Act 1889. The Board of Education was set up. County Councils could levy a 1d. rate for technical education.

Legislation of 1891 made elementary education free.

Legislation of 1893 and 1899 raised the school leaving age to 11 then 12.

Balfour's Education Act 1902. Local authorities were empowered to provide elementary and secondary education, superseding the old School Boards.

Legislation 1918 raised the school leaving age to 14.

Education Act 1944. Fees in state secondary schools were abolished. Elementary education was reorganised into infant and junior schools, secondary education was graded into modern, grammar and technical schools. The school leaving age was raised to 15.

Doubtless schoolchildren of today would have better things to do on their school holidays! Another entry dated 24 September 1917 shows that the children had put the grounds to good use, with sales of potatoes amounting to £5.2s. An entry in the school log for the year 1919 mentions that one family (named) found to have dirty bodies and clothing was to be 'excluded till clean'!

In 1938 the school became a junior school, the senior pupils receiving their education at Okehampton. During the early years of Bridestowe School pupil teachers along with monitors, who later perhaps became pupil teachers, were employed as assistants. The master's wife or sister acted as sewing mistress as well as providing support with the infants. Later managers engaged ex-pupil teachers or supplementaries as assistants, staffing at the school generally consisting of the master and two adult assistants.

As seen from the plans of the early school (page 82) the sewerage system was rather crude; a stream running under the toilets of both sexes carried away effluent material. This system was to be in operation for nearly a century as it was not until 1940 that changes were planned. Mr Ash, a builder of Blatchford Ash, Okehampton, was asked to survey the school and provide a plan and estimation for a new drainage scheme. Ash quoted the sum of £167.10s. for the new drainage scheme and water supply to the lavatories.

Letters between the Revd Fairhurst and Canon Hall of the Exeter Diocesan Council of Religious Education refer to the problem of financing the new sewerage scheme as planned. Indeed, Canon Hall, in a letter dated November 1940, stated that during:

... this crisis the Bishop's Appeal Committee does not want to expend a large sum of money at the moment. If the sanitary authority presses urgently let me know.

It is not clear when the work was eventually executed.

In January 1951 the field behind the school known as Denbole Meadow was sold to the Devon County Council for £280. Part of this land was eventually used as a site for new classrooms and a playground.

One final observation of much interest is a plan of part of Bridestowe village that lies amongst the documents relating to the school extension in 1862. The plan indicates a piece of land at the foot of Parsonage Road that lay adjacent to the Royal Oak Annex opposite South Ball Farm, as a proposed site for the school. Whether this was to be kept in mind as an alternative site bearing in mind the objections to the original site is far from clear. If the school had indeed been rebuilt on this proposed site the schoolchildren could have taken strolls along 'Madam Put's Walk', which lay alongside Parsonage Road, to the bottom of the garden belonging to the old rectory.

One final note should be made of another school, to many probably unheard of. From an advertisement that appeared in a newspaper in 1856 we discover that Revd Alexander Watson was using the Rectory House to run a school called the Rectory School:

Master was the Revd W.H. Jackson BA, Fellow of Durham University, First Classman, late Classical Scholar, Bishop of Durham, Latin Prose Prizeman, etc etc. The commodious rectory house with the beautiful grounds by which it is surrounded has been adopted to the purposes of a select school for instruction in the several branches of a liberal education, and for the formation of the character of the Christian Gentleman, and in which elder pupils are prepared for the Universities or the Civil Service examinations; and younger pupils are prepared for the Public schools for the Military College at Sandhurst, for Woolwich and Addiscombe, and for direct appoints to India and to the Army. The dormitories are furnished with single beds for each pupil, and the classrooms are replete with all educational apparatus. The air is most salubrious and the house is supplied with hot cold and shower baths. There is a good gymnasium and extensive play and cricket ground. French German Music Survey Drilling and Fortification Drawing are taught by resident masters. Drawing and, if required, dancing, by professors, who attend every week.

Joanne Ball (11 years) serving Mr Ernie Barkell, an ex-pupil of Bridestowe School (93 years), at the Wednesday lunches for old-age pensioners, July 17, 1984. (Bridestowe School)

Class of 1989, Bridestowe School.
Left to right, back row: *Jessica Clements, Gideon Pritchard, Lee Jutson, Dominic Hardy, Sylvia Palmer, [Gaveth] Wilkins, Dean Holland;*
3rd row: *Glen Wain, Rosemary Lucas, Simon Gilbert, Cris Leonard, Iain Bateman, Melanie Colmar, Ian Bickle;*
2nd row: *Rachael Hardy, Chris Woolley, Andrew Lucas, Dafydd Thomas, Ashley Symmons, Graham Down;*
front row: *Michael Bateman, Clare Wilson, Lisa Holland and Kerry Jutson.*
(Bridestowe School)

Retiring teachers, 1968. Presentation at the Parish Hall to Mrs Cynthia Lavis by Howard Barkell upon her retirement from Bridestowe School. Mrs Nellie Milnes, head, also retired at this time.
(Howard Barkell)

Terms (to be paid in advance) from 50 to 120 guineas according to age etc. Pupils requiring a separate room 30 guineas extra. The School will re-open on Tuesday 6 August. For references to parents of former pupils and for further particulars address Reverend Alexander Watson, The Rectory, Bridestowe. Two Graduates of the English Universities would be received into the advertiser's family, to be prepared for the examination for Holy Orders and to be trained in School and Parochial Work.

Whether Revd Watson was successful or not has not been established.

SOURCES
Bovett, *Historical Notes on Devon Schools.*
Devon and Cornwall Notes and Queries, Vol XXXI.
Devon Record Office: Diocesan Records Moger Supplement 1
(Moger PR 510-510a)
Schoolmasters Licences.
2205A.
2380C/82.
Sellman, R.R., *Notes on some Devon Rural Schools, Vol 1.*
Trewman's *Exeter Flying Post*, July 1856.

Chapter 6

ST BRIDGET'S CHURCH

Hine informs us that the 'fine Norman archway' at the entrance to the churchyard of Bridestowe, which stands at the head of a 'fine avenue of beech trees' through which the church, dedicated St Bridget, is approached, 'rather raises visitors' expectations' with regard to the church. He goes on to proclaim that visitors are 'doomed to disappointment'. What then, led this particular commentator writing in the early 1870s to take such a lugubrious view of a church to which the dignitaries of Exeter Cathedral had been presented? However, it appears that it was not so much the edifice itself of which Hine disapproved, but rather the restoration to which it had been subjected. Hine writes:

Bridestowe Church. (Doug Gale)

The church is said to have been built in 1450, but nearly all the ancient features of the building have been concealed under all kinds of monstrosities in compo and cement. Like the west front of Lichfield Cathedral – Wyatt's masterpiece of shams – the tower has been most elaborately restored walls, windows, parapet, pinnacle, and all, in Portland cement! The original windows of the church in nearly all cases having been taken out and replaced by others of the most approved carpenter's Gothic type. The really finely proportioned arcades between nave and aisles have been carefully covered with a thin layer of plaster and the original moulding parodied. What were no doubt timber cradle roofs have been converted into coved plaster ceilings springing from compo cornices, such as one often sees round a three feet passage in some 'Myrtle cottage', and the decorations of the interior are so smart and antichurch like that they would appear to be almost fresh from the hands of a West End house painter, with a knowledge of ecclesiastical interiors limited,

say, to St George's, Hanover Square, or any fashionable church of the Georgian period. There is something very incongruous in all this, as though a Cockney church had been transplanted to the borders of Dartmoor. I am not aware when this building was so altered and defaced, or by whom, but on the tenor bell in the tower is this description 'these bells rehung and the tower heightened and beautified 1828'. This probably points to the time when the rest of the 'beautifying' was done. That was a bad time – a very bad time – what we architecturally call a 'Dark Age' when, notwithstanding the introduction of gas, deformity was commonly mistaken for beauty in things aesthetic. Only one or two fragments of ancient masonry have been suffered to remain uncovered; one of these, a portion of the chancel arch on the eastern side, which appears to be of Early English character, and an original stoup attached to the first pier of the nave as you enter at the south porch. The church had formerly a very elegant rood screen, and a south rood turret. There is a low screen now at the entrance to the chancel, which is, no doubt, a part of the original high one. The squint has also been restored in plaster.

From the above notes we know that Hine is unable to distinguish his lime trees from his beech, but it must be said that he certainly knows how to display his feelings of disapproval. To be fair to Hine, he was not alone in expressing such a vie of St Bridget's.

Others have commented that 'the church went through a disembowelling of the worst description' and that it 'was restored by that method of removing much of interest and substituting plaster'. Of an inscription on the tenor bell, it was claimed:

... these bells enlarged, and the tower heightened and beautified, 1828. This assertion, however, legible as it was, we could not assent to, even had the whole peal, in their 'heightened' position, dinned the information into our ears with their ponderous tongues.

Main entrance to church (containing arch from the old church upon removal of the poor houses), 1920s.
(Doug Gale)

Although the church has suffered from over-zealous restoration, all is not lost; there are accounts of the church before all the many changes took place and we find that with the passing of time, attempts were made to remedy the wrongs which had been applied to the church.

There have been three churches within the parish of Bridestowe. Early on, in AD1180, the advowson of the church was granted to the Priory and Convent of Plympton by John Fitzduke, the Bishop of Exeter. This was later to be vested in the See of Exeter. The living of Bridestowe was considered to be good, the rector being lord of the manor of Bridestowe Sanctuary and the rector of the Parish Church of Sourton, which was annexed to Bridestowe as a daughter church.

As seen earlier, the foundation of the church was based in Celtic times; it may have been built of wood but little is known of the structure in this era. Also noted earlier, the church was dedicated to St Bridget, or, as sometimes known, St Bride,

who was an abbess and a patroness of Ireland. She died in Kildare early in the sixth century. The translation of her remains along with those of St Patrick and St Columba, to the Cathedral of Down, took place in the year 1186.

A second edifice was constructed on the same site, near where the present church stands. More is known about this second church, as revealed in an account by Revd Coryndon Luxmore written in March 1830:

The old church remained in the churchyard and was converted by the addition of chimneys into a Poor house. After thirty years' exertion to get the nuisance removed I succeeded. It was completely the shell of an old church, its roof being circular, and very curiously put together. A Saxon arch divided the chancel from the body of the church, I have placed it at my own expense at the principal entrance to the churchyard. The foundation of the tower was extremely curious, being circular, six feet deep, and built of thin stones from the moor, placed edgewise without mortar. I found in the ruins of the house a small silver coin of Henry VI.

Although the removal of the second church is to be regretted, we can be thankful that Revd Luxmore had the foresight to save the archway.

Use of the second church was probably discontinued in about 1450 when the present church came into use. Unfortunately, it is unclear whether the third church was built due to an increase in population, or to create more space for elaborate ceremony.

Surprisingly, we have to wait until the thirteenth century before we come across any information regarding everyday worship from documentary evidence. It is from the register of the Bishop of Exeter, Walter Bronescombe, that we begin to learn of the first recorded rector who lay at the head of a long line of incumbents that served at St Bridget's. Bishop Bronescombe's itinerary shows that:

On the Tuesday after the Feast of the Exaltation of the Holy Cross (16 September 1259) there was a Visitation of the Church of Bridestowe, as is given in full of the Register of Visitations.

Upon his visit the Bishop found that the living of St Bridget's was void whereupon the following day he committed the vacant possession to the charge of Thomas de Radeleghe, in the name of Nicholas de Plimptone, at the presentation of its true patrons, the Prior and Convent of Plympton. Nicholas de Plimptone was admitted by the Bishop to the Rectory by proxy, on 30 October 1259, becoming the first rector of Bridestowe to have his name on record. The custody was to

Pathway from main entrance to church lined with lime trees, 1920s.
(Doug Gale)

terminate on the following Easter Day (24 March 1259/60).

Master Roger de Toriz, or Thoriz, was instituted to Bridestowe on 27 October 1266. Prior to his institution to Bridestowe, and, indeed, during his rectorship, Toriz led an active life, being high-minded and scholarly. As he was granted various appointments within the Diocese of Exeter it is very doubtful whether he spent much time, if any, at his living in Bridestowe.

Roger de Toriz died on 29 April 1274 and was buried in a place most befitting someone of his position. Amongst the chantries in Exeter Cathedral is 'one chauntrye called Torryge' that had been named Toriz as a lasting tribute to Dean Roger by Bishop Peter Quivil.

Gilbert de Titinge, or Tytingge, was instituted 'on his promotion to Bridestow' on 24 September 1274. After a period of five years Titinge resigned his 'promotion' for Bishopsteignton.

Master Andrew de Kylkenny, or Kilkenny, was instituted to Bridestowe on 30 December 1279. Whilst at Bridestowe he was granted a 'licence to study theology for five years (9 October 1281)'. He succeeded to many positions within the Exeter Diocese, including the Bishop of Exeter's Official and his Proctor in Convocation. Andrew resigned Bridestowe in 1282 on being collated as Canon of Exeter on 22 November 1282.

Master Henry Kylkenny, Subdeacon, was instituted to the Rectory of Bridestowe on 6 September 1282. Only a few days after his institution to St Bridget's, Henry had been granted a licence of non-residence for five years to study Canon Law, 'with permission to put out his Benefice to farm meanwhile'.

As the registers of Bishop Bytton are not extant it is impossible to say for sure who succeeded Henry to the Rectory of Bridestowe. However, in Bishop Stapledon's Register we find a Letter of Dimissory and two licences of non-residence. These refer to three rectors who worked at Bridestowe.

Ralph de Knovyle may have been Henry Kylkenny's successor; from a licence of non-residence we see that Ralph was rector in December 1312. He had been granted a year's absence in which to study.

Master Gilbert de Knoville appears likewise from a licence of non-residence as being the rector of Bridestowe in 1321. On 15 December of that year he also had been given a year in which to study. Master William de Beare appears in a Letter of Dimissory as the rector in 1325. He was to have a number of dispensations for non-residence in order to study. An entry dated 1331 in the Bishop's Register reads:

Ashcombe. Item 3 November, the Parisian Master William Beare, rector of the Church at Brittestowe, as a priest, obtained a licence to study both in England and abroad for a whole year, with the customary edict and proviso.

In 1333 William was granted:

... a licence of non-residence until 3 November 1334 so as to study with the proviso that he should return to the aforesaid Church once a year, especially during Lent, so as to attend to the needs of the parishioners committed to his care; he should in no way omit this, if he can possibly be there.

On 12 September 1336 a further dispensation was given to him for study purposes provided that he 'return to his Church during Lent'. His studies led to him becoming a Bachelor of Canon and Civil Law by 1333, in which year the Dean and Chapter of Salisbury employed him as an advocate.

During William's time at Bridestowe a licence from the King dated 18 February 1338 granted the appropriation of the advowsons of Bridestowe, Bratton Clovelly and Ilsington to Bishop Grandison, for his College of Ottery St Mary. In fact, only Ilsington was so appropriated. Edward III issued a further licence which empowered Bishop Grandison to allow the Priory and

Convent of Plympton to appropriate the Benefice of Bridestowe. This Royal Licence never took effect. The pension of £6.13s.4d. that the Prior and Convent of Plympton received from the rectory of Bridestowe continued until the Dissolution of the monasteries in the sixteenth century.

In 1342 William was without funds to repair his church. During a visitation from the Archdeanery of Totnes it was noted that:

The chancel is inadequate. The Antiphonar is worn out. The chancel, the Antiphonar, and defects in buildings and glebe fences can be repaired for twenty pounds. Sir William, the rector, had nothing for defects.

Bridestowe Church interior, 1920s. (Alan Pearn)

If Master William de Beare was without funds it leads us to the question when, or, perhaps more pertinent, if the defects highlighted were put in good order? Unfortunately there is no record of such work being completed.

Seven years after this visitation the Black Death took hold (1349–1352). One source states that Bridestowe had an institution to the Rectory during those years. However, this seems unlikely as there was no institution until 1360, and only William Beare is recorded as rector (although it may be possible to suggest that a curate died from the Black Death during this time).

William de Beare's death is referred to in a petition to the Pope in 1359, in which Bishop Grandison attempts to appoint a member of his household, one Guy de Ayschwylle, to the Rectory of Bridestowe. The position had become 'void by the death of Master William Beare'. However, it appears that the petition was unsuccessful as a different cleric is recorded in succession to William de Beare.

Henry Pyke is given as the next rector of Bridestowe in Bishop Grandison's Register; he was collated to the benefice on 26 August 1360. However, it seems his institution was questioned, as he petitioned the Pope for confirmation of his appointment, which he duly received. In 1350,

before taking this position, he was Subdean of Exeter Cathedral during which time he was referred to as 'being on the Continent'. The date of his return to this country is not known.

In 1366, Henry declared to his Bishop, his offices and their values:

To you, Venerable Father and my Lord in Christ, Lord Bishop of Exeter, I, Henry Pyke, Master of Arts and Bachelor in both Laws, by these present writings, clearly, distinctly and in detail, set out my benefices. And I declare that in your Church at Exeter I have received a Canonry and at the moment I hold office as a Canon and Prebendary, of which the fruits, receipts and benefits go no way beyond four pounds sterling according to the Tythes taxation. And I declare that the fruits, receipts and benefits of the Parish Church of Bristowe in your diocese, do not amount to more than twelve pounds sterling, according to the Tythes taxation.

Following the death of Henry Pyke, Bishop Brantyngham collated John Loffwyke, formerly Clerk of the Diocese of Lincoln, to Bridestowe 28 February 1373. John was the first in a line of 13 incumbents who were to serve the parish for laconic periods, spanning 34 years or more. It is unlikely that such a rapid succession of priests contributed anything to the parishioners' needs. The religious and spiritual aspects of church life must have suffered; it may even have descended into a low level of forbearance.

On 14 November 1374, on the petition of William Talbot, Bishop Brantyngham granted a licence to the inhabitants of Sourton, to hold the celebration of all ritual services, burial excepted, in their chapel. It was stated that no prejudice should arise to the mother church at Bridestowe. Two years after this, it appeared that John had failed his Sourton parishioners in that he did not administer the daily services to which they were anciently accustomed. The case of dereliction of duty brought by the parishioners of Sourton against Sir John Loffwyke was a long drawn out affair, which lasted over three years. It was finally resolved in the favour of the Sourton people, but by this time, Sir John had already departed for the Benefice of Marsh Gibbon.

Sir John Wayte, rector of Marsh Gibbon in the Diocese of Lincoln, was collated to Bridestowe in London on 10 September 1377, the day that he had exchanged with Sir John Loffwyke. Before the ink used to record his collation in the Bishop's register was barely dry, John Wayte exchanged his new position for another.

Sir Walter Aumeney, vicar of Godmanchester, was collated in London to the Rectory of Bridestowe on 29 October 1377. He remained at Bridestowe for eight years during which time he

---

Church Plate

The church plate as recorded by the Reverend Coryndon Luxmore in 1830 recites

A silver Flagon large and handsome, inscribed 'Ex dono Domina Honoris Calmady Ecclesia de Bridestowe 1639.'
A small silver Communion Cup.
A silver Salver inscribed 'Ex dono Edwardis Drewe rectoris in usam hujus ecclesia 1659.'
A small pewter flagon and dish are also mentioned.

From a report in the Transactions of the Devonshire Association we have

Chalice – A baluster stem cup. 160 mm. high; bowl with a sacred monogram, 96 mm. diameter, 81 mm. deep; foot, 96 mm. diameter.
Inscription: 'Bridestowe Parish. 1676' (pricked).
Marks: R N (Richard Neale) and London hall marks for 1655.
Weight, 9 oz. 6 dwt.
Paten – On stand, with gadroon border round foot. 251 mm. diameter, 65 mm. high; foot, 108 mm. diameter.
Marks: Maker's illegible, and London hall marks for 1692.
Flagon – A tankard with domed lid. 245 mm. high, 197 mm. to lid, 98 mm. diameter at lid, 144 mm. at base.
Inscription: 'Presented by S. C. Hamlyn Esq., of Leawood and Paschoe, Devon, Christmas, 1865, to the parish of Bridestowe, Devon.'
Weight, 29 oz. 3 dwt.
Marks: W D, trefoil over (Wm. Darkerall), and London hall marks for 1730.
Alms Dish – Now used as paten. A plain plate. 225 mm. diameter.
Marks: A L, mullet under in quatrefoil (A. Lowders?), and London hall marks for 1692.
Weight, 15 oz. 10 dwt.
The chalice, paten, and alms dish have had the sacred monogram in circle added as ornamentation in the early nineteenth century.

---

was subjected to a Clerical Subsidy as well as the Tenths and Fifteenths. Under the Clerical Subsidy, the benifice was 'valued at xij^li and taxed at v^s'. Taking the total benefices as a whole from the Clerical Subsidy we find that Bridestowe was set at the third highest rate of valuation while the tax was set at the highest rate.

As for the Tenths and Fifteenths, the tithing of 'Brictistawe' was set at 16s.8d., as was the tithing for Sourton. This gave a combined sum of £1.13s.4d. Out of an approximate total of just over 600 tithings for Devon, Bridestowe came within the top 20 per cent of contributors. If we combine Bridestowe's payment with that of Sourton, it represents the twenty-fifth highest contribution of tithe within the hundreds of Devon.

Walter Aumeney had apparently taken a period of non-residence without seeking permission from his bishop. As a result of his absence, the revenues of Bridestowe church were sequestered. Luckily as far as Walter was concerned the sequestration was relaxed. One can only presume that he had good reason for his absence from Bridestowe for three months later he had been granted permission to continue with his period of non-residence. Just over a week after knowing that his non-residence

was now above board, seemingly thanks to friends in high places, Walter left the church at Bridestowe.

Sir Thomas Hertforde, the rector of Lymine, Kent, exchanged his benefice with Walter Aumeney for Bridestowe, he being collated at London on 11 November 1385. Following this, Thomas de Prestone, the rector of Essendon, Herts, exchanged his benefice with Thomas Hertforde. Prestone was collated to Bridestowe at London on 29 November 1387. Prestone stayed at Bridestowe for four years but it appears that he was not in residence for much of this time. He was consequently subject to sequestration. From a letter dated 21 May 1389 we find:

Bridestowe; Sir Thomas de Prestone, rector–Sequestration relaxed; To the same Thomas a formal injunction that he return to his Church at Bridestowe, to take up personal residence, as he is obliged to by Canon Law.

By now, one begins to wonder why these men of the Church took up the rectorship of Bridestowe if they had no intention of residing in the benefice.

After being collated at Chudleigh on 5 July 1391, Sir Robert Derby, the rector of Smarden,

Kent, exchanged his benefice with Thomas de Prestone for Bridestowe. Derby stayed at Bridestowe for just six months. After him came Sir Robert Wantynge, rector of Fawley, Bucks, who exchanged his benefice with Sir Robert Derby for Bridestowe. He was collated at Clyst on 21 December 1391. Wantynge stayed at Bridestowe for six years.

Nicholas Bodeway, rector of Arreton, in the Diocese of Winchester exchanged his benefice with Sir Robert Wantynge for Bridestowe on 14 May 1397. A year later Nicholas was granted a licence of non-residence for one year to study at Oxford from 16 May.

Another one-year period of non-residence for study at Oxford was granted to Bodeway from 1 May 1399. From 3 October 1402, three years non-residency was granted to Bodeway for further study whilst he had yet another year from 3 October 1405. Nicholas Bodeway was not to return to Bridestowe as rector, having spent his whole period as incumbent to the parish studying at Oxford. One wonders whether the parishioners of Bridestowe at this time were suffering the dereliction that their fellow parishioners at Sourton had experienced a few years earlier.

Reginald Bryta, rector of Bratton Clovelly, exchanged his benefice with Nicholas Bodeway for Bridestowe on 30 October 1406. He exchanged his rectory for Dittisham on 30 September 1409.

In turn, John Prata, exchanged his rectory for Bridestowe with Reginald Bryta. Like his predecessors, he was also granted a licence of non-residence for one year from 20 June 1410, and a further licence from 23 December 1411 to Michaelmas 1412. The following year however, he exchanged his living at Bridestowe for one at St Pancras.

John Wykyngston, the rector of St Pancras, exchanged for Bridestowe on 24 May 1413. During his short incumbency Wykyngston was granted a licence for non-residence for a period of one year from 30 September 1414. Four months later he appeared at Westminster to show cause why he should not 'pay to John, Prior of Plympton, £10, being arrears of the annual pension of ten marks due from the living of Bridestowe.' Just five months after this hearing, Wykyngston was on the move. During the time that his period of non-residence was still in force, he exchanged the benefice of Bridestowe with William Weston, who was the rector of Deene, on 23 July 1415. During his brief incumbency Weston offered a 'competent salary' to Robert Franke, a Devonshire chaplain, to serve the Parish Church of Bridestowe. However, Franke refused this undertaking, which led Weston to appeal to the Bishop for a remedy. As a result a Commission was issued on 31 October 1415 that resulted in Robert Franke being warned:

... three several times that he proceeds within ten days to the work at Bridestowe, on pain of suspension. If he refused to submit, he was to appear in person before the Bishop, at Clyst.

The outcome of this event is not known but William Weston resigned Bridestowe a year later.

John Fosse was collated to Bridestowe by Bishop Stafford on 26 November 1416. This collation marked the beginning of a long period of stability – John Fosse remained at the church for nearly 40 years.

During this period, Bridestowe's third church was constructed – this being the edifice that now stands in the churchyard. During the building of the new church an objection was raised by the parishioners of Sourton, on being called upon to provide funds for the rebuilding of the nave. At Chudleigh on 13 February 1451:

... a ratification of a composition took effect between the parishioners of the mother church of Brigidestowe, plaintiffs, and those of the dependant chapel of Sourton, defendants, made after long suit and a judgement for the plaintiffs in the Exeter consistory court, an appeal to the Court of Canterbury and a remission to the Exeter court. The wardens and parishioners of Sourton are to contribute towards the rebuilding of the nave of Brigidestowe church (now actually in progress) 20 marks, and no more except out of charity; and henceforth, every year on or within four weeks of the dedication festival of St Brigid [1 Feb] they are to pay the wardens of Brigidestowe 2s.6d. towards the fabric, books and ornaments. They are to keep up and renew when necessary that part of Brigidestowe churchyard which they have always maintained. If the parishioners of Sourton refuse to pay the 2s.6d. at the Feast of St Bridget or refuse to maintain their sector of the churchyard, or refuse to observe St Bridget's Day or the Feast of Dedication then it will be lawful for the parishioners of Brigidestowe to go to law to recover the cost from each and every parishioner of Sourton. Provided that if the Sourton people are late in paying but willing to pay on some Sunday or holy day together with any losses or expenses the Brigidestowe people may have incurred by reason of the delay and in future are prepared to observe and keep St Bridget's Day then the legal prosecution must stop.

James Banastre was the next rector of Bridestowe but the date of his institution was not recorded. As such, it is not known how long he served as incumbent before he resigned.

Hamon Bothe, LLD, who was the rector of Morchard Bishop, was collated to Bridestowe on 8 December 1474. However, he resigned just two months later, in favour of St Clement Danes, London.

Richard Bothe was collated to Bridestowe on 9 February 1475. Alas, he died in 1477. Richard Stubbes was collated to Bridestowe on 16 February 1478. He served his parishioners for less than three years before he resigned. Next came Lawrence Ryell, who was collated to Bridestowe on 2 September 1480. Nothing more is known of this rector.

Ralph Oldham is the next rector of Bridestowe, from 1535. He is mentioned in the *Valor Ecclesiasticus* of Henry VIII, where we find his living valued at:

	£.	s.	d.
Glebe estimated at	5	0	0
Sheaf	12	0	0
Tithes of wool and lambs	6	0	0
Of hay	0	6	0
Other tithes and offerings	10	4	2
Deducting 6s.8d. for archidiaconal fees, synodical dues 3s.6d., and visitation fees to the Bishop, 2s.2½d.	0	12	4½
Nett value	32	17	9½
Tenths	3	5	9½

During Ralph's incumbency a commissioner's report in 1553 informs us that there were 'iij bells in the towre' at Bridestowe.

James Bond was collated to Bridestowe 23 September 1554. He died whilst still rector, on 25 November 1570.

Roger Evans was collated to Bridestowe on 23 January 1571. However, records show that six months later he was no longer at Bridestowe. Unfortunately, the reason for his departure remains unknown.

William Marston was collated to Bridestowe on 16 June 1571. Marston was also collated as Precentor of Exeter Cathedral on 19 December 1571. After leaving Bridestowe in 1575, he became rector of Silverton, and died in 1599.

Gilbert Germyn was collated to Bridestowe 29 July 1575. It is not clear, however, whether this collation came about at the time of William Marston's departure. Gilbert recorded details of the land attached to his glebe and the land that belonged to the sanctuary manor, in a glebe terrier. From an account of the Bidlakes, it seems Gilbert fell into dispute with some of his parishioners. Although this account is fairly damning of Gilbert's character, he cannot have been as unpleasant as the report would have us believe; he remained at Bridestowe for 36 years, until his death in 1611. Whatever the disposition of Gilbert Germyn at least he can be applauded for remaining in office for some time.

Edward Cotton, the next rector of Bridestowe, the son of Dr William Cotton, the Bishop of

Exeter, 1598–1621, held a number of positions within the religious hierarchy. The year of his collation to Bridestowe is uncertain, it was performed by his father on 30 October, either in 1611 or 1613.

It seems that Edward spent little of his time, if any, at Bridestowe. During the Visitations of 1630 and 1638, he was represented by his curates, James Tucker, for Bridestowe and Thomas Woodroofe, for Sourton. During the Civil War Edward followed the Royalist movement. In 1643 he was reported amongst others to have followed the army of Sir Ralph Hopton. Edward suffered the loss of his Bridestowe living.

William Knapman of Throwley, a Puritan Nominee, was placed to the living of Bridestowe by order of the House of Commons in 1647 following the sequestration of Edward Cotton. Through Knapman we appear to have the earliest extant record of the beating of the bounds of Bridestowe and Sourton Common. We find amongst the

---

Glebe Terrier Circa 1601

The Rectorie of Briddistowe wth the Chaple of Sourton annexed therunto.

1: *The Patron is the Lorde Bishopp of Exon /*

2: *Ther are no Implements belonging to the same /*

3: *The scantuarie groundes is estemade to be 36: acres or ther a boute whereof ther are 3: acres of meadowe and the rest eareable grounde /*

4: *The Scantuarie is bonded one the [easte] sydde wth one tenement called Westerleue and the lands of the heires of Digaporte and one the weste sidde wth the lands of one Mr Wythers one the north sidde wth the high waye and one the Southe sidde wth the lane that leadeth from Digaporte to Briddistowe Towne /*

5: *There are belonging to the saide Rectorie 12: acres of smale Woodes or ther about banded wth one River called Ledde (Lyd) Water / Smyth grounde Mr John Lanxfordes woode and Brymbleham woode /*

6: *Ther is appurtayninge to the same Rectorie a litle manr viz 5: tenements: 2: Cottages and 2: free tennements for the wch man.r the p'son payeth yearlie to her Maties Collector 6li: 3s.: 4d.: and the yearlie Rente wch the p'son receiveth of the saide manr is 6:li 4s. and 4d. and 3s.: of the 2: free tenements /*

Gilbert Germyn

THE BOOK OF BRIDESTOWE

Bidlake papers notes taken by Knapman, not only of the bounds of his own parish, but those of a number of others as well.

Upon the Restoration, William Knapman was ejected from the living of Bridestowe. It is important to note that although Knapman had the label of 'intruder' attached to his name, he should not be presumed to be someone unworthy of the priesthood. As confirmation of this, Knapman was, amongst others, chosen to preach in St James' Chapel Okehampton, during 1657.

William Hutton was collated to Bridestowe on 9 August 1661. The Visitations of Bishop Seth in 1665 reveal that 'Hutton hath Bridestowe his curate Clement Hatch Soorton his curate Palmer he resides at Northlewe'. Hutton was yet another rector who elected not to live at Bridestowe. He died in 1670.

Edward Drewe, another Exeter dignitary, was collated to Bridestowe on 4 November 1671. Less than a year later, on 3 September 1672, he succeeded to the Archdeaconry of Cornwall. On 25 August 1675 he became Chancellor of Exeter but resigned from the office the following September.

Edward was probably absent from his rectory at Bridestowe, paying a curate to act on his behest. From a letter we learn of one such curate, a Mr Rowe, who had served Bridestowe at one time, and the name of another member of the clergy who was hoping to succeed to Rowe's position upon his departure. The letter, written and signed by Nicholas Downe dated 9 October 1675, includes this:

... he had some weeks since been desiring the assistance of the Registrar to obtain his succession to Mr Rowe in the parishe of Bridestowe. The parish is still vacant and Mr Drewe (I am informed) do seeke of a Curate. Therefore I have presumed to renewe my requests and again to importune your helpe in the thing. Mr Pindarvis, to whom I have heard ye curacy of ye parish now voyd was offered, is a person of good quality and parentage, and so will not submitt to live a Curate. You knowe, sir, yt a wedge may not enter with one stroake and yet a second passage may be wrought.

It is unclear whether Nicholas Downe did become a curate at Bridestowe, but for certainty from his letter we can tell what calibre of man he was – desperate for the position, with the ability to abuse others in an affable tone.

A glebe terrier signed by Edward Drewe, which can only be dated to the beginning of the eighteenth century, reveals for the first time a description of the Parsonage house, outbuildings, gardens and the glebe lands. The house was built primarily of stone and covered with a shingle roof. The ground floor consisted of a hall, parlour, kitchen, dairy, porch, and an entrance. The first floor consisted of a chamber over the parlour, a chamber over the kitchen and another chamber over the dairy, a study over the porch and a gallery over the entrance. All of the chambers

Bridestowe Church, c.1912. (Doug Gale)

Glebe Terrier Circa 1700

A Terrier of the Glebe Land [House and] Mannor belonging to the Parsonage of Bridestow.

The Dwelling house the walls mostly built with stone and covered with Shin[g]le onlt the out houses being Thatcht contayning one Hall one Parlour one Kitching one Dairrey over the Parlour one Chamber over the Porch one Study over the Dairrey one Chamber over the Kitching one Chamber all parted with walls plaistered and one Gallery over the entry one Stable one Barne two Shipping one large Court at the coming into the house one Garden on the South Side of the Court one Orchard on the East Side of the Court all which Containe 1 acre.

Three little Meadows bounded on the east with one field called the Parsonage ham on the west with the highway leading to the Church on the North with Mr Calmadys lands & on the South with the Barne the Court the Orchard & the land leadding from the Court to the Ham containing 4 acres 1/2.

One field called the Close above the house 4 acres 1/2.

One field called the South Sentrey 8 acres.

One field called the Middle Sentrey 10 acres.

One field called the Clover Close 3 acres.

One field called the Ham 2 acres.

Two fields called the North Sentreye 13 acres.

Bounded on the east & south with the Tenement called West ..ise and Diggeport on the west with the highway leading from Diggeport to Bridestow Church on the North with the highway.

A Mannor containing Tenn Tenements the high Rent of which is Six Pounds Thirteene Shilling & fower pence which is yearely paid by the Rector unto the Kings Majesty as a fee farme Rent 06:13:04.

had plastered walls. The outhouses, which had been thatched, consisted of a stable, a barn and two shippons. All the buildings stood in grounds laid out as a large court. Upon entry a small garden lay to the south of the court whilst an orchard lay to the east, all of which amounted to one acre. The glebe land totalled 45 acres, an increase of nine acres from the terrier of Gilbert Germyn.

Death at the age of 70 ended Edward's rectorship of 45 years. Despite being absent for much of this time, he figured amongst the lean number of his peers who remained at Bridestowe for a great number of years. He was buried in Exeter Cathedral on 21 December 1714.

William Stuart was collated to Bridestowe on 20 April 1715. Stuart became the rector of Sowton Church in 1716, which appears to have been his principal incumbency. He was buried in a vault outside the east window of that church on 30 June 1734, having died at Bath.

Peter Burnaford, who was collated to Bridestowe on 10 October 1734, was the son of Thomas Burnaford of Lamerton. He served Bridestowe for 45 years, but for the majority of his rectorship he chose to reside outside the parish. He lived in the neighbouring parish of Lamerton.

A rural dean's visit in 1748 found a problem with one of the bells; it was cracked and could not be chimed. A year later the bell was in the same condition but extraordinary circumstances meant the bell could not be repaired. A contract had been made with a bell founder for 'new casting the said Bell, but before the Work was begun the man was taken up and put into St Thomas Ward' as a debtor. As a result, a contract was made with Mr Pennington of Lehant. The bell founder was 'to have it recast in two months time at longest'. On this occasion the offending bell was indeed recast.

A Church Rate

Bridestow parish September 20 1659
A Rate made by Henry Bidlake gent and John Powell esquire for the repairing of the church.

	s.	d.		s.	d.
Lewood	2	8	Nicholas Burrow	0	10
Bigger Crandford	0	8	....	0	4
littell Crandford	0	4	Longham & Allins Town	1	0
Cobhamweek	4	4	Thomas Leaman	1	4
Great Bidlake	2	8	Richard Tirball	1	4
Way	0	8	Joan Ebsworthie	1	4
Brambleham	0	6	John [Rowndell]	1	4
great close	1	8	Richard Youlden	0	8
Coombow	2	8	Bear[a]	1	6
Higher Stone	1	8	Edward	0	8
Lower Stone	1	8	.... Daw	0	4
Sprighill	0	10	Leonard Gubbin	0	4
Walter Hawton	3	8	Humphry	0	8
Blackabroom	2	6	John [Wilkery]	0	8
Millaton	2	0	Henry Hockaday	0	6
littell Bidlake	1	2	Richard	0	6
George Stitson	1	8	John Daw	0	2
William	1	4	Standon	0	8
John	1	6	Mr George	0	6
Walter	0	8	Storkmans temt	0	6
John Maddaford	1	4	Stephen William	0	6
Aser Walter	1	4	Robert [Rowndell]	0	6
John Walter	0	5	Tanners Meadow	0	2
John Gill	1	4	Denbole Parks	0	2
Smelland	1	0	[Warrens Well]	0	1

Bishop Frederick's Visitation of June 1764 required a number of questions to be answered by Peter Burnaford about his parish and the daughter church of Sourton. The questions that were asked can be gleaned from the answers he gave:

I do not reside personally upon my Benefice of Bridestowe, but in Lamerton, an adjoining parish being indulged to do so by favour of my late Lord Lavington on account of my age and bad state of health. My curate's name is William Preston. He lives in Oakehampton as he could not get a convenient or agreeable house to board or be tabled at in Bridestow and being a gentleman not of a healthy but tender constitution therefore hopes your Lordship will indulge him yr favour of non-residence until he is in a better state of health. He is not licensed particularly to Bridestowe yet having not been long curate, but is to a former cure in your Lordship's Diocese. I allow him 40 pounds per ann. and the perquisites, which are worth about five pounds more communibus annis.

I have no other Benefice than Bridestow, as Sourton is only a chapel annexed to it.

I am thro' age [in] infirm state of health incapacitated to perform divine service myself, and have been for several years past.

Looking towards the church entrance from Rectory Road, 1930s. (Alan Pearn)

Divine service is performed in ye Church of Bridestow with a sermon once every Lord's Day thro' out ye year ye same in ye chapel of Sourton. Two Sundays successively ye sermon is in ye morning at Bridestow and ye third Sunday ye sermon is in ye morning at Sourton when ye sermon is in ye afternoon at Bridestow, which is ye usual method of ye performance of divine service.

The Sacrament of the Lord's Supper is administered four times in ye year both at Bridestow and Sourton on ye three great festivals and also about Mich'mas on ye Sunday preceding or following that festival, at each church.

The number of communicants at both churches were 50 at Christmas last.

The children are catechised in ye summer season after ye second lesson in ye afternoon in both

churches on several Sundays.

The churches and chapels both of Bridestowe and Sourton are in good repair, and there are all things decent for divine service.

The terrier of ye glebe lands, houses etc is in my Registers Office of Exeter, a copy of which I have in my custody.

The number of families in Bridestow is about 60, and about ye same number in Sourton.

There is not any chapel but Sourton which is annexed to ye living of Bridestow and in your Lordship's collation or patronage. Divine service is performed in it by my curate, as above.

There are no reported papists, nor any meeting-houses for dissenting congregations; nor are there any dissenters of any denomination.

There is no publick school, but there is a private school in both parishes. There are no almshouses, hospitals or other charitable endowments yt I know of; but only two houses for ye poor people situated in the churchyard, and repaired at ye expense of ye parish. [There was no parochial library.]

There is a field about four acres in measure called the Parish Ham in Bridestowe lying near ye River Lyd in Lyddecombe valued at 50 shillings yearly rent, which is received by ye churchwardens and applied to ye use of ye parish, time immemorial, as I am informed.

The date of my collation is: October 10th 1734.

The date of my priests orders is Oct 20th 1717.

The number of catechisms that may offer themselves for confirmation may be about 30 as there was about that number confirmed by ye late Lord Bishop of [Terne] some few years past.

My Honoured Lord, as I cannot write very legible thro' a nervous disorder in my hands I doubt not but your Lordship will be pleased to admitt of my making use of ye hands of a neighbouring clergyman, and I am your Lordship's most dutiful and obedient servant.

Lamerton near Tavistock Devon April 2 1764.

Signed by Peter Burnaford.

Upon death and according to his wishes, Peter was buried at Lamerton. His will was proved on 22 January 1778.

Thomas Herberden was collated to Bridestowe on 1 May 1779. Whilst rector, Thomas was 'chaplain to the Bishop of Exeter', and had a dispensation from the Archbishop of Canterbury in February 1782 to 'hold the Rectory of Bridestowe, (value £300) together with the vicarage of Bishop's Nympton (value £190).'

Charles Thomas Coryndon Luxmore was collated to Bridestowe on 22 October 1786. He was part of the Luxmore family, descended from William, the eighth Earl of Glencairn, who settled in the Okehampton district in the seventeenth century. Some of the Luxmores became Mayors of

Okehampton and lived in the mansion house there called 'Fairplace'. From the start of his incumbency, and using the limited means at his disposal, Charles became a benefactor dedicated to improving the quality of life for his parishioners. They must have felt fortunate to have his services in the days when life, particularly for the poor, was very hard. He remained in the post for 59 years until his death in 1845.

Charles was elected as an Assistant Burgess of Okehampton before becoming Principal Burgess in 1787. He then became Mayor of Okehampton between 1790 and 1796. In 1792 Charles was chaplain of St James' Chapel in Okehampton and the master of the grammar school. As a parson schoolmaster he taught the youth of Okehampton, held two prayer sessions a day in the Chapel of St James, preached four session sermons a year and conducted a service at the election of the mayor.

On 1 November 1792, Charles married Caroline Putt, daughter of Reymundo and Lucretia Putt of George Street, Plymouth, at St Andrew's Church. Caroline was 'a young lady' who was 'possessed of every accomplishment and a genteel fortune'. Shortly after the wedding Mr and Mrs Luxmore 'settled' at Bridestowe.

Bishop Cary's visitation in 1821 resulted in a series of questions. Charles' replies reveal more details of his benefaction towards the people of Bridestowe Parish.

I am unsure of the number of families but a list will soon be returned by the overseers. There are no papists or dissenters amongst their numbers. I reside in the Parsonage House at Bridestowe.

I have another benefice at Lanteglos near Camelford which is served by Thomas Amory, the resident curate, but I do not know if he is licensed or not. I pay him 85 pounds per annum and he has the house and garden free of all taxes, as are the surplice fees. I also perform divine service at Sourton, a daughter church of the benefice.

Divine service is held on the Lord's Day once at Sourton and once at Bridestowe regularly at 11 and two o'clock with a sermon at each place.

As for the instruction of youth in religion in Bridestowe, there is a boys' school to the number of 50, likewise for girls. In Sourton a school for boys and girls upward of 40 in number, but there is no provision for religious instruction.

The youth are catechised at the schools in Lent but I have no funds for procuring books for such a number of scholars and cannot supply the whole – but as far as my means will allow it – I do it.

The sacrament of the Lord's Supper is administered four times a year in each parish.

At Sourton there were 74 communicants whilst at Bridestowe there were 75 perfectly different communicants.

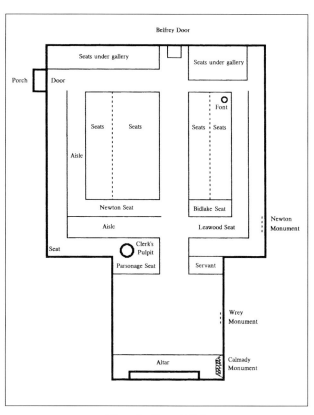

Church Plan 1830.
(Based on a sketch drawn by Revd Luxmore)

The only benefaction is one small field, value five pounds annually, given to the church now on a lease for a single life of which the churchwardens receive the chief rent. This benefaction is properly applied. There is a house for the reception of the poor, which was the old church. It is a disgrace to humanity as well as to the churchyard where it is situated.

There is no parochial library.

The parsonage house is in very good repair, as is the chancel and churchyard. Bridestowe church, however, is undergoing a thorough repair. Sourton church is in good repair.

I have a copy of the Terrier of the Glebe Lands from Domesday Book of the church etc. The only chapel is at Sourton as above.

My priests orders are dated 24 September 1786, whilst my institution is 28 October 1786.

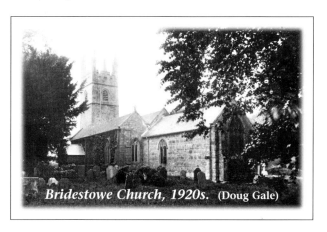

Bridestowe Church, 1920s. (Doug Gale)

We can see from the answers provided by Coryndon Luxmore to his Bishop that he attempted to supply books for the schoolchildren from his own pocket. This announcement is surely another statement of his charitable belief. Two other declarations he made are of much more interest however, namely, 'there are no dissenters' and 'the church is undergoing a thorough repair'.

It seems that it was not strictly the case that there were no dissenters in the parish. Amongst the Exeter Diocesan papers are some certificates from dissenting parishioners of Bridestowe, dated between 1811 and 1844. The earliest such certificate reads:

To the Honourable and Right Reverend Father in God George by Divine Permission Lord Bishop of Exeter. We whose names are hereunto subscribed do hereby certify that we have set apart a certain building in the town and parish of Bridestow in the county of Devon for the worship of Almighty God by certain of his Majestys Protestant subjects dissenting from the Church of England which we request may be registered pursuant to Act of Parliament.

2 November 1811 John Cloake, [Stn] Hockaday, Samuel Youlden, M. Chapman and Harriot Taylor.

In 1829 we find that:

... a house or building the property of Mr John White innkeeper... to be used as a place of religious worship by... Protestants (etc) and request a certificate.

It is not clear whether the property was one of the village inns or a private dwelling, but we can see that Bridestowe certainly had a number of dissenting parishioners. Indeed, by 1834 records show:

I John Scoble of the parish of Bridestowe Descenting Minister do hereby certify that a building has lately been erected in the village of Bridestowe to be used as a place of religious worship by Protestants.

The final certificate dated 1844 reveals that the dissenters called themselves the 'Bible Christians'.

It is unknown why Charles failed to report the dissenters amongst his parishioners in 1821 when there is much evidence that proves they were present.

When Charles mentioned the thorough repairs that were taking place at the church, he must have been referring to the nave and tower, as he reports the chancel was in good repair. Earlier it was noted that the heightening of the tower and the recasting of the bells took place in 1828, as were repairs effected by the liberal use of cement to obliterate many of the original characteristics

within the church. Other than extending the height of the tower and the hanging of a new peel of bells, we are not aware of any other alteration except for the making good of all stonework, not by restoration, but, as seen, by excess injury. A number of modern authors state that the peel of bells was increased at the time they were recast in 1828 from the three at the time of Edward VI, to the present six. This cannot be right, Polwhele gives six bells in 1791 'from the minister'.

Charles Thomas Coryndon Luxmore died on 10 August 1845 at the Rectory House of Bridestowe aged 90. John Buller was collated on 26 November 1845, but it seems that his appointment by Bishop Philpotts created some displeasure, due to the fact that the Bishop's eldest son had married into the Buller family. It was said of Buller:

This amiable gentleman was transplanted too late in life from St Just and Perranzabuloc, in Cornwall. Within a twelvemonth he paid the debt of nature at Plymouth 26 October 1846, aged 69 years.

Hinds Howell, the seventh son of Conrad Adams of Barbados, was collated on 12 December 1846. Prior to holding the incumbency of Bridestowe, Howell held that of Shobrooke, where (according to G. Oliver):

... he introduced tasteful improvements, and along with the attention he paid to his flock, we believe that the parishioners of Bridestowe have cause to congratulate themselves on possessing such a kind, intelligent, and zealous friend and pastor.

During the second year of Howell's incumbency the rectory house was rebuilt. One source based on hearsay claims the house had been destroyed by fire. However, the sworn affidavit of John Hayward dated 20 April 1847, offers a different reason for the rebuilding of the house:

The rectory house with the necessary offices thereto on the glebe of the Rectory of Bridestowe in the county of Devon has been built with improper materials, and is so much impaired by dry rot that it is necessary to take them down and rebuild them. The value of the old material therein is £130.

The Bishop gave his consent to Howell to commence the rebuilding of the Rectory House by John Hayward of Exeter on 26 July 1847. On studying the layout of the new house one may wonder why a parish priest would want such a grand residence. The Bishop also contemplated this very thought.

A visitor to Bridestowe in 1849 gives us an account of St Bridget's Church. This visitor, James

Bridge Davidson, penned prolific notes on the churches of Devon. On 23 August 1849 he wrote:

The entrance to the churchyard from this poor and dirty village is by a large semicircular arch which, if not of Anglo Norman structure is in the style of that period. It is ornamented with the billet moulding and rests on shafts with impost capitals carved with the chevron and... bend and lozenge mouldings.

The church consists of a nave about 48 feet long by 15 wide, a chancel about 30 by 12 feet, an aisle on the north about 48 by 8 feet, another on the south of the same dimensions, a porch of late date covering the south door and a tower at the western end of the nave about 70 feet high, finished by battlements and four square turrets with crocketted pinnacles. It contained six bells. The south door is under a plain arch of mouldings. The nave is open to the aisles by three wide heavy arches on each side, resting on columns formed by four attached shafts with intervening mouldings and plain moulded capital of the windows. Some are made by [ciriquefoiled] lights and tracery, all of modern erection of three lancet lights under pointed arches. The ceilings are curved and plain. The remains of a carved oak chancel screen exists in the ordinary style of the sixteenth century and over it in place of the rood loft are painted whole length figures of Moses and Aaron with the tables of the ten commandments. At the back towards the chancel is a large painting of the resurrection with several figures the size of life. The font is a high octagonal basin of stone on an octagonal column and base mouldings without ornament. A gallery is at the west end of the nave.

Davidson's report suggests that the church must have been at its most interesting prior to being plastered in cement. A particular point of interest was to the west of the nave, above the back seats. A gallery was in use for the singers where entrance was gained from a doorway just to the west of the south porch.

Seating for the congregation at his time was by family or estate 'high deal'. The pews were built and maintained by the individual families of the parish, who initially petitioned the Bishop for permission to erect seats for their estate. Being called 'high deal pews' one may wonder just how high these seats actually were. It may be that they were similar to those in the church at Staverton, which were subjected to ridicule, as the following lines show:

Here Squier came and sat the service through,
And Squier's lady, sons and daughters too,
And Squier's friends and sometimes his relations,
And Squier's staff (according to their stations)
I've heard it said the Squier felt remorse
That he was not allowed to bring his horse;
So dark and stable–like was Squier's pew
That maybe Squire did – and no one knew?

Top: *View from West Bridge to Church Entrance.*
(Alan Pearn)

Middle: *View of Church Entrance.* (Alan Pearn)

Left: *Looking up Station Road towards the Chapel (note the buildings beside the White Hart and the house beyond Chapel).* (Alan Pearn)

Family seats were the basis of a variety of disputes between the congregation and the church authorities. Furthermore it may come as no surprise that they were also the subject of bitter feuds between various Bridestowe families.

Davidson recorded monument inscriptions on his visit. On the floor of the chancel such a monument reads:

> Here lieth the body of Jone Nosworthye
> of Billacombe widow who died Janr AD1665
> An Anagram
> O none is worthye
> Approache yee mourners of the sable traine
> Unsluce your sorrows – oh let run amaine
> Hartes swelling fluids of grief command eache eye
> To melte into a dropping elegye
> And is doleful language and sad stile
> Let's carve our sister's monumental pile
> Then pollishe it with kisses that being done
> With an amazed silence let eache one
> Court fate like Niobe – he may become
> Companion as in life so in the Tombe.

In the churchyard an epitaph on one of the gravestones reads:

> Remember death, for die you must;
> As you are now, so once were us;
> As we are now, so you must be,
> Therefore prepare to follow we.

The parish stocks retained in the church are of an ordinary pattern displaying no special peculiarities, with accommodation allowing for three persons to be detained at any time. Stocks have been used for punishment since Saxon times, their use being primarily confined for misdemeanours of a religious kind, such as blasphemy, the breaking of the Sabbath or for drunkenness. In 1405 an act proclaimed that stocks should be provided in each town and village, their use generally fell into lapse by the early-nineteenth century. The miscreant placed in the stocks as punishment for an offence of a religious nature was kept in them until churchgoers had all left the church.

Returning once again to the incumbency of Hinds Howell we find that he had resigned from Bridestowe in 1855. In his place, Alexander Watson was collated on 20 July 1855, as relayed in a newspaper report:

Plan of Bridestowe Church 1866.

As an evidence of the anxiety of our Right Revd Diocesan to provide for the faithful pastors within his diocese who have long ministered in populous parishes with but very scanty incomes we have to record that he has presented the Revd Alexander Watson, the notorious Tractarian of St Mary's Church, Torquay, who held that cure for about four years at the pittance of

---

The Religous Census of 1851

From the Religious Census of 1851, which was taken on Sunday 30 March we find that there were four groups of religious gatherings in Bridestowe. We have:

The Anglican 'Episcopal Church' *where eighty people attended the morning service whilst two hundred and twenty people attended the afternoon service. Eighty children attended morning Sunday school whilst eighty also attended the afternoon Sunday school.*

The 'Zion' Bible Christian Chapel, *which was erected in 1830 and had twenty free sittings, eighty other sittings and standing room for fifty, saw one hundred and ten attending the afternoon service whilst one hundred and twenty people attended the evening service. There did not appear to be a Sunday school for children at that time.*

The Wesleyan Methodists, *who did not have a building exclusively for religious worship, had an attendance of twenty-five people at an evening service. There did not appear to be a Sunday school.*

The 'Ebenezer' Baptist Chapel, *which was erected in 1833 and had one hundred and forty free sittings, saw twenty people attending the morning service whilst thirty people attended the afternoon service. Again, there did not appear to be a Sunday school.*

Above: *Revd Fairhurst flanked by H. Dennis and E. Barkell (churchwardens) 'found guilty of begging for the bell fund', 1936.*
(Joan Calmady-Hamlyn)

Middle: *Ground floor plans for the Revd Clarke's new Rectory House.*

Below: *Top floor plans for the Revd Clarke's new Rectory House.*

£300 a year, to the rectory of Bridestowe one of the richest which his lordship has at his disposal... Watson was going to work wonders, by converting the parish and all around – who were mostly Bible Christians as they are called. It being stated that indeed, this numerous sect may be called the National Religion for that vast district.

Shortly after his collation Watson chaired a Vestry meeting where a proposal was put forward to increase the number of seats within the church. It may be that Watson wanted extra seating in order to accommodate new converts.

By 1857 Watson had a harmonium placed in the church, the choir wore surplices and daily services took place. All this was at a cost over which Watson got into great difficulty and was obliged to leave. He seems to have been a man of high ideas having set up a 'select school' at the rectory. Watson, it seems, had exchanged for Bedford Chapel in London and became bankrupt. He died aged 49 on 1 December 1865.

Charles Whitley Clarke, on coming to Bridestowe in 1858, quickly settled the debts run up by his predecessor. Whether Clarke was

the benefactor is far from clear, but he was described as a:

most courteous gentleman and was a kind of a Squire Parson and was in every way a gentleman by birth being looked upon in his case as very superior in life.

Soon after his arrival in the parish, Clarke requested consent of the Bishop to build a new parsonage house. The Bishop commissioned a report on 22 July 1855 to make enquiries before he acquiesced to Clarke's request. The Rectory had burnt to the ground on 14 March 1855.

Having settled in his new abode Revd Charles Whitley Clarke proceeded to refurbish the Parish Church, beginning in 1866. Clarke petitioned the Bishop with a view to making major alterations and improvements to all parts of the building. He had argued that the internal arrangement of the church was not convenient, and that it was disfigured and considered unsuitable for worship by reason of the high pews. The bulk of the work that was required to improve Bridestowe Parish Church involved re-seating the nave with pine benches with ornamental ends. The rights to the high deal pews had been freely surrendered. At this time it was said that the ground plan of Bridestowe Church 'is very unlike our Devon churches. The great length of chancel and absence of chancel aisles give it a character that is unusual in our churches.' The work completed at St Bridget's enabled parishioners to sit in comfort. Revd Clarke remained at Bridestowe for 24 years; he left in 1882 for the rectorship of Wallington, Hertfordshire, where he died on 23 February 1913 at the age of 91.

William Hinton Drake was collated on 2 June 1882. During his rectorship changes were to take place at the behest of the Bishop. It appears that the mother church was again slighting Sourton. However, Drake died on 15 December 1888 aged 68, and so never saw the outcome of the Bishop's plans, which resulted in Bridestowe losing its daughter church in Sourton.

John Loveband Francis was collated to Bridestowe in 1889 whereupon he was confronted with the divisions within the parish. The first indications of the separation are gleaned from a letter, written by a former rector of St Bridget's, in response to a request from Exeter Diocesan Officials. In a letter to the Archdeacon of Exeter on 26 December 1888, Revd

Left: *Rectory House, 1930s.* (Doug Gale)

Below: *Fête at the Rectory House. Revd Francis seated to left of table next to woman in hat with Mr Westcott to his right with hat in hands.* (Alan Pearn)

Bottom: *Plan of the Proposed Reseating 1866.*

Hinds Howell highlighted some problems that had been experienced, which furthered the argument for the separation of the two parishes. It must be remembered, of course, that at this time the mode of travel was by horse or on foot so some of the predicaments presented by Howell, although trivial to us, were real to him. Howell wrote:

When I went to Bridestow I soon found that work as hard as I could, I could not do all that was wanted single handed [for even] *after I had two curates I seldom ever had a dinner with my family, and so I began with one curate and afterwards I had two up to the time of my leaving in 1855. It was not so much that the population was over large but that the population, then nearly 2000, was scattered over 10,000 acres and when cases of illness occurred in outlying parts of the two parishes it took all ones time to attend both in one day. You will see by and by why I trouble you with these details but up to the time of* [my coming to Bridestowe], *the previous rector (with a slight interval) had been there 70 years and one service was given at Bridestowe and one at Sourton. I held two services in each church besides all the usual Holy Day services and all were family attended.*

Separation of the two parishes was the obvious answer to enable full attendance of the two 'flocks'. A petition headed 'Scheme for the separation of the Chapelry at Sourton and constituting it a separate Benefice' dated 12 February 1889, tells of all that was involved in the make up of the church living from the Bishop of Exeter to the Lord Bishop of Canterbury. However, the scheme made no provision for providing living accommodation for the rector of Sourton upon separation at this time. A letter dated 18 February 1889 from Vincent Calmady Hamlyn at Lincoln's Inn, London, to the Bishop in part reads:

As far as a site for a vicarage is concerned, I will certainly co-operate gladly with the Woollocombe trustees. I am bound to say that neither they nor I can probably give the land. I certainly have no fervour to do so but I doubt not that a comparatively nominal sum for the purchase would get over our legal difficulty.

Hamlyn was to eventually give a piece of ground upon which to erect a dwelling for the new arrival to Sourton.

The separation process seemed to take too long for some people. However, it was a significant development; after all it was a division of a cure of souls that was thought befitting as a seat for the dignitaries of Exeter Cathedral.

There is no firm record to indicate the date at which the separation actually took place. The orders were probably forthcoming in May 1889. With the division accomplished Revd John Loveband Francis began to administer to his new cure. It was claimed that Revd Francis was:

... active and zealous and deservedly popular among the clergy and laity of the neighbourhood. As a devoted churchman and one who never flinches from speaking

Above: *'God the best Maker of all Marriages combine your Hearts in One'. A triumphal arch erected over the West Bridge for one of the Calmady-Hamlyn family. The small boy in the centre of the picture has a 'hoop and stick'; a police sergeant stands at the church gate. A similar arch to this was erected in May 1878 for Shilston Calmady Hamlyn's daughter when she was married but with 'Happiness to the bride and bridegroom' as a motto. At this time cocoa-nut matting was laid from the church gates to the porch. Two hundred school children lined the matting, the little girls having in their hands bunches of flowers with which they afterwards strewed the path.*
(Joan Calmady-Hamlyn)

the truth as to the sin of schism – he has more than once had to encounter the anger of the 'dissenting brother,' but honesty and sincerity always beat in the long-run, and no one at least more highly respects a clergyman who teaches and preaches Catholic truth than those who conscientiously differ from the faith and practise of the Anglican Church.

We have seen previously that the 'National Religion' for the district was that of the 'Bible Christians' so it is not surprising, perhaps, that he had to deal with the 'dissenting brother.' Not only did the Revd Francis work on his new parishioners, he also set to work on his new church. It seems that the restoration work carried out by Revd Clarke was considered 'well intentioned' but was 'by no means a success.' From a citation dated 7 March 1890 further work needed to be undertaken, including to re-seat the chancel, provide a new lectern, altar, reredos, and altar 'footpace'. The chancel was to be improved and new stone windows were to be inserted in the nave and aisles to take the place of the cement ones, along with other remedial work.

The eventual cost of the restoration work was estimated to have reached £620. It was money well spent, as at last here was a church with its chancel furnished and decorated to splendour. An account written in 1891 claims:

In this church is a large mixed choir who sing with much taste and precision; there is a weekly Eucharist, and saints and holy day services; the parishioners attend in goodly numbers and have helped their rector pecuniarily according to their means for the restoration.

During January 1896 Revd Francis petitioned Bishop Edward Henry for permission to pull down and remove the poor houses adjoining the churchyard.

After serving as rector for 38 years the Revd Francis retired from his clerical duties in the year 1927. He was presented with a motoring coat and an illuminated address, bearing engravings of the interior and exterior of Bridestowe Church, containing 153 names of subscribers. Having thanked the subscribers and expressing grief at leaving Bridestowe he said that he hoped the mutual goodwill that existed between him and the parishioners would be extended to his successor. On 27 December 1933, the *Western Morning News* reported his death; he was 89 years of age. His funeral took place at Bridestowe and he was buried beside his mother. The report reads:

It is no light task to speak of John Loveband Francis – Devonian of Devonians. Born at St Giles in the Wood Vicarage 10 February 1844. He was Rural Dean of Okehampton in the days of Bishop Frederick Temple who was once heard to say 'I like Francis because he doesn't always agree with you.' He gave his whole soul to the Parish of Bridestowe where his ample means enabled him to occupy the huge rectory and bring up his three sons and five daughters.

Richard Sydney Davies, the vicar of Kingsbridge, was collated to Bridestowe towards the end of 1927. Two years later, along with his churchwardens, Charles Frederick Drielsma and John Rendle Westcott, Revd Davies petitioned the Bishop of Exeter for a faculty to install a new organ in St Bridget's Church. It was proposed to dispose of the old positive organ and erect a new pipe organ. The estimated cost was £350, which would be defrayed by 'donations and parochial effort'. The new organ was duly installed, and the Revd Davies resigned Bridestowe for the living of Upottery in 1934.

Christopher Sedgewick Fairhurst found that the living of Bridestowe was worth £480, whilst the glebe land was now a mere ten acres on his collation in 1934. During his incumbency a faculty was sought to restore the bell frame and do various repairs in the tower and to recast one bell. The newly hung peel of bells was reported on 2 October 1936:

Top left: *Methodist Chapel Sunday School.* Left to right, lady standing at left: *Mrs Down;* back row: *Marcia Leach, Mrs Violet Mortimore, Mrs Iris Pearn;* 3rd row: *Marcia Heathman, Pamela Lake, Roger Heathman, Rodney Richards;* 2nd row: *?, ?, Mervyn Down, Alan Pearn;* front row: *?, Jennifer Richards, ?, Shirly Heathman, Keith Down.*
(Brian Maddaford)

Top right: *New Year's Eve Ringers, 1960.* Left to right: *Ernie Chapman on 5, Harold Phillips on tenor, Frank Pike on 4, Jim Barkell on treble, Arthur Mudge on 2, Sam Chasty on 3.*
(Howard Barkell)

Above left: *'Variety Stall' at the church fête held at the Rectory September 1929 during the incumbency of the Revd Davis. Miss Tickell is standing up behind the stall.*
(Derek Northcott)

Above right: *Revd Francis.*
(George Lavis)

Bottom right: *Ern Barkell standing to the left of the bell with a workman to the right during the bell and tower restoration work, 1936.* (Alan Pearn)

After a silence of several months, occasioned by repair and renovation work, the bells of St Bride's Church, Bridestowe were rung once again. Some time ago it was discovered that the tower was in an unsafe condition, and that the six bells were badly in need of attention. An appeal for financial help was made. One of the bells has been recast and the remainder have been cleaned and re-tuned. The tower also has been strengthened. Formerly the bells occupied very cramped quarters on one level, but now they have been rehung in two tiers, which it is hoped will improve their tone. The cost of the work, which took five months, is £300. Subscriptions come from within the parish where all denominations have responded. The Bishop of Crediton dedicated the bells at a service conducted by the Revd Fairhurst. Presiding at the public luncheon in the Church Institute, which preceded the ceremony, Lord Carrington said the occasion was a very happy one for the parish. His first introduction to the bells of Devon, he said, took place at Exeter some time ago when he stayed at a hotel in the Cathedral Yard. 'It seemed to me that they started to ring the bells there at about half past four in the morning, and didn't stop until ten o'clock at night,' he commented. He trusted the Bridestowe ringers would not be quite as zealous as this.

Top left: *Plan of the proposed partial restoration, 1890.*

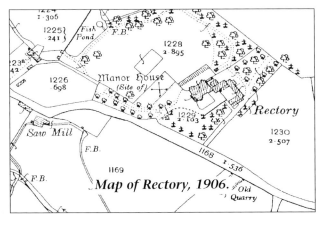

Map of Rectory, 1906.

With the restoration of the church bells completed Revd Fairhurst resigned in 1944. Richard Davis Holden was collated to Bridestowe in 1944 and resigned in 1951. Henry Kent Kingdom was collated in 1951, with Sourton in 1953. He resigned both in 1957.

Children affectionately knew Revd Kingdom as 'Pop' Kingdom. Many a happy hour was spent at the rectory playing games inside the house or in the large grounds. Fond memories of Sunday school outings, which, even in the 1950s, were a real treat – going as far away as Exmouth seemed to be like visiting the other side of the world. 'Pop' Kingdom was a great organiser of pantomimes, minstrel shows, fêtes and jumble sales. He also loved to play cricket. Under 'Pop', children enjoyed regular attendance at Sunday school and perhaps as they grew older, were told off for talking in the choir stalls during the sermon.

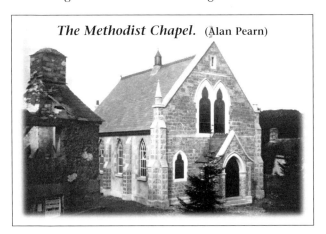

The Methodist Chapel. (Alan Pearn)

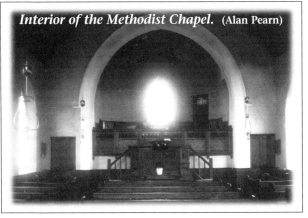

Interior of the Methodist Chapel. (Alan Pearn)

Alexander Hunter was collated to Bridestowe in 1957; he resigned in 1963. During his first year, one of the screens in the church was restored to the memory of Sir Giles Sebright. The total expenditure for the work was sponsored by the Bridestowe Branch of the Church of England Men's Society.

In 1962 Revd Hunter, along with the churchwardens, petitioned the Bishop of Exeter for a faculty to re-roof the nave and north and south aisles of the church. A Licence of Faculty was granted on 22 August 1962 to carry out the work as specified in the petition.

The Rectors of St Bridget's Church

	Thomas de Radeleghe
	in charge.
1259	*Nicholas de Plimtone*
1266	*Master Roger de Toriz*
1274	*Gilbert de Titinge*
1279	*Master Andrew de Kylkenny*
1282	*Master Henry de Kylkenny*
	Master Ralph de Knovyle
	occurs c. 1312
	Master Gilbert de Knoville
	occurs c.1321
	Master William de Beara
	occurs c.1325
1360	*Master Henry Pyke*
1372	*John Loffwyke*
1377	*John Wayte*
1377	*Walter Aumeney*
1385	*Thomas Hertiforde*
1387	*Thomas de Preston*
1391	*Robert Derby*
1391	*Robert Wantyngge*
1397	*Nicholas Bodeway*
1406	*Reginald Bryta*
1409	*John Prate*
1413	*John Wykyngdon*
1415	*William Weston*
1416	*John Fosse*
	James Banastre
1474	*Hamon Bothe*
1474	*Richard Bothe*
1477	*Richard Stubbes*
1480	*Lawrence Ryell*
	Ralph Oldham
	occurs 1535
1554	*James Bond*
1571	*Roger Evans*
1571	*William Marston*
1575	*Gilbert Germyn*
1613	*Edward Cotton*
1647	*William Knapman intruder*
1661	*William Hutton*
1670	*Edward Drewe*
1715	*William Stuart*
1734	*Peter Burnaford*
1779	*Thomas Herberden*
1786	*Coryndon Luxmore*
1845	*John Buller*
1846	*Hinds Howell*
1855	*Alexander Watson*
1858	*Charles Whitley Clarke*
1882	*William Hinton Drake*
1889	*John Loveband Francis*
1927	*Richard Sydney Davies*
1935	*Christopher Sedgewick Fairhurst*
1944	*Richard Davis Holden*
1951	*Henry Kent Kingdom*
1957	*Alexander Hunter*

In November 1964, a year after Revd Hunter had resigned, the *London Gazette* published:

The benefice of Lydford, the benefice of Bridestowe and the benefice of Sourton shall be permanently united together and form one benefice with cure of souls under the style of The United Benefice of Lydford with Bridestowe and Sourton but the parishes of the said benefices shall continue in all respects distinct.

On 3 April 1967, the Ministry of Housing and Local Government, announced that under the Town and Country Planning Act 1962 the Church of St Bridget had been included in the list of buildings of special architectural or historic interest. The arch at the entrance to the churchyard was also included on the list.

At the end of the nineteenth century the separation of Sourton from Bridestowe took place. Then just 73 years later Bridestowe was once again united with Sourton, but this time with the additional Benefice of Lydford. To quote Revd Francis upon his first visit to Bridestowe on 11 February 1889 is perhaps the best way to complete the history of Bridestowe Church, the once home of Exeter Cathedral dignitaries. He reported to his Bishop that 'church life' was 'at a lamentably low ebb.'

SOURCES

Ashworth, E., *Exeter Architectural Society Transactions Vol. 4.*

Devon and Cornwall Notes and Queries. Vol. XXVII.

Devon and Cornwall Record Society (ed.), *The Episcopal Registers of the Diocese of Exeter 1420–55.*

Wickes, M. (ed), *Devon in The Religious Census of 1851.*

Devon Notes and Queries. Vol. III.

Emden, A.B., *A Biographical Register of the University of Oxford to AD1500.*

The *Exeter Diocesan Gazette* October 1909.

Foster, J., *Alumni Oxonienses 1500–1714 Vol.1.*

Hine, J., *Notes on Some Moorland and Border Churches in Devon.*

Hingston-Randolf, Revd F.C. (ed), *The Episcopal Registers of the Diocese of Exeter 1257–1419.*

Oliver, G., *Lives of the Bishops of Exeter* and *Monasticon Dioecesis Exoniensis.*

Reynolds, H., *The Ancient Diocese of Exeter.*

Transactions of the Devonshire Association.

Trewman's *Exeter Flying Post* (various references).

West Country Studies Library:
    Cresswell MSS.
    Burnet Morris Index.
    Fulford Williams H., MSS.
    MS Devonshire Churches.
    Davidson MS Church Notes – West of Devon.
    Newspaper cuttings.

Chapter 7

INDUSTRY

Various forms of industry – some perhaps only to an exploratory degree – have taken place in the parish of Bridestowe but the only activity to remain is that of agriculture. There were, of course, the tailors, carpenters, blacksmiths, saddlers, innkeepers and shopkeepers that kept Bridestowe self-sufficient but many of these have disappeared along with the diverse commercial enterprises that once thrived.

Remains of the larger commercial activities such as lime quarries, mines and the peat works are extant, whilst other enterprises are not so obvious. Clues to an area's industrial history can often be found in place-names – for example, the Tan Yard. Perusing a good map produced during the early-twentieth century will also yield evidence of previous workings, particularly of small stone quarries.

FARMING

At the time of Domesday there were just a few farms. Other holdings appeared later, which swelled the ranks of the farmers in the parish. Today, as at the time of Domesday, we only see a small number of farms dotted about the parish. The economic climate has resulted in farms becoming fewer in number, but bigger in size, and farmers no longer need to employ a number of people to work their farms – very different to the agricultural methods of the past.

A lease produced in the eighteenth century gives an insight into what was required of the leaseholder. The lease of 1763 taken up by James and John Pellow for 21 years from Arthur Tremayne shows that Way consisted of:

... all that Messuage or Tenement Barton or Farm and premises called Way situated and lying in the Parish of Bridestowe aforesaid, together with all houses, edifyces, buildings, barns, stables, court-lages, gardens, orchards, lands, meadows, pastures, foodings, moors, commons and commons of pasture, ways, paths, watercourses, easements, profits, comoditys, advantages and appurtences.

Arthur Tremayne reserved for himself all rights to work and dig any mines of tin or other metals and quarries of stone that happened to be on the land. Likewise, he was able to cut down and work up all the timber trees and young saplings of oak, ash, elm, beech and sycamore standing, growing or to stand and grow upon Way.

The Pellows paid a yearly rent of £46 by equal quarterly payments. As part of this contract, they had to bring onto every acre that was tilled 50 bushels of good coal-burnt stone lime of double Winchester measures, or 40 horse teams of small lime. Alternatively 300 horse teams of good dung could be spread to improve the soil. After every such dressing they were permitted to take a maximum of three crops of corn or grain. They were not to mow clover grass more than once during the term of the lease and were not to plough, till or break up any of the meadow ground. The selling or carrying off of any dung, ashes or other spoil made on the premises was not permitted. However, they were able to spread this material to facilitate good husbandry.

Refreshment at harvest time, Newtake, 1930s.
Left to right: *Lew Dawe, Bill Davis, George Lavis, Fred Brooks, Mrs Brooks.* (George Lavis)

Above: *Mowing the hay.* Left to right: *William Lavis, Thomas Lavis, Bill Lavis, William Otto Lavis.*
(Brian Lavis)

Below: *Bill Lavis with his horses.* (Brian Lavis)

Sufficient repairs to sustain and maintain the hedges, ditches, gates, posts, bars, stiles and fences had to be carried out. Towards these repairs, rough timber was supplied by Arthur Tremayne. Any thatch on the houses that was in need of attention had to be repaired, but Arthur Tremayne provided 50 nitches of good rood every year. To recompense the Pellows for the repairs they did to the hedge around the moors called Way Moors, £2 was deducted from the first year's rent. Both parties were obliged to maintain the hedges and fences. Arthur Tremayne paid all the rates, taxes, outgoings and impositions assessed except the great and small tithes and the house and window tax. The Pellows were indemnified from any apprentice that was bound. The lessor kept the dwelling house and outhouses in good repair, although he was not obliged to work on the thatch.

TINNERS

Although tin mining did not take place in Bridestowe there were, amongst the inhabitants of the parish, men who were subject to stannary laws due to their occupation as tinners. They possibly worked at the stream tin works that lay between Great Nodden and Coombe Down and to the east of Southerly Down. The works has long since been disued.

The Devon County Dairy School April, 1927.
Man in hat: Bill Hutchins.
(Brian Lavis)

Tin mining on Dartmoor seems to have begun in the twelfth century in which period official records of tin mining emerge. Tin was not extracted from a mine by a shaft but by streaming. Ore, in the form of heavy black stones and sand, lay in beds found either at surface level or to a depth of up to 40 feet. The miners would wash the material that collected in the waterways especially created for the purpose, and in so doing, separated the ore from the waste. Next the ore was smelted – it was mixed with peat and burnt on a low heat over a hole in the ground. This reduced the ore to metal.

A tax of 2s.6d. per thousandweight had to be paid on the tin before it could be put on sale in a recognised market town – Lydford, Tavistock, Plympton, Chagford and Ashburton. If a tinner set to his labour on private land the only restriction over him was that he had to either give the lord of the manor a percentage of the tin, or a cash equivalent.

During 1201 laws decreed that tinners might freely and without hindrance dig for tin at all times and in all places both on the royal moors and in private lands of bishops, abbots, earls and other lords. They could divert streams of water and dig peat wherever and whenever fuel was required for smelting. There were some rules that the tinners had to obey with judges on a yearly circuit to deal with offenders. Lydford Castle was built in 1195 expressly to incarcerate those who offended or interfered with the stannary laws. Tinners at this time stood apart from the ordinary system of law; they were dealt with by their own warden who treated them favourably.

In 1373 there were 151 recognised tinners in the stannary of Tavistock but these numbers became swollen by the addition of diverse people who falsely claimed to be tinners in order to evade payments of the tenth and fifteenth taxes. Tinners were only 'above the law' so long as they were engaged in digging tin under the active protection of the Crown.

Small Holding, New Standon, about 1928.
Left to right: *Ivy Maddaford, Joyce Maddaford, Marion Maddaford.* (Brian Maddaford)

Of interest is an 'Order for contribution to the Queen's service by foreigners and tinners' from the Justices of the Devon Quarter Sessions under Elizabeth I. The document reads:

Upon a general complaint made unto this Court that divers of the principal inhabitants of sundry parishes within this county have of late time very fraudulently interested themselves in some tinwork under colour thereof to be protected and discharged against the general and necessary charges for the service of her Majesty, wherewith they have in former times been rated and taxed, together with the rest of the inhabitants of the parish. It is therefore thought fit by this Court, and so ordered, that such as are newly crept in to be tinners, at any time within six years last past, of purpose to exempt themselves from any charge of her Majesty's service, or have at any time contributed with the foreigners within six years last past, and which have not been ancient tinners, or to whom any tinwork is not descended or acquired by marriage, shall from henceforth pay to all services of her Majesty with foreigners, as before their so making themselves tinners… shall pay all such charges as formerly have been imposed upon them.

From 1328 the stannary jurisdiction in Devon was separated into four divisions which were headed by Plympton, Ashburton, Chagford and Tavistock. Tinners had their own parliament that sat at Crockentor, in the middle of Dartmoor. At the start of the sixteenth century each tinner carried his metal to the stannary town nearest his mine where it was coined and duty was paid at the standard rate of 1s.6¾d. per hundredweight of 120 lbs. From an abstract of the Coinage Rolls for June 1523 we find the names of some of the Bridestowe tinners, the quantity of metal coined by each and the amount of duty paid by them. Under the Tavistock entries are:

John Knyght of Brestow with two hundredweight and six pounds of metal paying 3s.2½d. duty.
Thomas Row of Brestow with two hundredweight and a quarter of metal paying 3s.6¼d. duty.
William Walter of Batshyll with two hundredweight and ten pounds of metal paying 3s.3¼d. duty.
Walter Borrogh with one hundredweight of metal paying 1s.6¾d. duty.
John Cornyshe with one hundredweight, one quarter and ten pounds of metal paying 2s.1d. duty.

Records show that on 27 October 1600 a parliament was held at 'Crockerntorrie before Sir Walter Ralegh and 24 Jurates' amongst whom representing Tavistock was Peter Ebsworthy.

Gathering in the hay. Left to right: *Ivy and Frank Maddaford.* (Brian Maddaford)

The Wordens at work. (Alan Pearn)

Steam engine and threshing machine. (Alan Pearn)

Harvesting Time, 1946. Left to right: *George D., Tom R., The Irish Guardsman, Will L., Capt. O., Chris P., Cynthia H.* (Brian Lavis)

SLATE QUARRYING

An account of the excavations at Okehampton Castle reveals the existence of a tentative slate quarry at Bridestowe. In 1422 'the purchase of 100 stone-tiles (presumably slates) for the houses within the castle and their carriage from Bridestowe' was recorded. It is also stated that 'none of the roof slates identified geologically during the excavations came from Bridestowe' although 'slates found in the excavations' had been 'identified as coming from the immediate vicinity of the site', that is, the site of the castle.

What then, are we to make of these observations? It may be that the slates had been purchased locally by a tradesman at Bridestowe, stock piled, and then sold on to the castle authorities at Okehampton. There seems to be no further evidence to suggest there was a slate quarry at Bridestowe. The only other possible link is that in Bridestowe a field called Denbole Park (where the additional school classrooms now stand) is mentioned in 1653. This may be significant in that in Cornwall many fields are named in a derivative form of the slate quarry of Delabole in the parish of St Teath. If some other evidence had been forthcoming it might be possible to say for certain that slate quarrying had occurred in the parish.

WOOL AND CLOTH

By the eighteenth century Tavistock had become the nucleus of a considerable serge-making centre, which contributed towards the economy of the country. Settlements scattered about the edge of Dartmoor had fulling mills, or tucking mills as they were known in Devonshire, which were powered with water from local streams. In some localities the water had to be diverted to the mill via a leat. Bridestowe had a tucking mill; amongst the Bidlake papers is a lease which shows that William Lange of Sourton, Tanner, had taken:

... a house standing by Bidlake Mill with a herb garden adjoining the 'townplace' land lying on the north side of the tucking mill under the mill leat, and a meadow lying under the 'townplace'.

This mill, probably quite basic in design, may have just been a building containing tubs for scouring the woollen cloth. Through use of soap and fullers earth, this process cleansed the cloth of oil or grease. In the West Country stale urine was also used as the scouring agent. Once clean the cloth was pounded with heavy wooden hammers driven by a water wheel to promote thickening or felting of the cloth. It was then partially dried and stretched on racks or tenters.

At the turn of the nineteenth century a newspaper advertisement recorded:

To be let by private contract a dwelling house with a garden and

necessary outhouses, and a new building adjoining and now erecting which can be furnished in a stile to make it very convenient for a person in the woollen line, situate in the very pleasant town of Bridestowe adjoining the great western road, Okehampton to Launceston, and a never failing stream of water. Bridestowe is admirably situated for a person in the woollen trade it being surrounded by gentleman farmers that keep very large flocks of sheep, the produce of which trade can several times in the week, be conveyed by the public waggoners, which stop at Bridestowe. Apply to John Newton of Stone House.

Whether this advertisement created any woollen business is unknown – certainly in 1850 when *White's Directory of Devonshire* appeared, no such business was listed at Bridestowe.

Sheep shearing at Crandford. (Brian Lavis)

PEAT WORKING

On Dartmoor peat was used in place of coal. A charter of Henry III granting the right to take peat from the moor referred to it as coal, whilst people in the eighteenth century who cut peat and sold it were known as colliers. Peat was used for industrial purposes such as for smelting tin, as well as for domestic fuel by almost everyone living on the moor. It was also cut and carried to the fringes of the moor where it was sold – in itself a minor industry.

As a commoner, a peat cutter from Bridestowe had the right to cut peat on the moor from early times. Peat cutting was carried out between the end of April and early September probably at Rattlebrook Head or Kitty Tor. It was customary to keep to an established tie that could be worked for a number of years until the supply became exhausted. The peat worker used three special tools for his work. A triangular shovel called a budding iron was used for cutting the peat whilst a long knife trimmed heather roots and a semicircular tool with one of its prongs turned up at right angles was used to lever the cut turf out of the tie. The peat was carried in panniers on horses or donkeys to the vicinity of the worker's home. It was then ricked and later thatched after being dried.

In 1878 the Duchy of Cornwall granted a licence to the West of England Compressed Peat Company Ltd to work a square mile at Rattlebrook Head with the right to construct a tramway. The company aimed to convert peat into fuel by a process of hydraulic compression. Although it lay in the parish of Lydford about half a mile outside Bridestowe and Sourton Common, the peat operation nevertheless had some effect on Bridestowe and its occupants.

In September 1878, the High Sheriff of Devon, Shilston Calmady Hamlyn, used a silver spade to cut the first sod of the railway which was to serve the peat works. The railway, of standard gauge, connected to the London and South Western Railway at Bridestowe in 1879. From Bridestowe station the line followed a steep route to the peat works, ascending nearly 1000 feet along its five-mile length. After leaving the station at the Okehampton end of the down line, the peat railway crossed the Okehampton to Tavistock road, according to Roche:

... over a makeshift level crossing and swept up in a great curve to Nodden Gate on the edge of the moor behind the Fox and Hounds. Thence it came out on the lower slopes of Great Nodden high above the Lyd Valley. In half a mile the line swung north-east through a deep cutting and out to the northern flank of 'Plum-pudding Hill,' close to below the summit and some 600 feet above Bridestowe station, visible far below. A sheep-track was crossed by a granite overbridge and the line ran on a low embankment on to the lower slopes of Corn Ridge. Here there was a reversing point ('the junction,' as we grandiloquently named it complete with points lever, corrugated iron hut and derailed truck) thence the railway started off again in the opposite direction, climbing even higher, crossing the infant Lyd near its source just beside the primitive clapper known as Lydda Bridge, skirting the slopes of Woodcock Hill and passing within feet of the rocks of Gren Tor, till it swung outwards again, now 1000 feet above the distant Bridestowe and turned the most spectacular corner of all. The line now entered a deep cutting through the col between the tor and Woodcock Hill and actually ran down a steep gradient to reach its terminus.

Before the railway was mechanised in its later years, horses drew the trucks.

The railway, however, did not guarantee the success of the peat works. In 1880 or thereabouts the peat works failed, and over the next 20 years a number of unsuccessful attempts were made to resume operations. In the 1890s a German scientist, it is reputed, was said to have perfected a plant to extract alcohol, but whilst some success was achieved for a time, the scientist died and his secret with him. Work started again at Rattlebrook in 1901 until the First World War, with eight or nine men being employed to cut the peat. Although the work was not continuous, local people were glad of the employment, the men making a daily climb from their villages in all weathers. On a piecework basis, the pay was 2s. per journey, and 17s. per week at other times.

A great problem at Rattlebrook was the drying of the peat, which had a high water content. Large ovens, using charcoal, were constructed but they were not very effective. A pressing process was abandoned because much of the peat was squeezed out along with the water. Various attempts were made to put the peat to different uses but its high water content always presented difficulties.

In 1921 the Prince of Wales visited the works at Rattlebrook Head, after which he descended to Bridestowe station on the railway. The station was eventually removed in 1931.

In 1936 the Duchy granted a licence to Holford Process Ltd, of London, to work 360 acres of peat at Rattlebrook for the production of oil, charcoal and other chemical products. March 1947 saw a national fuel crisis and the Ministry of Fuel and Power considered the possibility of peat from Dartmoor being used in the home and in industry.

However, the idea was rejected as uneconomic.

The Christow Manufacturing Company was given permission to take peat for agricultural purposes in 1952 but this also proved to be unsuccessful. Then in 1955, Messrs Renwick, Wilton and Dobson leased the peat works for horticultural purposes but this proved to be uneconomic due to the distance of the peat works from the road.

Some of the peat was used at the 1956 Royal Show for bedding flowers and shrubs in the display pavilion. This was to be the last venture for the Rattlebrook peat works. In 2001, only heaps of rubble, rusted metal and portions of partially demolished walls remain at Rattlebrook but the track of the railway can easily be traced.

MINING

Remains of mines that came into being during the early-nineteenth century are located on the edge of the parish of Bridestowe which abuts the moor. It is these mines that probably inspired the author of *White's Directory of Devonshire* in 1850 to refer to Bridestowe as an 'improving village'. At that time, when the mines were in operational order, it must have been an indication to the villagers that they were in for better times. Employment was probably at an all-time high, which of course brought various benefits to the community. The population rose to 1128, which in turn generated passing trade and employment for trades people and other workers. Needless to say the mines did not stay in operation and as a result the villagers' prospects declined.

The Bridestowe mines lay along the peripheral region of Dartmoor. The area was a rich source of minerals, capable of yielding lead, silver, zinc, copper and arsenic to name but a few commodities. In the 1850s the mines of Dartmoor, West Devon and Cornwall between them produced over half the copper used worldwide. Vancouver reported that:

In the parish of Bridestow a lode of copper has lately been discovered within six or seven fathoms of the surface: the ore is generally combined with spar. A soft or

earthy ore of copper has also been found in the same parish; but the extent of these bodies, or whether on further search they may be found worth attending to, is left to future investigation and inquiry.

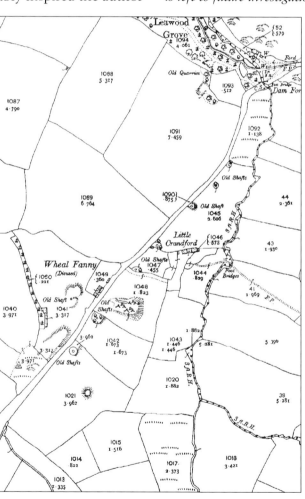

Map of Mining at Crandford.

One of the mines in the parish was known as Wheal Calmady (wheal is an old Devonian and Cornish word meaning mine, and is often the prefix to a Christian name). It seems to have been started as early as 1806 when 'four shares of that promising and valuable copper mine' were for sale. This mine was situated on Leawood Down and had been leased to 'Pethick and others' for 21 years. Other than this, nothing seems to be known of this mine.

However, another, called Wheal Hamlyn, was started in 1850 but its exact location is unknown. The workings are said to have lain in an abandoned limestone quarry, the lode on which the workings stood was large, extending one and a half miles over Water Gate, Great Close, Burley Wood, Combebow and Combebow Downs, the property of Mr Calmady Hamlyn. The mine was regarded with great interest in its day – a correspondent in August 1850 ventured to suggest that the lode was the largest in the kingdom, being 30 feet and of native copper, 'green' (malachite), sugar spar, gossan, prian and mundic. An adit went 100 fathoms into the hill and a shaft was sunk into the lode at 17 fathoms. A powerful water-wheel for working machinery was near to the mouth of the adit. In 1856 after a period of inactivity the mine was restarted. The quantity of carbonic acid gas in the mine was so great at times that candles were extinguished, and the men were only able to work for half an hour at a time.

John Simmons, a mineral agent to the Duchy of Cornwall, provided a further account of the mine a few years later whereupon under the management of a Cornish mine captain a considerable quantity of bulk sampling was raised giving a produce of about 2½ per cent copper. This was insufficient to pay for the working of the mine.

Again, after remaining idle for some time another party started a deep adit at the foot of the quarry where the copper stains appeared strongest. It was promising but never opened up, and shortly after it was once again abandoned. The mine never yielded its full potential of copper.

Wheal Fanny possibly named after the wife of Calmady Pollexfen Hamlyn lies adjoining the road near Crandford Farm (its position can be seen on the 2½-inch Ordnance Survey map). Wheal Fanny originally formed one sett along with Tor Wood Mines near the Lake railway viaduct in the parish of Sourton. The workings, however, lay over a mile apart. It is thought that Wheal Fanny originally opened for copper in around 1822, and some five years later a lead lode was discovered. The work continued intermittently until 1836, by which time the engine shaft was 30 fathoms deep. The adit portal lay west of the road, which crosses Crandford Brook at Dam Ford. It extended in a south-westerly direction for about 300 fathoms where it connected with Engine Shaft. The adit also connected to Hitchen's Shaft.

The mine had a period of idleness but was reopened in 1851. A 40ft by 4ft water-wheel was used to pump the mine but it proved insufficient to cope with the water. In September 1852 a 36-inch steam engine was erected. However, due to one of the largest shareholders experiencing money difficulties, work was suspended and the sett and materials were advertised for sale by auction in July 1854.

A letter penned by George Henwood in 1857 stated that the mine never had a fair trial. He wrote: '... all that mass of gossan which has never been sunk through is not there without something else being beneath.' With the aid of a 70-inch engine 'the lode being large and the water quick' he considered that the mine should be reopened but the letter had no immediate effect.

Renamed the Leawood Mine work resumed in April 1864 (the name came from the seat of the mineral owner, Shilston Calmady Hamlyn). In the next eight months the adit was cleared for 200 fathoms, the shaft timbered, and an engine-house erected in which a 60-inch engine from Harvey's of Hayle was installed. The mine employed 28 people and the prospects were said to be very encouraging, both for copper and lead. Despite this the mine was abandoned in 1868 with no recorded production. The chimneystack was felled around 1900. The walls of the engine house, built of local stone with granite quoins, still partially stands.

There is evidence of two other mines but there is little detail on them. A mine called Wheal Newton was in existence in 1850; this was probably situated between Millaton House and Stone Quarry where shafts are shown on the 25½-inch OS map. Additionally, *White's Directory* for 1850 makes mention of a mine called Wheal Mary which may refer to the disused shafts shown on the 25½-inch OS map at Battishill Down, just off the Okehampton to Tavistock road.

Blacksmith's shop at Poole Hill. (Doug Gale)

LIME QUARRIES

Spoils from lime-quarry workings lie at Combebow and Water Gate. Combebow Quarry appears to be the earlier of the two and the first real insight into it can be found in a document dated '1170'. At this time the technique of lime burning was described:

After the stones are quarried and broke with a large maul to a portable size fit to be lifted on a small horse, they are carried upon the kiln bed, and there broke with small mauls to a size fit for burning, none of which should exceed three pounds weight. Wood is then to be laid on the ground under the grating at the bottom of the kiln on which a layer of small culm is laid, and then a layer of limestones, and so on. Alternately with the culm and lime-stones till you get eight or nine tiers high, when the fire is to be lighted, and when the wood is consumed, the lime-stones in the middle of the kiln will natu-rally sink. A small quantity of culm is then to be added, and the limestones in the kiln brought to a level with the long poker. This being done a layer of culm is put on, and on that a layer of limestones, and which is alter-nately repeated, till the kiln is three quar-ters full, which will be in the course of four or five days, at the end of which time some lime will be produced. Then the shifting bars are to be introduced across the top of the three fixed bars at the bottom of the kiln; this the limeburners say saves a considerable quantity of culm. The kiln is now to be gradually filled with a layer of culm and limestones alternately, when it is considered to be in a full state of burning, and will generally produce between 60 and 70 Winchester bushels of lime a day. This however depends in some measure on the wind which prevails at the time, for the higher the wind is, the greater will be the quantity of lime produced. The breaking of the limestones, when brought on the kiln head, to the size proper for burning, is performed by two men who constantly attend by day, in order to keep the kiln well supplied with stone, and to remove its produce, which is done every morning. The culm made use of for burning the lime must be of the smallest kind, and should there be any stones in it, a skreen must separate them from it. The proportion of culm for burning, is about 7 Winchesters to 25 of lime.

In November 1770, the letting was agreed for:

... all that messuage or tenement, with the lyme kilns and quarry thereunto belonging, called or commonly known by the name of Combebow and Combebow Lyme Quarry.

Any person agreeing to accept the lease had to abide by certain conditions, but details of the quarry do not appear to have been recorded. John Newton and William Gubbins, both of Bridestowe, contract-ed and agreed for the quarry with Leonard Gubbins on behalf of Warwick Calmady. After this, Escott and Pitts held the lease of Combebow Lime Quarry for 14 years from 1807, whilst from 21 February 1822, Richard Palmer of Lifton and John Palmer of Bridestowe leased it. The tenants were to deliver to Calmady Pollexfen Hamlyn:

... good stone lime as required at the same rate as other customers, unless the price shall exceed ⅓d per bushel, when only ⅓d will be paid by Calmady Pollexfen Hamlyn, who may have four cartloads a

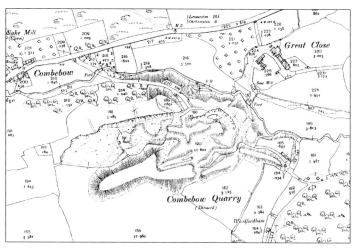

Above: *Map of Combebow Quarry.*

Below: *Map of Stone Quarry.*

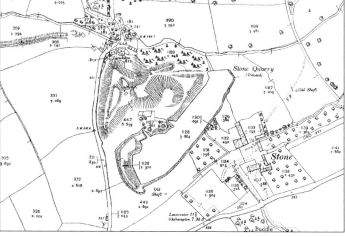

day when the kilns are working, and not to wait more than one hour at a time on one days notice. The lease takers are to grind all wheat, barley, oats and other grain, beans and pease at the mills belonging to Calmady Pollexfen Hamlyn, called Leawood Mills.

It seems business was not to be lost to Bidlake Mill just over the road. It is difficult to say when the Combebow Quarry ceased as a working quarry, but from the rates set for Bridestowe in 1841 we find that a person called Palmer and someone called Ham were responsible for paying the same. Upon looking at the entries in the various directories for Devonshire it is probably fair to say that the Combebow Quarry was in operation up to the end of the nineteenth century.

In 1839 a full description of the Watergate Quarry was detailed by the person who held the lease, in the hope of raising a new mortgage to enable the erection of a steam engine in order to increase the quarry's output. The lease provides a valuable insight into the nature of the quarry, some of which is outlined below.

The premises at Water Gate were about 14 miles from Launceston on the London road from Launceston to Okehampton. They covered an area where the limestone extended under a surface of 28 acres, 26 of which were still unworked. There were four kilns on the premises with very extensive railways, inclined planes, an adit level and a water engine with a wheel of 12hp. All of this was necessary machinery for working the wagons and the railways up the inclined planes and for pumping the water up to the adit level. The working gear in and about the premises cost £1000. The quantity of lime burnt and sold in 1838 amounted to 13,000 bushels, at 6d. per bushel. The lime was chiefly used as manure and the farmers paid their bills once a year (usually in the middle of

February of the following year) for all lime bought between January and December. A discount was usually allowed for prompt payment. The farmers fetched the lime and there was no soliciting for custom. About 10,000 bushels of limestone were worked but not burnt. It was considered necessary to sell 30,000 bushels in order to cover all costs. Once this had been achieved, any further sales that were made contributed to profit, after deducting fuel for burning.

In 1833 the sum of £3500 was paid for the lease and since that time through to the time of writing all the available profits have been exhausted in extending and improving the works. The annual expenditure consisted of the rent of £110 taxes, wages averaged £60 per month about 40 hands being employed. The cost of culm, timber and iron for the previous year amounted to £580.

The lessee wanted to be able to increase his working power by erecting a steam engine, as during three months of the year the water power was only sufficient to work the wagons on the railways and inclined planes. The steam engine would cost about £450 and when erected would enable the lessee to gain an increase of 20,000 bushels of lime, bringing the annual amount to 50,000.

Records do not reveal whether this larger steam engine was erected but if we accept that the quarry was in full operation in 1880 and consider the following entries in the directories then it seems plausible that the engine was indeed erected.

Above: *Tramway Entrance (?), Stone, 1992.*
(Howard Barkell)

Left: *Lime kilns, Stone Quarry, 1992.*
(Howard Barkell)

1850: Gill and Rundle, Lime Burners.

1866: Palmer and Ham, Stone and Lime Merchants. A good business is done in lime and stone.

1878: George Vicary, Captain of Stone Quarry. In the parish are two quarries of lime and stone, in which an extensive business is carried on, and employment offered for a number of hands.

1883: Palmer and Crocker, Lime Merchants.

1893: John Durrant Palmer, Farmer/Lime Merchant.

The quarry of Water Gate is known today as Stone Quarry. It is shown on the 25½-inch OS map with extensive workings. Anyone travelling along the road from Cross Lanes to Way Cross can quite easily see the kilns.

STONE QUARRIES

If one studies the 25½-inch OS map it is possible to see numerous small stone quarries within the parish of Bridestowe. It is highly probable that the stone from such quarries was used in the construction of the highways by waywardens rather than any other venture. It was easier and more cost effective to open up a new quarry near the site of the road works, rather than transport stone from quarries some distance away. Under the Turnpike Acts stone for the construction of a highway could be taken from anywhere. This act caused Philippa Bidlake to write for advice from her brother-in-law, John Heirn, an attorney, when she was confronted with such a situation. Her letter, dated March 1786, recites in part:

Last Thursday the waywarden of Bridestowe with the man who has taken the turnpike road to repair called here and very submissively desired leave to go upon Bidlake Down for some materials to repair the roads. I let them know I had no right to give leave as there were others equally concerned, nor should I give any till I had acquainted you of it. The turnpike fellow said he had a paper signed by the justices to go upon any person's ground where there had been a quarry. Before I asked to see his paper, he told me he could not part with it, for t'was what he had [access] to. I desired a copy of it which he brought soon after, and which I've inclosed to you and withal desire to know what answer I shall return them when they come again which perhaps will be very soon.

As is often the case we only get to learn a part of the story. It is not known what advice was given to Philippa Bidlake, if any, nor whether the way-warden took stone off the estate of Bidlake. Nevertheless, the incident gives some insight into the power of the waywardens.

Removing the tree after the storm at Leawood.
(Joan Calmady-Hamlyn)

TANNERS

The small area within Bridestowe village known as the 'Tan Yard' gives an indication that the tanning trade had once taken place in the parish. Additionally, the Court Book of the Manor of Bridestowe Sanctuary shows a field called 'Tanners Meadow' in the occupancy of John Crossman in 1650. William Sloley is mentioned as a tanner in 1738, as is Arthur Edgecumbe in 1789. Furthermore, in 1796 we find:

To be let by private contract, for a term of years, from Lady Day next, a very good Tan-Yard now in work, a good dwelling house and gardens, convenient outhouses and ground, thereunto belonging, in the parish of Bridestowe. For further particulars apply to Mr John Newton of Bridestowe, where the taker may depend on having good encouragement in taking the same.

A further notice appeared 40 years later:

This is to give notice that the partnership lately subsisting between James Palmer and John Bevan of Bridestowe Tanners is this day dissolved and that the business in future will be carried on by John Bevan. All persons who stand indebted to the aforesaid are requested to pay the amount of the same to either of the above and all persons having any demand on the said Palmer and Bevan are desired to present their accounts that the same may be examined and payed.

Bevan, it seems, attempted to continue to make a go of the Bridestowe tanning works, but he became bankrupt in 1848.

The only surviving references to tanning in Bridestowe are those of a non-productive nature – in other words we learn only of the existence of the tan yard and its occupiers. The preparing and working of leather at Bridestowe was probably fairly basic. Oak bark was more than likely ground in pounds or water mills, as the chief tanning agent used in water to soak hides and skins in the tanning pit. The mixture in the pit was known as 'wooze'. Imported tanning agents were 'sumach' and 'valonia'.

TIMBER

In 1808 Vancouver reported for the Board of Agriculture that:

In a small, though remarkably fine grove of Scotch and silver fir on the barton of Bridestow, there is a tree of the latter species rising a little above the rest, which girths at five feet from the ground, ten feet ten inches, and reckoned sixty-five feet in height, great timber measure. At this distance from the ground its leading shoot appears formerly to have been crippled, and to have spread into a small broomy top, which are the only limbs produced upon it, the shaft being all the way perfectly clean, and free from branches. This is by far the finest tree of the sort ever viewed in England by the author of this report.

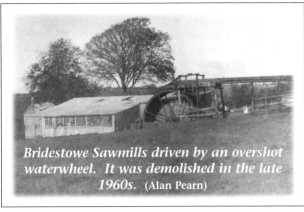

Bridestowe Sawmills driven by an overshot waterwheel. It was demolished in the late 1960s. (Alan Pearn)

Does Vancouver's observation show that the growing of timber at Bridestowe was of any significance? A grant dated 1462 reveals:

... all the timber and all the trees growing in the wood called le Rodewode lying in the north part of le Rode. Richard Milward clerk, Thomas Holeway and Henry Holeway were to cut down the timber and trees before the feast of St Peter ad Vincula 1465, and carry it away before the feast of St Michael. A consideration of 40s. was to be paid to William and John Holeway for each acre of wood, of which five marks were to be paid on the feast of St Peter and Paul, five marks was to be paid on the feast of All Saints, and the remainder on the following feast of All Saints. Witnesses being Thomas Shilston, Thomas Rede and Thomas Nobell. Dated at Lydford the 30th of May, 1462.

A newspaper report that was published ten years prior to Vancouver's report, reveals that timber being grown in vast quantity was up for auction on Saturday 29 April at three o'clock at the White Hart, Okehampton:

A great quantity of fine oak, ash, sycamore, and elm timber trees now growing in Eastlake Wood and on Eastlake Farm and the contiguous lands in the parish of Bridestowe, a small distance from Okehampton and on the High Road to Plymouth Dock, consisting of 9290 oak, a part of large dimensions, the remainder very suitable for builders, carpenters, coach wheelwrights and lath [tr]eaders. And 755 ash, sycamore, elms. The whole of the timber is marked and numbered and to be felled before the end of the year 1798, and cleared before the end of 1799. For viewing apply to George Westlake at Bridestowe of whom printed catalogues may be had 14 days preceding the sale, also at the Kings Arms, Bodmin; White Hart, Launceston; Place of Sale; Post House, Callington; Fountain, Plymouth Dock; Messrs Trewman and Son Printers, Exeter; Messrs Goading and Co Printers, Sherborne; Messrs Skinner, Dyke and Skinner, Aldersgate Street, London.

It was probably hoped that the oak would be wanted for ship building hence the mention of the 'High Road to Plymouth Dock' and the number of outlets available for catalogues.

Upon Brembleham in 1890 '100 timber trees marked and numbered with white paint' and 'about 16 acres of good coppice 26 years growth' were up for auction on behalf of John Newton of Stone. In 1804 'six acres of coppice wood (tithe free) of about 23 years of growth now standing in Parsonage Wood' was up for sale.

'Capital Navy and building timber' was to be sold at the Royal Oak Inn, Bridestowe on 1 March 1810. 'In one or more lots 140 capital oak trees with tops and bark now standing on Leawood, Great Close and Combebow Estates' where the 'trees are of large diameter situated for removal a quarter of a mile from the turnpike road.' Viewing or particulars of the timber could be gained from the 'Hind at Leawood House or Mr Gould Surveyor at Okehampton or Mr Marshall of Pascoe'.

In 1813 Calmady Pollexfen Hamlyn sold to John Buckingham of Lifton:

... 80 oak trees with tops and bark numerically marked with white paint now standing on Coombow and Great Close Estate along with 20 ash trees also with their tops and bark.

The oaks were sold for £300 and the ash £55. In 1848 an advert to 'shipbuilders, timber dealers, wheelwrights, coopers, turners and others' reported 'a very important sale of oak, ash, sycamore, elm and other timber trees, pollards, poles and coppice woods' for 'auction at the White Hart Inn Bridestowe on Monday 21 February'. The sale included 708 oak, 518 ash, 32 sycamores, 26 elm, 2 chestnut and 2 lime timber trees, with their tops and bark, and coppice wood.

It might be thought advantageous to see such a mix of trees in today's times as there are so many conifers. However, today's forests are managed, with replanting being a continuous event.

CORN MILLS

In 1582, Gilbert Germyn, the rector of Bridestowe Church apparently 'kypeth yn his hands the comon great Mylls of that p'ishe'. This is the only solid reference we have to these 'great Mylls', likewise, knowledge of the other mills discussed below can only be gained from incidental mentions in various documents.

Other mills in Bridestowe are Bidlake, Leawood and Stone. Leawood Mill, the last to be erected, is mentioned in a legal document of a case brought at the Devon Assizes in 1653 before 'the Keepers of the Liberty of England'. It seems that in 1652 John Harris brought a bill against John Toker of Bridestowe in a plea of trespass. Harris, it was reported:

... complayneth of Toker for that whereas hee the said John Harris the first day of August in the yeare of our Lord 1552 was and yett is seized of an ancient water Corne Mill with the appurtenment in the parish of Bridestowe called by the name of Stone Mill. And whereas from the tyme whereof the memory of man is not extant unto the contrary a certain ancient water course did in the p'ishe aforesaid rune and ought to rune and passed to the said mill for the driving of the wheels thereof there. Notwithstanding the aforesaid John Toker purposing and maliciously intending to him the said John Harris in the use and occupation of the said ancient water corn mill and to cause the same to be wholly useless and unprofitable for want of water to drive the wheels thereof. The said John Toker together with Henry Case of Bridestowe, labourer, the five and twentieth day of August in the Yeare of our Lord 1552 did divert and turne the ancient water course from its ancient course unto another water corne mill in the parishe of Bridestowe newly erected and called by the name of Leywood Mill for that the said

ancient water course could not in [its] ancient course rune as it was formerly [accustomed] to rune. And the diversion of the said water course from the tyme aforesaid untill the three and twentieth day of October then next following did confinne by means whereof the said John Harris of one hundred pounds. And thereupon hee brings his suite... the said John Harris by his attorney aforesaid as the said John Toker by Henry Langford his attorney... Therefore lett a jury thereupon come together and sworne who doe say upon their oaths that the aforesaid John Toker is guilty of the trespass within mentioned as the said John Harris hath within complayned against him. And that assesse the damage of the said John Harris besides his costs and charges by him about his suite in this behalfe. It is considered that the said John Harris recover against the said John Toker his damages of 40s. by the jury assessed. And also [£6] 10s. for his costs and charges to the same John Harris, which said damages in the whole doe amount unto £8.10s.1d.

Whilst the damages awarded were far short of the £100 as claimed by Harris, the fact that damages were awarded at all proves that Toker did indeed divert the water required to operate Stone Mill.

The legal document in all its length is wanting in one important area – it does not tell us the name of the 'ancient watercourse' that was diverted. If we look at an OS map one can only assume that it was Crandford Brook. However, the River Lew runs into the Crandford Brook below the Sporting Green so it seems surprising that the corn mill at Stone was unable to continue operating. As such, it seems fair to suggest that perhaps Toker did not completely cut off the supply of water from the Crandford Brook, but merely dug a leat to divert some of the water to power the new mill at Leawood; thus the water at Stone was not always of sufficient strength to work the mill.

If this was the case it would make sense that the sum awarded was less than a tenth of that quoted as being lost through lack of working time at Stone.

A lease of 1655, between John Harris of Hayne, Dame Cordelia, his wife, and Shilston Calmady of Leawood shows that 'the natural watercourses near the mansion house of Leawood, and Leawood Mills' was let at the yearly rent of 4d. This proved the Leawood Mill was eventually powered by water legally being used under lease.

Little is known about the day-to-day running of the mills in the parish, other than the fact that the lessee was obliged to take any grain grown on the land to the mill (which belonged to the landowner). There appears to be little or no information regarding when the mills ceased working.

SOURCES

Devon Record Office: 189M.
                      1292M.
                      29/Box 11.
Hamilton, A., *Quarter Sessions From Queen Elizabeth To Queen Anne.*
Hamilton Jenkin, A.K., *Mines Of Devon: North and East Of Dartmoor.*
Harris, H., *Industrial Archaeology Of Dartmoor.*
Higham, R.A., *Okehampton Castle.*
Higham, R.A., Allan, J.P., and Blaylock, S.R., *Excavations At Okehampton Castle, Devon, Part 2.*
Devon and Cornwall Notes and Queries Vol. XXV., Vol. XXXVI.
Roche, T.W.E., *The Withered Arm-Reminiscences of the Southern Lines West of Exeter.*
Transactions of the Devonshire Association, 1949 and 1950.
Trewman's *Exeter Flying Post* (Various references).
Vancouver, C., *General View of the Agriculture of the County of Devon* (1969 ed.).

Chapter 8

PARISH ADMINISTRATION

VESTRY MEETINGS

Originally established for the management of ecclesiastical affairs from the fourteenth century, Vestry meetings consisted of male ratepayers of the parish who carried out civic functions. The Vestry met to agree 12-month appointments of churchwardens, overseers of the poor, waywardens, constables and other officials. A notice of an intended meeting was posted on the church door and signed by either the incumbent or the churchwardens. By common law the chairman of the meeting was the minister of the parish; if he were not present a chairman was to be elected by majority vote.

Two churchwardens were normally appointed at Easter – one for the people, the other for the minister. The latter were 'the proper guardians or keepers of the parish church'. At times nominees endeavoured to decline office as a salary was only paid on the very odd occasion. Until 1964, common law compelled any parishioner chosen as warden to serve office. When one considers the nature of the churchwardens' work, it is understandable that some people chose a fine rather than the duties, some of which are outlined in the chart on page 128.

The office of overseer of the poor was established by the Poor Laws Act of 1597/8, and was made compulsory by the Poor Relief Act of 1601. Each Vestry appointed at least two persons selected from the parishioners to the office of overseer, which was unpaid. Their duties were to levy a poor rate and supervise its distribution to the poor. In 1834 most of their duties were transferred to the Guardians of the Poor, although the overseers still had to assess and collect the poor rate. Eventually the office of overseer was abolished by the Rating and Valuation Act of 1925.

The Highway Act of 1555 established waywardens, or, as they were sometimes known, surveyors of the highways. This post was also unpaid, but was appointed by the parishioners. After 1691 the waywarden was appointed by Justices at their special 'Highway Sessions' from a list of holders of land and inhabitants supplied by the parish. Three times a year he had to view and report upon road conditions to the justices. Days were to be fixed whereby statute labour was to be performed and fellow parishioners were to be supervised in their odious task of repairing the roads. The compulsory office of waywarden was under a monetary penalty if not performed by the elected person. This office, after that of the constable, was perhaps the most unpopular in the parish.

The constable was nominated at a Vestry meeting held at the end of February or the beginning of March. This office stems from early-manorial times and is probably the oldest of all parochial positions. He was almost wholly responsible for the maintenance of law and order within the parish and his powers of arrest were frequently exercised; the staff of his office were sometimes posted to the outside door of his house as a sign of authority. He could take in charge anyone who had committed a felony or a breach of the peace and could place that person in the stocks, the roundhouse or the cage. Alternatively, the wrongdoer could be held at the constable's own house until he or she could be brought before a magistrate.

Vestry meetings up and down the country were run by common law, each parish having its own interpretation of what that law should be. As the results of the meetings seemingly fulfilled the criteria required to sustain the parish, it was left well alone to carry on with its business.

Vestries at Bridestowe were held in the White Hart and Royal Oak, although the village school became a venue for later meetings. The business of the meetings was recorded in minute-books – of the two that are extant one covers the period 1829–58, the other 1859–1923. The contents of the Vestry minute-books demonstrate the diverse aspects of parish business with which the Vestry meetings dealt. Details of various meetings include an account book dated 1859–1903, an earlier overseer's account amongst the Bidlake papers and an undated account amongst the Calmady-Hamlyn papers, which indicates payments to the poor. A notice fixed to the church door at Bridestowe in 1866 informing the parishioners of a forthcoming

Vestry meeting ran:

Notice is hereby given that the Annual Vestry Meeting for this parish will be held at the White Hart Inn Bridestowe on Thursday the twenty fifth day of March 1886 at 9am for the purpose of nominating Guardian Overseers and Waywardens for the year ensuing. Also to transact any other business in connection with the above named parish that may be brought forward, the ratepayers are requested to attend.

The style of entry in the Vestry minute-book follows a set pattern throughout. The initial entry for each meeting (a copy of the notice of the intended Vestry meeting) is followed by a list of the ratepayers present and the name of the person in the chair. The business of the meeting as it took place was then entered. This included resolutions, whether passed, nominations, whether elected, and other decisions that had been made during the meeting.

Family documents and the numerous entries in the Vestry books are of great social interest but they are too prolific to enter here. We will though, look at the binding out of two poor children as apprentices.

Devon Constabulary House, 1930s. (Brian Maddaford)

Turning to minutes of a Vestry meeting held on 16 October 1811 we find:

We the Churchwardens and Overseers of the poor at a Special Vestry held this day which was published in the church 29 September last for this purpose do agree that Margaret Barkwell a poor child of the said Parish of Bridestowe, nearly nine years of age, and now under a relief shall be bound as a parish apprentice to William Lee for an estate known by the name Buddlebrook, in this said parish. Value at £20 per annum being an estate that is farthest back in the said parish and the said William Lee being a person very capable of maintaining such apprentice. But should the Honorable Bench of Justices have any objections to bind the said apprentice to the said

William Lee, they are most humbly desired to set forth their reasons why they refuse to do so.

Signed: John Newton, Chairman
William Palmer, Overseer
Thomas Pugsley, Overseer

The following is a shortened indenture, of an earlier date, which gives an insight into the conditions set for a parish apprentice and her mistress. We have:

This indenture made 20 April 1763 Witnesseth That Henry Glover Church Warden of the Parish of Briddistow And Henry Voyzey Overseer of the Poor of the said parish, by and with the Consent of his Majesty's Justices of the Peace whose Names are hereunto subscribed, have put and placed, and by these presents do put and place Elizabeth Major a poor child of the said Parish, apprentice to Philippi Bidlake for an Estate called Great Bidlake in the parish of Briddistow with her to dwell and serve from the day of the date of these presents until the said apprentice shall accomplish her full age of 21 years or day of marriage according to the statute in that case made and provided. During all which term the said apprentice her said mistress faithfully shall serve in all lawful business according to her power, wit and ability; and honestly, orderly and obediently, in all things demean and behave herself... the said Philippi Bidlake the said apprentice in good housewifery shall teach or cause to be taught. And shall and will, during all the term aforesaid, find, provide and allow, unto the said apprentice, competent and sufficient meat, drink and apparel, lodging, washing and all other things necessary and fit for an apprentice. And also shall and will so provide for the said apprentice that she be not any way a charge to the parish... during the said term. [The following sentence was crossed through but has been included here for interest] And at the end of the said term, shall and will make, provide, allow and deliver unto the said apprentice double apparel of all sorts, good and new (that is to say a good new suit for holy days, and another for working days).

Elizabeth was to be well provided for but no doubt she had to work hard. It can only be hoped that she enjoyed a better life at Bidlake than the one she might have had to suffer as a poor child.

Although 1923 is recognised as being the last date in the Vestry minute-books, the meetings actually terminated between the late 1880s and the early 1890s. This was due to the Local Government Act of 1894, which stated that where in rural areas the population was over 300, elected Parish Councils were to be formed. An entry in the Vestry minutes-book dated 4 December 1894

Payments to the Poor

Bidlake Account (in part) reads:

Hundred de Lifton Parochia de Briddistowe The Accounts of William Bidlake gent: Allexander Ebsworthie and Richard Harris Overseers of ye Poore of ye p'ishe of Briddistowe for one whole yeare last past made ye xiiij^th daye of Aprill: 1612. Payments were made Unto

Edward Whith... for keeping Peeter So[x] the sonne of Edmonde So[x] for one whole yeare	38s 4d
For Clothe to make a Coate for said Peeter So[x]	2s 3d
For a paire of Shoes for said Peeter So[x]	7d
For makeing same So[x]'s Coate	4d
For a Shroude for Edmond Cotten	3s 10d
Unto William Heywoode for keepinge of a Base child of Thomas Cuddis for 33 Weekes	17s 11d
For a Coat for the said Base child	2s 10d
For amendinge of Shoes of the said Base child	4d
For a paire of Shoes for said Base child	11d
For a Shirt for said Base child	12d
For a pair of Stockinge for said Base child	7d
For a Smock for A... Bennett	2s

Calmady-Hamlyn Account (undated but probably early to middle 19c.) reads:

Ann Walter	*3 weeks pay*	*7s 6d*	*Richard Bond*	*7s 6d*	
Mary Collings	*3 weeks pay*	*4s 6d*	*Drew Friend in need*	*1s 0d*	
Joan Walter	*3 weeks pay*	*3s 0d*	*Shoes for William Roberts*	*8s 0d*	
John Palmer	*3 weeks pay*	*12s 0d*	*Canvas thread and Buttons for John Matters*	*1s 2d*	
Dorthy Daw	*3 weeks pay*	*7s 6d*	*Mary Gerry in need*	*1s 0d*	
Elizabeth Collings	*3 weeks pay*	*6s 0d*	*Dun Palmer for tending Ann Matter*	*1s 6d*	
William Ball and Whife	*3 weeks pay*	*12s 0d*	*Dun Palmer for tending Ann Matter*		
Joan Maiours		*7s 6d*	*last month omitted*	*2s 0d*	
Joan Roberts		*4s 6d*	*Payed Robert Broad part of Elizabeth*		
Grace Bond		*6s 0d*	*Ayreses rent*	*10s 6d*	
Joan Maiours Child		*5s 9d*	*William Smallacombe in need*	*12s 6d*	
Elizabeth Brewer		*3s 9d*	*Paid for mending Elizabeth*		
Mary Down		*3s 0d*	*Ayreses Bedstead*	*2s 6d*	
Thomas Ackfords Maid		*6s 0d*	*Mary Norish for her children in need*	*6s 0d*	
Mary Gerrys Boy		*3s 9d*	*Roger Daw in need*	*5s 0d*	
Chris Knights Base Child		*3s 0d*	*Grace Ayres in need*	*3s 0d*	
Drew Friend		*1s 6d*	*Elizabeth Reddicliffe in need*	*2s 0d*	
Mary Bickel		*4s 6d*	*Mr Davy omitted Sussana Friend in need*	*6s 0d*	
Mark Lake		*12s 0d*	*Payed Mr Davy two journeys to Dolton four*		
Mary Coombe		*4s 6d*	*days expenses on the road for himself Mary*		
Elizabeth Ayreses Boy		*6s 0d*	*Matter and James Ousborn*	*£1 7s 0d*	
John Lakes two children		*9s 0d*	*Meat and liquer for James Ousborn at*		
Mary Ackfords Base Child		*9s 0d*	*my house*	*2s 6d*	
Jane Jordans Base Child		*3s 0d*			

gives due notice for the election of Parish Councillors. Minutes of Parish Council meetings were kept in a book for that purpose.

Looking back at the activities of the Parish Council, it can be seen that improvements did occur within the village although perhaps to those of us living today the changes may appear to be of little consequence. Some problems which were presented to the initial councillors, it seems, are still being debated today; services, such as the cleaning of the village and the delivery of mail. When changes are made it is presumed that they will be to the advantage of the parishioners, but alas, that is not always the case.

Nevertheless, most of the people living in Bridestowe must surely have experienced a greater quality of life as a result of the development of its governing system.

SOURCES
Devon Record Office:
    2750A. Vestry and Council Books.
    1292M.
    189M.

Typical Churchwardens' Duties:

To manage parish property and income.

To represent the views of parishioners.

The provision of facilities for worship and the allocation of pews.

To encourage parishioners to attend church and to ensure children are baptised.

To attend the Archdeacon's court.

To account for the expenditure of the church rate.

To assist in the compilation of the parish register.

To supervise the education and relief of the poor in collaboration with the overseers of the poor.

To report any failing in the duty of the incumbent.

To maintain the parish arms and pay the local soldiers.

The control and extermination of vermin.

To present offences within the cognizance of the church courts.

Typical Constable's Duties:

The supervision of Watch and Ward as specified by the Statute of Winchester, 1285.

The upkeep of the stocks and lock-up.

The inspection of alehouses/suppression of gaming houses.

The apprenticing of pauper children.

The supervision/removal of itinerant strangers/beggars.

Collaboration with other officials in the relief of the poor.

The collection of the county rate/any special national tax.

The maintenance of parish arms and training of local militia.

The care of the parish bull.

The presentation of parishioners often absent from church.

Assistance at shipwrecks in the locality.

The apprehension and detention of suspected criminals, the arrest of escaped prisoners.

The suppression of riots and unlawful assemblies.

Collection of child maintenance from fathers of illegitimates.

Is this the Red Lion?

Chapter 9

A VILLAGE MISCELLANY

LAW & ORDER ON THE MANOR

A Court Baron, or, as it eventually became known, a Customary Court Baron, was a manorial court that enforced the customs of the manor. It was the property of the lord of the manor and as such was a private jurisdiction generally presided over by the lord's steward. Court business concerned escheat, the reversion to the lord or the Crown of an estate when a tenant died without heirs, where the heir had not obtained majority and where the tenant had committed an offence which incurred the forfeiture of his estate. Surrenders and transfers of land, and the rights of the lord and tenants were also subject to the jurisdiction of the court. Originally, the Homage or Jury at the manorial court meetings had to consist of at least two freeholders, but with the decline of this form of tenure, copyhold tenants formed the Homage and the Court Baron became a Customary Court Baron. Such a court was held at Bridestowe.

The Incumbent of the Parish Church was the lord of the manor of Bridestowe Sanctuary and Parsonage and we find that two court books of this manor are extant and date from 1575 to 1898. The books give the series of the lords of the manor as William Marston, Gilbert Germyn, Edward Cotton, William Knapman, William Hutton, Edward Drewe, William Stuart, Peter Burnaford, Thomas Herberden and Coryndon Luxmore of whom we are well aware.

The earliest book dated from 27 April 1575, contains mainly Latin text until 1735 where-upon entries appear in English. The first book is referred to as 'a curious record' by George Oliver, a Roman Catholic priest, in a letter dated at Exeter 6 May 1853. What certainly is curious is that there are no indications as to where the court was held other than to say 'within the said manor'.

Whether the lord of the manor of Bridestowe Sanctuary had the power of 'infangenethef', that is, the power to hang one's own thief if caught in one's own territory, or 'utfangenethef', that is, the power to hang him wherever caught, is not made

clear. Before the hanging of a thief it seemed that he had to be caught 'handhaving or back-bearing', that is, with the stolen goods upon him. The 'loser of the goods' had to be the person who was to prosecute the thief.

On each manor, the reeve was to gather all such rents, revenues or other yearly profits and give a true account at the end of the year. The affeerors (officers appointed to assess penalties for proven offences) were to well and truly tax, assess and affier (assign) all the amercements presented in court. The foreman of the jury was to enquire and make true presentments of all such articles and things directed. The business of the court consisted of two parts. The first related to those items for the lord's benefit. The foreman of the jury was instructed:

If any of the Customs, Rents, Franchises, Royalties, Services, Evidences, Rent Rolls or Court Rolls of the Mannor be concealed or withheld, you are to Present, and by Whom.

If any Encroachment be made upon the Lord's lands without Licence, you are to Present, and by Whom.

If any Tenant takes away the Lord's Game, Hawke, Hunt, Fish, or Do other Trespass in this Mannor without Leave of the Lord, you are to Present, and by Whom.

If any of the Tenants of the Mannor be Dead, whose Death is not yet presented, and by what Tenure He held his Lands, and what is to come to the Lord thereby, as an Herriot or otherwise, and who is next of Kin of such Tenant, you are to Present, and by Whom.

If any Tenant hath Committed Forfeiture by Waste or Otherwise, you are to Present, and by Whom.

The court also dealt with items concerning the tenants and the foreman of the jury was instructed:

If there be any Common in your Mannor, and a Tenant take Common that hath none, or having Common keep more than his number, or put in Cattle that are not Commonable, or otherwise abuse the Common, you are to Present, and by Whom.

Proceedings of the Court of William Knapman held on 27 September 1653

The free tenants present were the heirs of Dinham and the heirs of Sir Shilston Calmady who are to do suit at Court twice by the year at 'Roodemas' and at 'Michaelmas'.

The tenants in possession were Shilston Calmady, John Youlden, Richard Youlden, William Storkman, John Storkman, John Crosman, John Toll (dead), William Prouse in right of Penelope his wife, Agnes Ebsworthy spinster, George White in the right of Johan his wife, William Gill, Reginald Hawkey.

John Crosman William Gill Edward Gill	}	tenants for one tenemt caled Stondon in Stondon by copy accordinge to custome	rent xviijs a best beast for a Herryott
John Toll Henry Toll and John Toll his sonne	}	tenants for on tenemt caled Sleekers lyeinge in Sowerton otherwise Sowertowne	rent xxs a best beast for a Herryott
Richard Youlden and Mary his wife	}	tenants for one tenemt caled North ball in the towne of Bridestowe	rent xxs a best beast for a Herryott
William Storkman Johan Storkman Henry Crosman	}	tenants for one tenemt caled South ball in the towne of Bridestowe	rent xxs a best beast for a Herryott
William Prouse for the life of Penelope his wife late wife of George Parsons and George Austin	}	tenants for two tenemt caled North ball and Bridgehays in Bridestowe	rent xxvjs viijd a best beast for a Herryott
George White for the life of Johan his wife	}	one house or cottage in Bridestowe	rent xvjd a best beast for a Herryott
Reginald Hawkey Martha Knapman Mary Knapman	}	tenants for one house and one meadowe caled Denboles parke in Bridestowe	rent viijs a best beast for a Herryott
John Crosman Elizabeth his wife Ann Crosman	}	tenants for a house and peece of land lyinge nere the churchyarde	rent xvjd Herryott vs

The Jury Made their Presentments:

They present the death of Sir Shilston Calmady a free tenant of the manor who holds one tenement called [?] in the town of Bridestowe now in the tenure of William Ebsworthy of the lord of this Manor by the [?] and there is due to the lord for a [rent] sixteen pence, that Josias Calmady his son is the next heir.

They present Richard Yolden to be Reeve for the year following.

They present the death of Peter Ebsworthy who held according to the Custom of the Manor one tenement called Denboles Park upon whose death there was a best beast due to the lord and the tenement upon his death fell into the lords hands.

They present the death of Katherine Ebsworthy who held one house and meadow at the west bridge end in Bridestowe upon whose death there is a best beast due to the lord and that Agnes Ebsworthy is next tenant.

They present the death of Grace Gill widow who held one house and parcel of ground in Bridestowe upon whose death there is five shillings due to the lord for a heriot and that William Gill her son is the next tenant.

They present the death of the said Grace Gill who also held one house and a piece of ground in Bridestowe upon whose death there is five shillings due to the lord for a heriot and that the premises upon her death is in the lords hands.

They present the death of the said Grace Gill who also held one house in Bridestowe called the smith shop and upon her death the premises fell into the lords hands.

They present one house to be in decay to wit fallen unto the ground in default of George White in the right of Johan his wife he hath time to repair the same until Michaelmas 1654 upon the pain of three pounds at the request of the said George White.

They present the death of George Parsons who held one tenement called North Ball Bridge Hayes upon whose death there was a heriot due to wit a best beast and that Penelope the now wife of William Prouse is next tenant.

They present the Hind fold to be in default of the lord of the said Manor.

If you have any By-Laws broken, you are to Present, and by Whom.

Mentioned in the court books (which cover some 323 years in all) are various properties belonging to the Bridestowe Sanctuary and Parsonage Manor. Many of the names of the tenements of the lord of the manor will be familiar, but few will have heard of the tenement commonly called the 'Red Lion', also mentioned in the court hearing of 1653.

Among the various presentments made to the court we find that on 3 January 1576 the wife of John Horewyll junr of Lydford was presented for having entered the lord's wood, and there cutting down certain young trees growing and carrying them away. Thomas Pearce of Lydford had been guilty of the like offence as had John Craneberry. On 10 May 1581, John Craneberry and Thomas Pearce were presented for repeating the said offence and left to the lord's mercy.

On page 14 of the earliest court book William Taverner was recorded as having been fined five shillings for making a dunghill in the highway. In 1613 Balls Meadow, North Ball and Bridhayes are mentioned and in 1623 Sleekers Farm in Sourton is listed. In 1650 John Crossman is mentioned as being tenant of one house and Tanners Meadow. On 29 December 1653 William Ebsworthy is presented for 'makeinge a dung hill on the Commons beelonginge to the tenants within the said Mannor', and also 'for fodderinge and feedinge of cattle there to the damage of the tenants awarded agt him'. At the same time William Gill was presented:

... for contemptuously refuseinge to come to the lord's court beeinge lawfully summoned according to the custome contrary to the custome of the said mannor therefore he is fined x^s.

In 1690 the customary tenant of the White Hart was Agnes Fursman, a widow, along with Thomas Wyatt and Agnes, his wife of Tavistock.

Tenements (and sometimes their tenants) mentioned in 1700 include: Balls Meadow, North Ball (Alexander Douslian), East Ball, South Ball (Homiris Crossman), Tanners Meadow (Thomas Wymott), Standon (William Mason), The Stables (Josias Calmady), Red Lion (William Nicholls) Broadhayes (Bridhayes), Denbole Park, The Green, Blacksmiths Shop, Coombe Houses, Cottages (William Pengelly), Cottage (John Crossman).

On 2 March 1735:

... to this court came Gillin the wife of William Newton of Bridestowe and received from the Hand of the Lord a certain parcell of land or ground containing thirty yards or thereabouts being part of the Waste of the Manor commonly called the Green near the White Hart in Bridestowe in order there to erect and Build a Dwelling house containing two ground rooms and two Chambers over the same and to make a Herb garden of the remaining part of the said granted parcell of Ground.

On 20 November 1739 'at the west end of the west bridge in the town of Bridestowe a house commonly called or known by the name of the sign of the White Hart', was let for three lives 'on a fine of forty two pounds' and 'a yearly rent of eight shillings'. On 17 May 1756 the death of Richard Williams, a customary tenant for the Red Lion was presented. On 11 August 1779 Andrew Hockaday was presented for 'building a house without the liberty of the lord thereof', whilst some seven years later on 4 October 1786 mention is made of a William Hockaday of Bridestowe, blacksmith, paying a rent of one shilling per year for a blacksmith's shop. In November 1794, the manor pound was presented as being in need of repair. As for the 'Red Lion', the last entry in the court book appears in 1801. When this hostelry was demolished does not appear and there is no mention of it in the Tithe Schedule of 1841.

The last entry for a Court Baron was made at the house of James Joyce in 1895 but there is little written substance. This is not the closure one might expect for such an important occasion, the end of what was an important era. Thomas Moore, a New York lawyer, is the present holder of the title 'Lord of the Manor of Bridestowe Sanctuary'.

❋ *Village Views* ❋

Top left: *The Launceston Road looking towards West Bridge.* (Alan Pearn)

Top right: *Bidlake Vean, 1930s. At one time this was the home of Sylvia Calmady-Hamlyn.* (Author)

Below: *The clapper bridge behind the Sporting Green, c.1990.* (Susan Cann)

Bottom: *The bottom of Poole Hill without the petrol pumps, c.1990.* (Susan Cann)

Above: *The White Hart is on the right but the Post Office has been levelled to make way for a bus turning area. If only the planners had had hindsight!* (Doug Gale)

Below: *The butcher's shop, S.A. Worden & Sons. Left to right: Bill Heathman, Lilly Worden, customer (?).* (Alan Pearn)

❆ *Village Views* ❆

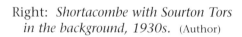

Top left: *Bridhayes Cottages.* (Doug Gale)

Top right: *The Old Post Office.* (Doug Gale)

Left: *Accommodation as well as a Butcher's Shop, 1950s.* (Doug Gale)

Right: *Shortacombe with Sourton Tors in the background, 1930s.* (Author)

Below: *Fore Street, 1950s.* (Doug Gale)

❧ *Village Inns* ❧

Left: *The Royal Oak, 1960s.* (Doug Gale)

Middle: *Fox and Hounds, 1920s.* (Doug Gale)

Right: *White Hart, 1940s.* (Doug Gale)

THE CIVIL WAR

During the English Civil War, Bridestowe was to bear witness to a skirmish at nearby Sourton Down but some four months prior to this action the village would become the setting for a mutiny. On 30 December 1642, the Royalist troops under Sir Ralph Hopton were in Exeter and being short on supplies called upon the city defended by Parliamentarians to surrender. The summons was ignored as the city was well prepared for a siege and a relieving force was close to hand. On the night of the 31st the Royalists attacked the city to no avail, being forced to retreat. On the way back to Launceston the Cornish Foot, 'dispirited and underfed', became rebellious and broke into mutiny at Bridestowe. With no little difficulty, their commander, Hopton, managed to rally his men and led them back to Cornwall.

In the days leading up to the Sourton Down skirmish a Parliamentarian army under the command of Major General Chudleigh occupied Okehampton. On 21 April 1643, a Friday, the Parliamentarian army of Devonians consisting of 1000 foot and 200 horse left Okehampton and marched towards the Cornish Royalist army headquarters at Launceston, commanded by Sir Ralph Hopton. Saturday saw Chudleigh advancing to Lifton and on Sunday he crossed the River Tamar at Polson Bridge where he met scattered opposition. This was soon overcome and Chudleigh's army moved quickly towards their main objective, Launceston, where stiff opposition was met. At five o'clock in the afternoon Chudleigh received help from 700 London Greycoats of Colonel Merrick's regiment from Plymouth. These troops, under the command of Lieutenant-Colonel Sir Shilston Calmady, did little to ease Chudleigh's problems in doing battle with the Cornish, and eventually he was forced back across the river into Devon. Chudleigh and his men returned to Okehampton where they were quartered.

On Tuesday 25 April Sir Ralph Hopton moved east with his regrouped men, hoping to join forces with the King's army for a spring campaign. That Tuesday some 4000 foot and 500 horse advanced into Devon, through Lifton and on to Bridestowe where they were quartered before moving on to Okehampton. As Hopton's men were putting out their guards a friend from Okehampton informed them of a growing weakness within the opposition quartered in Okehampton. This news encouraged the Cornish leader to attempt a surprise attack on the enemy, so he marched towards Okehampton.

The Cornish were on the western part of Sourton Down before the night closed in and were put in order for a night march to do battle very early the following morning. The Cornish, it was said, 'appear'd upon view the hansoms't body of men that had bene gotten together in those parts all that warr.'

Unfortunately for Hopton's fine-looking troops, many of them volunteers and raw recruits, Chudleigh decided that the safest defence was a swift offensive move – in this case an ambush. About 108 men, being three troop of horse and divided into six groups of 18 men, were scattered around Sourton Down. The Devonians attacked from six different directions making as much noise as possible in order to disguise their numbers. The Cornish were routed at the very first assault; the Parliamentarians were able to disrupt the entire vanguard of Hopton's army. The Cornish though stood their ground and, expecting a second charge, were not altogether mistaken when Chudleigh charged their ranks again. With this Chudleigh withdrew his exhausted men to Okehampton as the enemy were growing more effective in opposition.

The Commanders of the Cornish army did not think it fit to advance that night so made good their ground. A violent thunderstorm soon persuaded them to withdraw to the security of Bridestowe. Of this storm Vicars wrote:

One thing is remarkable, that as soon as our horse charged it grew darke and it thundered and lightned in a very terrible manner, and the thunderclap brake just over their heads and then raine extraordinary, and it was a very great winde and hard weather all that day and night.

From Bridestowe the Cornish retreated to Launceston. Such a severe blow dealt by inferior forces was a major coup for the Parliamentary cause. The London pamphleteers could not find sufficient words to praise the Devonian valour and resolution and pointed significantly to the storm as a providential gesture which made the victory complete.

It would be some time before Bridestowe saw such drama unfold before their eyes again. Fifteen months later royal personages passed through the village upon their travels; Queen Henrietta Maria (after giving birth to Princess Henrietta at Exeter on 16 June 1644) left the city in a pitiful condition for fear of her safety on 30 June. She travelled on a litter without her baby via Okehampton and Launceston to reach Falmouth on 14 July where she embarked upon a Flemish man-of-war. She probably passed through Bridestowe on 3 July as a manuscript dated 1 July at Okehampton records 'Queen Mary came hither with a great many and stayed two nights.'

During his war campaign King Charles stayed at the village of Bow on the night of 29 July 1644 and proceeded to Okehampton on Tuesday the 30th, staying at the house of John Rattenbury. On the following day the King and his party travelled through Bridestowe and on to Lifton, being accommodated at the Parsonage there (not, as tradition might have it, at Great Bidlake) along the way. Upon returning into Devon the King travelled via Tavistock moving on to Okehampton where he once again lodged in the house of Rattenbury, leaving the following day for Crediton.

The roles of Calmady and Bidlake family members during the war have been covered in Chapter 2, but mention should also be made of a common soldier from Bridestowe who played his part in the conflict. The following 'maimed soldier's petition' has survived the ravages of time:

To the right Worshippfll and Honorable his Majesties Justices of the peace for the County of Devon aforesaid and the Generall Sessions of the peace to be holden for the said County.

Anno Regni Rogis Jacobi 2di nunt Anglie...

Cortio Annoy Doninj 1687

Humbly Sheweth The Humble Petition of Thomas Prost of Bridestowe in the said County Husbandman.

That yo. Petitioner being a Souldier in his Majesties Service King Charles the first of Blessed memory under Captaine Bidlake in the Regiment of

the Honorable Sir Nicholas Stanning declares and haveing Received severall dangerous wounds suffered long imprisonment for his loyalty, and being now above sixty years of age and unable to gett his Liveing, and haveing never deserted the said Service. May it therefore please your Honours the pr[sents] Considered to order such pension for the releife of yor Petitioner as to yor Honours shall seem fit & yor Petitioner shall ever pray.

Wee believe the contents of this petition true Nicholas Harreys Tho. Wood Arthur Tremayne.

Wee whose names are hereunto subscribed Inhabitants of the parish of Bridestowe within mentioned doe certifie your honors that the within named Thomas Prost your poor Petitioner by Reason of the wounds and hurts he Received in his Majesties Service King Charles the first of Blessed memory is soe much disabled in his body that he cannot gat a livelihood for himself and his poor family as formerly he hast done by Reason of wch he has been of late chargeable to our said parrish Wittness our hands the Two & twentieth day of June Anno R Regis Nimo Anglice Cortio Annoys Donij 1687.

Thomas Loman Overseer
Leonard Gubbins
Walter Nicholls
[Peter] Walter
William Loman Church Warden
James Newton
John Tickell

VENVILLE MEN

In centuries past, as common land Dartmoor has proved to be a most useful commodity to the people sanctioned to use it, albeit at a price in the form of obligatory service and monetary payment. A brief history of Dartmoor shows that as a Royal Forest it was subject to a system of austere laws that were relaxed when King John granted a Charter on 18 May 1204, which apparently allowed for the deforestation of Devon up to the metes and bounds of Dartmoor and Exmoor. Men were relieved from attending forest courts and it was further conceded that no man should lose life or limb for breach of the forest laws. Any man convicted for a breach of the forest laws was to be heavily fined whilst for default of payment of that fine a term of imprisonment for a year and a day was to be imposed. Release from such a sentence was obtained upon pledges for good conduct otherwise a man was to entreat the realm of England.

On 10 October 1239 Henry III granted to his brother, Richard, Earl of Cornwall, the manor of Lydford together with the Forest of Dartmoor. The forest became a chase. A century later, in 1337,

Edward III granted the manor of Lydford with the Chase of Dartmoor to Edward, the Black Prince, Duke of Cornwall, upon which Dartmoor became a part of the Duchy of Cornwall.

A writ dated 13 June 1240 to the Sheriff of Devon had instructed him to summon a jury of 12 knights to determine the boundaries of the Forest of Dartmoor and among the jurors was Hugh Bollay, who might well have been a member of the de Bolley family who held the manor of Bridestowe.

During the reign of Henry VIII, a diagram drawn at the bottom of a document in all probability was meant as an aid to show the relationship between Dartmoor Forest and adjoining areas. The diagram consists of a circle containing three others, each in turn inside the other, sharing a common centre point. The outer circle represents the whole of Devonshire. People living in the area between the outer and second circle were known as foreigners or wreytors. They had rights on the Commons of the forest except for the inhabitants of Totnes and Barnstaple who were excluded. The area between the second and third circles contains the lands which are said to be in Venville, whilst the area between the third and inner circle is the 'Waste', called the Commons of Dartmoor. Finally, the innermost circle represents the Forest of Dartmoor upon which were the copyhold tenants who were forest men.

Bridestowe, along with 22 other parishes bordering the Forest of Dartmoor lies within the area said to be in Venville. Owners and occupiers of land in Venville were known as Venville men who paid Venville rents. From an account of rents for 1505–6 we find that the parish of Bridestowe paid two shillings. Men also owed suit to the manor court of Dartmoor held at Lydford Castle. They had rights of free pasture on the Commons of the forest and men in Venville could also take from the forest all they required for fuel, building, hedging etc, save green oak and venison. Birkett believed that these rights could be 'exercised on and throughout the Forest and Commons of Devon irrespectively of forest, parochial or manorial bounds.' He continued:

The Venville tenants must pay their Venville rents to the Duchy, and may only depasture during the day; but if they wish to depasture at night they must each pay an additional 3d. per anum to the Duchy. The Venville Tenants, the owners and occupiers of all land in respect of which Venville rents are due pay

those rents. In some cases these rents are paid by the Overseers of the Poor in respect of the whole of the land in the parish, in other cases by the tenants of specific farms, manors or vills.

He further explains that 'levant and couchant' means that a man could turn out upon the commonable lands as many head of cattle, horses or sheep as he could support in winter 'by the produce of his holding during the year'.

Indeed, there is evidence of the Bidlakes using the Commons to depasture their livestock. It also seems probable that one of their early ancestors, Ralph of Combe, also partook of his right to use the Commons, but seemingly he did not abide by the law for he was 'fined 12d. for having his dog in the forest in fence time.'

Back in 1236 Henry III had granted the tithe of the herbage of the Forest of Dartmoor to the Chaplain at Lydford. The tithes, however, were not always forthcoming, as amongst others, the Revd David Birchinsha, instituted in 1688, found to his disapproval. He began a lawsuit against the non-payers but this took so long to settle that it had to be continued by the Revd Thomas Burnaford who had exchanged with Birchinsha in 1701. That same year, Stephen Reddicliffe of Bridestowe, a 50-year-old weaver, appears to have given evidence in the case.

RIGHTS OF WAY

A map, c.1609, showing 'the way to Deartmoore forest, the Comen of Devonshire' for those wanting to drive livestock onto the moor for grazing, doubtless sketched as an aid to dispute an allegation of trespass, forms the basis from which we can build upon a picture of further disagreements between the Bidlakes and Ebsworthys. The disagreement in question seems to have surrounded one party refusing to let the other proceed over his land to drive his animals onto Dartmoor to participate in his Venville rights. Paul Ebsworthy who was occupying Stone had brought pleas of trespass against John Bidlake and later against both John and his son William, albeit they claimed a right of way over Ebsworthy's land. It would seem that the pleas of trespass were to be heard at the Devon Assizes in Exeter. The suit taken against John Bidlake began on 20 March 1608/9 and continued until 20 March 1610/11, whilst the plea of trespass brought against father and son began on 20 June 1611, continuing until 'the vijth of february last'.

The map measures approximately 30" by 22½", it is of a very simple but clear application and sets out the layout of the area of land over which the trespass was said to take place. It was perhaps

drawn in order that judge and jury, if unfamiliar with the area, could follow the evidence presented to the court.

The map is nearly divided into two equal portions by the Okehampton to Launceston Road. Okehampton, at the upper left, is represented by a cross sitting on the top of a tower to show the church, whilst Launceston has a castle for a landmark. Further churches on the map indicate Bridestowe, Sourton, Thrushelton, Tavistock and Brentor where the church is drawn perched on the top of a very steep hill. A castle represents Lydford. Other roads shown lie between Bridestowe and Lydford and from Way Cross to Lydford, this latter crossing the Okehampton to Launceston Road at Cross Lanes.

Bidlake House, labelled Wester Bidlake, is represented by a house lying within an enclosure, trees in rows form Burley Wood whilst Dartmoor and the Commons of Devon are identified by 'sugar loaf' mountains at the top of the map. The map was sketched to lead the reader to 'Wester Bidlake', through the Great Close (the area of land that is the subject of the trespass plea) and on to the 'Comons of Devonshire'. As the scale of the map differs in the main portion from that of the outer limits (which are reduced) the map carries a note:

from thee westergate of the great close to the cross-lane is paces measured by paces going 712 from the crosslane corner to ye east gate of yt close is by like measure pases 465 westergate of ye great close as the way in the close lieth to ye eastergate ys by like measure pases 648.

A well-written narrative was drafted by John Bidlake to add weight to his defence against trespass. It consists of five different copies of notes that appear to have been written successively as additional information came to hand. At first John writes to show how his title to Bidlake came about. He starts off with the grant of Warren de Sacville of Bidlake to Ralph of Combe and continues with the succession of Bidlake until the point at which Paul Ebsworthy brought the plea of trespass. The note is too lengthy to quote in full, but parts are of interest. From the time of the marriage of Katherine Bidlake with John Cooke:

Bidlake had ben occupied by one Robert Friende (her farmr thereof) and wthin some fower yers after havinge fully stocked his grounds prposed as his ancestrs to putt some shepe & cattle to Deartmore

yerlie & to dryve theym thorough the great close as the way lieth Robt Ebsworthie then holding it [denied] him both that way & thereupon the mattr being heard amongst friends was omitted and was contynually used and so have the heirs of the said Henry Bidlake till this action brought by Paule Ebsworthie.

In 1565:

The grant for the hedwere to Bidlake mill leate was made & ye same leate finished & mylls reedified towards wch besides the 4 mill stones yt were made in Deartmoore many other great moore stones were brought over the great close to yt from out of Deartmoore or Comen of Devon & divers rode & went to those mills wth their corn over the said close as fro' Sourton p'ishe Raddon Rise & Bridsto p'ishe & Walter of Fernworthie, Beare Stannan Cobham Weke & Blackbrome.

A list of shepherds to Henry Bidlake for his 'shepe kept in Deartmoore vide his account booke for shepe' tells us that 'Edmond Caddyn was shepheard Ano Dni 1563.' At this point the writing is partially obscured by a fold in the paper but it would seem that Caddyn had at least used a route from Wester Bidlake to Dartmoor via 'Borley' (Burley Wood). Continuing with the list of shepherds:

Scouts 50-year Reunion (on Dartmoor) Walk, 6 August 1949 – 6 August 1999. Left to right: *Neil Barkell, Jack Crocker, Tony Johnston, Brian Maddaford, Norman Gale, Howard Barkell, Douglas Gale.* (Doug Gale)

John was shepheard Ano Dom 1573 (yn the life of Peter after Caddyn 3 yers) and so continued untill Ano 1578. Roger Friend was shepheard Ano Dom 1578 (after the death of Petr Ebsworthy 2 yers) & so contynued untill Ano 1585. Both Caddyn and John drove ye shepe always over the great close.

John's notes clearly indicate that Wester Bidlake had been in the hands of the Bidlake family for nigh on 350 years, and that whilst occupied by Wester Bidlake the family had made use of their Venville rights upon Dartmoor, not only by grazing their sheep there but also by taking

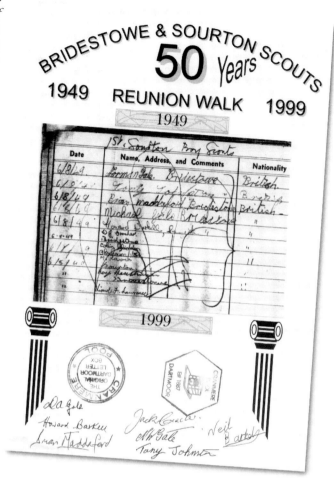

stone for building work on the family residence and the mill at Combebow. Further notes show continuing use of the 'Great Close'.

Lastly, to reinforce his claim, John quotes a much earlier case of a similar matter that had arisen. From an entry of the court roll of the Manor and Forest Court held at Lydford in 1471 Henry Cole had been found:

... guilty of closing the way from Bidlake to Cobhamweek and thence to Dartmoor to the grave injury of other tenants, thus illustrating long standing rights of way to the moor.

PARISH CHARITIES

From an inquiry held at Bridestowe on 21 February 1912 we learn of two charitable institutions benefiting the parish. Taking the oldest charity first we find that in pursuance of an inquiry into Charities in England and Wales in 1824 a field called the Parish Ham, or, as sometimes known, Church Land, was held in subvention towards the Parish Church. The Commissioners appointed for the 1912 inquiry used the report resulting from the above inquiry of 1824 as a basis for their own findings from which we find that the Parish Ham was the only charity in existence at that time.

In essence the 1824 Commissioners reported that the Parish Ham had belonged to the parish for many years, but only one document was presented to the Commission officials relating to the field. The document, a lease dated 8 April 1765, had been demised to Richard Friend. In their capacity as churchwardens Ebsworthy, Tapson and Richard Harvey, along with Shilston Calmady and six other parishioners of Bridestowe said to be Feoffees of the field, had granted the lease for a

term of the life of Richard Friend and the life of his son Richard Friend junior. A consideration of five shillings was to be paid along with an annual rent of thirty shillings, this to be applied for the use of the Parish Church. The lease was to take effect after the death of Agnes Cole.

At the time of the Commissioners' report in 1824 it was said the annual value of the field, which consisted of about three acres of land, was about £4, with a chief rent of 16d. payable to the lord of the manor of Cobham Week. Richard Friend junr, who was still living at the time of the report, paid the annual rent of 30s. to the churchwardens. This money contributed to the repairs of the church.

Minutes in the churchwardens' account book which dates from 1791 refer to a lease dated 26 May 1582 in Mr Hamlyn's possession, this indicates that the Parish Ham existed in the year 1582.

On 13 July 1866 the charity commissioners set up a scheme for the running of the Parish Ham by trustees. A span of 30 years is to pass before once again we find the charity commissioners holding an inquiry into the Parish Ham charity. This took place in the church school at Bridestowe 21 February 1912, it was attended by the Reverend J.L. Francis, Mr C.H. Calmady Hamlyn, Mr T. Sly, both churchwardens, and Mr J.H. Barkell. The inquiry report dated 6 March 1912 reveals that the field, which formed the basis of the Parish Ham charity, had been sold under the authority of the charity commissioners dated 16 December 1898. Although the actual date of sale and the name of the purchaser are not given, we are informed that the sum paid was that of £112.

The second charity, which originated in 1862, was the land given by the rector from the Manor Sanctuary to enlarge the village school. From the Commissioners Report of 1912 we find that:

By Deed of 2 April 1862, the Revd Charles Whitley Clarke, Rector of Bridestowe... under the Authority of the Schools Sites Acts, freely, voluntarily, and without valuable consideration granted to the minister and churchwardens for the time being of the parish of Bridestowe a piece of land with the buildings thereon, situate in the village of Bridestowe, bounded by a farmyard then occupied by William Bickle, farmer, on the east by a cottage occupied by John Bickle, labourer, on the west by a piece of land occupied by John Bevan, on the south and on the north side by the high road leading from Okehampton to Launceston, running through the village of Bridestowe, the premises being parcel of the manor of Sanctuary of Bridestowe... upon trust for a school for the education of children and adults or children only of the labouring, manufacturing and other poorer classes in the parishes of Bridestowe and Sourton, and for no other purpose, the schools to be

at all times open to the inspection of Her Majesty's Inspectors of Schools, to be controlled and managed as follows... the principal officiating minister for the time being of the said parish shall have the super-intendence of the religious and moral instruction of all the scholars, and may use the premises for the purposes of a Sunday school under his exclusive control... the selection, appointment and dismissal of the schoolmaster and schoolmistresses and their assistants... shall be vested in and exercised by a committee consisting of the principal officiating minister... and five other persons, being contributors in every year to the amount of 20s. each at least to the funds of the said school, and communicants of the Church of England as by law established... the master or mistress of the school to be members of the Church of England, with usual provisions for administration and conduct of business... the dismissal of any teacher on account of defective or unsound instruction of the children in religion may be referred to the Bishop of the diocese whose written decision thereon shall be final... and with a power to the committee in the month of March in each year to appoint a committee of not more than four ladies, being members of the Church of England, to assist them in the visitation and management of the girls' and Infant schools, which shall remain in office until the first day of the same month in the following year, when it may be renewed.

The second charity needs no further explanation here save to say that religion clearly was to play a part of school life. Unlike other parishes though, Bridestowe had no charity for the support of the poor and needy.

THE SPORTING GREEN

From the court books of the Manor of Bridestowe Sanctuary we find that the Sporting Green was originally known as Tanners Meadow. It was first mentioned in an account of head rents within the court books dated 1846, due to the Sanctuary Manor. An abstract from the account reads:

Liberty given to James Lintern and John Lintern of Coombwick to cut granite in the sporting green and Ben Major To pay 1d per year for putting turf, wood etc on sporting green as customary with Mr Luxmoore.

Initially it would seem that conditions under which the lord of the Sanctuary Manor let Tanners Meadow to the parish as a sporting green were quite simply that the parishioners were to main-

tain its upkeep. On 5 May 1884 it was resolved that the sporting green, as it was now seemingly

Sporting Green Event, 1950s. The gent leaning on his stick is Mr Northcott. (Derek Northcott)

Clay-pigeon shoot at the Sporting Green, c.1950.
Left to right: *Revd H. Kingdon (known fondly as
'Pop Kingdon' to the kids), John Chapman, Harold
Phillips, Ernie Chapman, Frank Harris, John
Hambly, Stuart Hannaford, Mary Dennis, ?, Reg
Huggins, ?, Bill Gale, ?, Maurice Gloyn, Mabel Gale,
?, Henry Dennis, Bob Pyle.* (Howard Barkell)

Fête at the Sporting Green, c.1950. Left to right:
*Derek Palmer, Norman Woodman, Howard Barkell,
Michael Gale, ?, Clifton Towl.* (Howard Barkell)

known, was to be put into 'fair and decent order'. Execution of repairs to, and erection of, fences, gates, styles, etc. was to be carried out by seven ratepayers as a committee who were also to collect contributions and subscriptions with the view of keeping the Sporting Green in good repair from year to year. During 1895 the Reverend Francis was to let it at a nominal rent to the Parish Council. The commoners met and approved of the PC accepting the rector's offer. In September 1898 the Sporting Green was the subject of an argument; the commoners felt that the PC and the Revd Francis should present the question of sporting rights to be argued before an arbitrator.

From evidence given at the arbitration it was thought probable that the claim of sporting rights arose as the greater part of the cottages in the village, before they were sold for the Redemption of Land tax, belonged to the Church. The rector had allowed the cottagers to use the Green for

their pigs, and no succeeding rector had exercised his right to close the Sporting Green against the parishioners. He had also permitted children to play on the Green. Evidence also showed that each rector had let it for pasture and had exercised their rights of ownership by locking the entrance gates. The Court Rolls easily proved the freehold and there was nothing therein to support the claim of any sporting rights of parishioners on the Green. To help prove the rector's case extracts from Court Rolls identifying the Sporting Green as Tanners Meadow were shown.

The arbitrator found in the rector's favour but to prevent any further argument the rector agreed to lease the Sporting Green to the PC at a nominal rental. Tanners Meadow, it would seem, was a natural place for children to play and the place where parents carried out animal husbandry in a small way, no succeeding rector having the heart to turn them off.

VILLAGE GOSSIP & ARGUMENT

As documented in Chapter 2 we know that William and Agnes Bidlake were involved in disputes with Gilbert Germyn, the rector of Bridestowe. They, however, were not the first of the Bidlakes to become embroiled in disputes; Peter Ebsworthy also came in the Bidlakes' line of fire. He was cited 'for usurpinge of place in the Church, being a man of no discent, or parentage, and claiminge a Seate unfittinge for a man of his ranke or position.' Furthermore 'next for his wief abusing of my weif in goinge to the Communion, by blowes and afterwards with disgracefull words'. Next came Paule Ebsworthy:

... for layinge of violent handes upon my weif in the Church yard, and his weifs scouldinge, Katherine Ebsworthy using these words before the Parson unto his sister, Peter's weif, that her sister might be ashamed to suffer such to goe before her as my weif was.

These tribulations, to be brought before the Bishop, had developed out of what can only be described as two families, who, for whatever their reasons, did not see eye to eye, hanging out their dirty washing for all to see.

❊ *Entertainment* ❊

Right: *Bridestowe School Pantomime, 1940s?* (Author)

Below: *School Concert, 1934.* Left to right, standing: *Grace Cox, Jack Westcott, Marion Maddaford;* sitting: *Miss Moyse, Ida Lake, Pam Towl, Edie Voyzey.* (George Lavis)

Below left: *The Prince (Frank Chope) and Princess (Marion Maddaford) outside the Royal Oak, Bridestowe Carnival. This is thought to be 1937.* (Brian Maddaford)

Below: *Bridestowe School Pantomime, Sleeping Beauty, probably in 1935.* Left to right, back: *Barbara Gale, Eric Crocker, ?, Peggy Meadows, Dudley Ellis;* centre: *Marion Maddaford, ?, Ida Lake, Bill Hutchings, Lenord Chasty, Joy Maddaford, Ada Jeans;* front: *?, Pam Towl, Iris Sleeman, Greta Towl.* (Brian Maddaford)

On 12 April 1807 an alleged disturbance of the King's peace erupted at Combebow. A spectacle of feuding and jealousy was taking place between the sons of two prominent Bridestowe families. Indications of acrimony between the parties involved appeared in a letter dated 27 December 1806, which set forth a hint of possible civil action to be pursued in the courts at Exeter by Calmady Pollexfen Hamlyn against John Newton. The author of the letter, Thomas Luxmore of Fairplace, Okehampton, had written to Calmady Pollexfen Hamlyn:

I have just been in company with Mr Packer of Bow and hearing he had made use of unwarrantable language respecting you I took the liberty (at your request) to appeal to him in the subject and to know the reason why he had made use of your name otherwise than that of a Gentleman, he appeared at first much startled at the accusation and candidly and fairly told me that neither directly and indirectly had he ever spoken ill of you to Mr Newton, nor to any other person or persons whomsoever he never having any just cause or reason for so doing.

Prior to the letter we have further evidence that not all was well between Hamlyn and Newton for on 3 September 1806 Newton was given notice to quit and yield up his possession of all the premises at Combebow by March 1807. It seems that Newton had failed to keep to the conditions of his lease.

The letter written by Luxmore and the notice for Newton to vacate Combebow might not seem evidence of any great malice between Hamlyn and Newton, but a legal brief dated 23 July 1807 tells us more of the events which led up to the disturbance at Combebow on 12 April.

The brief headed 'In Trespass and Ejectment—this was to be heard at the Devon Lammas Assizes, 1807' shows Calmady Pollexfen Hamlyn to be the plaintiff's land holder with the principal defendant being John Newton. The brief was written on the behalf of the plaintiff's lessor and we do not have access to a similar document written on behalf of the defendant; we do know, however, that Newton was adamant that he was innocent of all allegations made against him.

Initially, Calmady Pollexfen Hamlyn had demised to Richard Ro[z] on 10 April 1807 certain premises with their 'appurtenances in the parishes of Bridestowe and Thrushelton', that is, the premises at Combebow which Newton was given notice to quit. Richard and his assigns were to hold the premises until the end of a seven-year term and by virtue of the demise Richard entered the premises and became possessed thereof. Two days later on April 12, John Do[z] with:

force and arms entered into the premises at

Combebow consisting of twenty dwelling houses, twenty courtlages, fifty outhouses, ten lime quarries, ten lime kilns, five hundred acres of lime rock and five hundred acres of land whereby Richard was then ejected from his farm within the premises by John who committed other wrongs to the great damage of the said Richard, against the peace of the lord the king.

Following on from the incident a complaint was made to Thomas Bridgeman Luxmore, Attorney, whereby injury and damage to the value of £100 had been sustained by Richard during his forced ejectment from the premises at Combebow, therefore he was to bring a suit against his attackers. Calmady Pollexfen Hamlyn initiated proceedings.

Added to the brief at some time after the main body of detail had been written was the statement that the defendant 'being a very rich purse proud man valued not his money in this dispute.' Also, much personal altercation had taken place between Hamlyn and the defendant, although this was to be ignored in the dispute, as was the defendant's abusive language towards Hamlyn who, as a gentleman and acting magistrate for the county, was to take other measures to silence the defendant. With this statement came the end of the declaration on behalf of Hamlyn but not the end of the affair.

A dramatic turn about by the defendant Newton as to his position prior to the cause being tried at the ensuing Devon Assizes 28 July 1807 was to take place. On July 23, the defendant's attorney Mr Hawkes made a statement that in part read:

Mr Newton agrees to give up the quarry and premises at Christmas next to Capt Hamlyn or his assigns. Mr Newton was not to do any wilful waste or destruction upon the premises from this time and was to make satisfaction for any that may have been done within five days from Ladyday 1802. Such damages, if any, to be estimated and agreed upon by two surveyors one to be named by each party. Mr Newton to pay the costs of Mr Hamlyn's solicitor that may have accrued. Dated 23 July 1807.

No doubt John Newton's turn around was made upon receiving sound advice from his legal representative that his case was hopeless. The above agreement was not to herald the end of animosity between the two men however. A second brief dated 12 September 1808, again prepared on behalf of the plaintiff, sets out the details for an ensuing case to be heard in the courts at Exeter. Calmady Pollexfen Hamlyn, plaintiff, was to bring a suit for damages against John Newton, defendant.

It seems that on this occasion Newton was in disagreement about the level of tax which had been set against him by Hamlyn whilst acting in

❋ *Entertainment* ❋

Top left: *Bridestowe Carnival, HMS Horse, 1935. Left to right, standing: Greta Towl, Tricie Towl, Pam Towl, Joyce Maddaford, Claude Weeks; sitting: ?, Marion Maddaford, Alf Lee at the horse's head.* (George Lavis)

Top right: *Bridestowe Carnival, Robin Hood, 1935(?).*
Left to right, standing: *Dorothy Hutchings, Lilly Worden, Iris Worden; sitting: Jane Hutchings, Violet Worden, ?, Daisey Worden.* (Alan Pearn)

Above: *Bridestowe Carnival, 1935(?). Left to right, children at front: ? Gorman, Gladys Jewell, ?, ?, Joan Philpott, Phyllis Barkell, Dorothy Hellier, Marie Philpott, Roy Parsons, Audrey Philpott, Doreen Gale, Gracie Baskerville, Barbara Gale (with broom); stewards: ?, Irvine Kidd, Dick Burnham; lady in hat, Mrs Maddaford; mounted parade leader, Bert Tucker.* (Howard Barkell)

Above right: *Stewards at Bridestowe Carnival, c.1935. Left to right: Sam Chastey, Dick Burnham, Cecil Kidd, Charlie Broad, ?, Bert Crocker.* (Brian Maddaford)

an official capacity. Although Newton took steps of appeal against his tax bill it appears the procedure was not enough to pacify the hostility felt towards Hamlyn. In order to denigrate his victim Newton exercised slanderous behaviour in an attempt to get Hamlyn to respond in ungentlemanly fashion.

The brief informs us that Calmady Pollexfen Hamlyn was a gentleman of considerable fortune and altogether possessed of landed estate to the amount of £3000 a year. He was also possessed of other landed estates in the funds and otherwise upwards of £6000, of which he was now about to realise in freehold estates. As a Captain of Grenadiers in the North Devon Militia he saw nine years' service from which situation he resigned upon his marriage, some three years hence. He was now an acting magistrate for the county, a commissioner of property, and assessed taxes. The plaintiff, it was said, was 'well known and respected by the nobility and principal gentry of the county.'

The defendant was also a man of considerable fortune. He was a farmer, limeburner and engaged in many trades. He had upward of £1000 a year landed estate and a considerable sum of money. It was said to be common knowledge that the defendant had 'been the terror of the neighbourhood'. From his great overflow of money 'not one shilling [did] he expend but for the worse of purposes'. He kept about himself 'a gang of fellows (of which William Rule was alleged to have been one) who were ready for all kinds of mischief at any time'. He never forgave and never forgot when he had resolved to injure and overpower any man, however poor. On public occasions he uttered such 'horrible falsehoods' and 'shameful language', as any man of common feelings was unable to bear.

At a Parish Vestry meeting, Newton publicly said that the plaintiff was a 'Damned Rascal, Scoundrell and Knave' and from the onset of the meeting the plaintiff did not speak to the defendant but later on Newton in a most violent manner started 'hollering' so that he could be heard out in the public street, repeatedly informing all present at the meeting: 'I do not value thee Hamlyn more than the dirt of my shoes. Thou art a Knave, a Rascal, a Scoundrell, a Damned Scoundrell', this being repeated over and over again. Amongst the people attending the Vestry meeting was Mr Chapman, who, on returning home, relayed the incident which had occurred between Hamlyn and Newton to his wife. A statement provided by Mrs Chapman reads:

When Mr Chapman came from the vestry he told me that there had been a terable sceane in the vestry between Mr Hamlyn and young Newton. I asked him concerning of what he sed Mr Newton sed that Mr Hamlyn had got a parcel of men at his home til midnight and fed them to purjer themselves to swear a false statement against him at the last assize which was young Osborn and young Blatchford. Mr Chapman remarked the culeness of Mr Hamlyn all the time and could not think how he done it as he did.

With counsel's advice taken into consideration it seems the cause was heard on 17 April 1809 in the courts at the Castle of Exeter. The resulting verdict was an award of £30 damages to Calmady Pollexfen Hamlyn with an apology from the defendant through his counsel.

A CONSISTORY COURT HEARING

On 13 May 1766 John Newton petitioned the Bishop of Exeter for seats within the church of Bridestowe for his estate called Higher Stone. Within a week the petition was accepted by the Church authorities and they granted a licence of confirmation to Newton on 19 May. This sequence of events, which, upon first sight, appears to be straightforward and of little consequence, was to set the background for a dispute with subsequent upheaval for a number of elderly folk of Bridestowe and other surrounding parishes. Ebsworthy Tapson who occupied Lower Stone, therefore a close neighbour of John Newton, was to set in motion a process that continued for a year. Tapson made objections to the granting of the licence of confirmation to Newton as he also claimed rights to the seats in question. Tapson's objections were to be eventually heard by the Bishop of Exeter in his consistorial court which dealt with matters of an ecclesiastical nature and, like any other court, the process of Church law was not a matter which was to be rushed through with any great promptitude.

Following on from the petition of Newton we find that Tapson had moved quite swiftly; he had obtained legal representation to present his objections to the Consistory Court at Exeter on 27 June 1766 whereby a lengthy submission was put to the court.

Tapson stated that he was an inhabitant of Bridestowe and owner-occupier of Lower Stone for which he paid all parochial rates. Tapson claimed that he was legally entitled to 'one sitting for a man and another for a woman in the very seats

❧ *Entertainment* ❧

Top left: *Mervyn Down at Millaton, c.1957.*
(Alan Pearn)

Top right: *Bridestowe Carnival, 'Not Wanted Any Plan', 1935. Left to right: Wally Ellis, Hubert Ball, Clifford Dawe, Fred Weeks, George Baskerville, Amos Baskerville, Percy Bickle (Model T Ford Truck).* (Sam Ball)

Middle left: *Black and White Minstrel Show, Parish Hall, 1950s. Back row includes: Howard Barkell, Bill Squires, Amos Baskerville; middle row includes: Wally Wyatt, Ted Hayden, Jim Barkell (white face), Ern Barkell, Frank Cloke, Frank Harris, Revd H. Kingdon; front: John Wyatt, Brian Lethbridge.*
The girls probably include: Ann Jewell, June Jewell, Barbara Harris, Phyllis Cann and Carol Shuttleworth. (Howard Barkell)

Middle right: *Keith Down at Millaton, c.1957.* (Alan Pearn)

Above: *Bridestowe Pantomime, 1950s. Left to right, standing: Wendy Short, Ann Jewell, Phyllis Cann, Jean Barker, ?; sitting: Brian Lethbridge, June Jewell.* (Sam Ball)

now Petitioned for by John Newton' as the owner occupier of Lower Stone and had for 'time out of mind possessed and enjoyed one sitting for a man and another for a woman in the said seats'. It appears that Tapson's suit did not proceed beyond the presentation of his objections as five witnesses called upon to substantiate his claims were unwilling to participate in any proceedings. To overcome his dilemma Tapson bought the full rigors of the court to bear by applying for a compulsory witness order, which was issued on 22 August 1766. The order summoned Roger Maddaford, Roger Daw, John Hockaday and Ann his wife of Bridestowe and Sarah Fry of Coryton to the Consistorial Court at Exeter on Tuesday 9 September to testify the truth of what they knew in the matter to be heard.

The named witnesses in the citation, whose ages ranged from 53 to 75 years, must have been in a state of trepidation after being served with a notice to attend court. Here we have five people who had initially refused to act on Tapson's behalf, now being compelled to attend court at Exeter, take an oath and become part of a system, which, no doubt, would be most foreign to them – not one of them was capable of performing the simple act of signing his own name. Furthermore, a journey of some 30 miles was to be taken on horseback which was to take them away from their homes for four days.

Tuesday 9 September 1766 was the day on which Tapson's cause was to begin in earnest. Furlong, his Proctor, opened the cause by exhibiting the Bridestowe rate book to show that the estates of Higher and Lower Stone were rated alike. He then proceeded to produce Tapson's witnesses.

The first to appear was Roger Maddaford, a 62-year-old yeoman. He told the court that he was 'born and had his usual abode in Bridestow from his Nativity'. He said that Tapson was an inhabitant of Bridestow who had been in possession of Lower Stone as owner-occupier for the last ten or eleven years, paying considerably to the parochial rates. Maddaford informed the court that 'since his remembrance being upwards of forty years', the owner-occupier of Lower Stone had claimed and enjoyed the right of a sitting for a woman in one of the seats which had been deemed and reputed to be a right, but knew of no right of a sitting for a man.

Uptram, Proctor for Newton, subjected Maddaford to an interrogation. Different people occupied Lower Stone. Samuel Keen was the owner of the mills, the Mill Green, the eastern part of the mansion house and some quarry pits. Joseph Sercombe was Keen's servant. The rest of Lower Stone belonged to Tapson who rented out part of the western ground to Nicholas Tapson. The western part of the mansion house, the barns,

cellars, offices and four fields were in the occupation of Tapson. Maddaford said he did not know if the seat did or did not belong to Lower Stone. He said he signed a paper brought to him by Newton's son, John, which he believed may have been the petition but as he could not read, nor had he ever heard the contents of the paper so signed by him read, he could not say whether it was the petition or not.

The second witness, Roger Daw of Bridestowe, yeoman, aged 63 and upwards, gave his evidence much along the lines of Maddaford. The third witness, John Hockaday of Sourton, blacksmith, aged 75 or thereabouts, said he was 'born in Soreton a Chapelry belonging to Bridestow' where he had resided for the previous 25 years, but for several years before, but for how many he did not remember, he lived in Bridestowe.

The final witness, Sarah Fry of Coryton, aged about 53, said she was 'born in Bridestow where she had lived for more than 30 years from her nativity' but she now lived at Coryton. Her husband, William Fry, had rented Lower Stone and continued as tenant during their intermarriage, being about six years. During that time she had normally sat in one of the seats now petitioned for without any denials, as had frequently Mary Fry, a former wife of William, who sat in the same seat. Mary Fry, sister of William, who had lived with her brother as housekeeper, had sat in the seat for more than 'sixty years back'.

On completion of Sarah Fry's evidence a two-month period was to lapse before court proceedings continued. On 7 November 1766, Uptram, acting for John Newton, made comment to the court on the evidence as given by Ebsworthy Tapson's witnesses. He said that no credit ought to be given to the witnesses who had lied, were friends of Tapson who had influenced them and enemies of Newton. Aged persons of Bridestowe knew that the man's seat was erected and built or repaired by some or one of the Nichols family who had been former owner-occupiers of Higher Stone.

The next stage in the hearing of the cause was to be the appearance of Ebsworthy Tapson. He appeared at the court on 14 November and was cautioned as to his position; he was to have his evidence ready for the next court. His case was quite lengthy. Tapson said that full faith and credit should be given to the depositions of the witnesses who had appeared for him, a denial was made of the accusation that they were friends and under his influence. He believed that the seats petitioned for by John Newton did not entirely belong to Higher Stone. As owner-occupier of an estate, or, at least, the greater part of an estate called Lower Stone for which he paid parochial rates, he was entitled to one sitting for a man and

❧ *Entertainment* ❧

Top left: *Bridestowe Pantomime*, Snow White
and the Seven Dwarfs, *1950s.*
Left to right: *?, A. Wyatt, J. Rodd (?), ?, D. Gale, T. Cann, R. Ellis, G. Daniels.* (Sam Ball)

Top right: *Bridestowe Wesley Guild Pantomime*, Sleeping Beauty, *1972.* Left to right, back row:
*C. Palmer, C. Lobb, D. Bray, H. Pearn, R. Maddaford, B. Bray, J. Down, H. Barkell, S. Pearn, I. Pearn,
S. Lobb;* sitting: *R. Perkins, L. Down;* front: *G. Yates, D. Heathman, J. Maddaford, K. Heathman,
W. Elsworthy, J. Gale.* (Brian Maddaford)

Below: *Bridestowe Pantomime*, Cinderella, *1950s.* Left to right: *Ann Jewell, Carol Shuttleworth,
Author, Brian Lethbridge, Barbara Harris.* (Author)

one sitting for a woman in the seat now in controversy, which he believed had for 'time out of mind' belonged to Lower Stone.

Next up in court were the witnesses for John Newton who gave their evidence on 30 December 1766. Like their fellow witnesses, they were quite elderly and were cited to appear.

We find that the first witness to appear, Andrew Hockaday, a blacksmith aged 75 or thereabouts, had lived in Bridestowe for upwards of 50 years, and for more than the previous half century could remember the occupiers of Higher Stone making use of the said seats. Hockaday said he remembered Walter Nichols as occupier of Higher Stone, his family had made use of the seats now petitioned for, for some 50 years. The man's seat had been erected before his remembrance. It was a firm oak seat and it had not been repaired by anyone. Liberty had been given to Mr Mavin, a schoolmaster, by Tapson to sit in one of the seats.

Under interrogation Hockaday said he knew the nature of an oath and the danger of perjury and that he was cited to appear to give evidence. He had known Ebsworthy Tapson from his infancy, he being a parishioner of Bridestowe for some 50 years. Nicholas Tapson was one of the singers who sat in the gallery along with the other singers.

The second witness, Robert Redstone, a lime burner, aged at least 78, said he believed the two sittings in question belonged to the occupier of Higher Stone.

The third witness, Agnes, wife of Henry Crossman, aged about 60, said that soon after taking over Lower Stone, which he was to occupy for 30 years or more, William Fry did, in her presence and hearing, apply to Elizabeth, wife of Walter Nichols the occupier of Higher Stone, for liberty to sit in one of the seats in question to which Elizabeth readily gave her consent.

The fourth witness, John Collins, a 30-year-old yeoman, during his evidence in chief added that he heard Walter Nichols declare that he had repaired the man's seat. Under interrogation Collins added that Nicholas Tapson was a singer who sat in the gallery. Other than those two points Collins' evidence was much the same as the earlier witnesses.

The fifth witness to appear was Philip Mock of 'Soreton', husbandman aged 70 years and upwards. Mock said that he remembers Walter Nichols who was owner-occupier of Higher Stone sitting in the seats in controversy, along with his son Walter and their respective families. All previous owners of Lower Stone as before mentioned had never claimed a right to the seats as far as he, Mock, could remember.

The sixth and final witnesses to appear for Newton was Thomas Roberts, a yeoman, aged 70 years and upwards, who had lived in Bridestowe

for some 60 years. His answers were generally the same as given by the previous witnesses and he made his mark to endorse his depositions.

The outcome of the court's finding was read out on 8 May 1767. We find that 'the Judge having first had a Hearing of this Cause and duly weighed and considered those Merits and Circumstances thereof' declared that it did not appear that the seats ever belonged to the estate called Lower Stone, or that the said Ebsworthy Tapson 'in virtue and right thereof hath any right to the two seats or any part thereof.' John Newton and other occupiers of Higher Stone 'in virtue and right thereof had for time immemorial' made use of and sat in the said seats quietly and peaceably 'thereby a Licence for Confirmation of the said seats was to be granted to Newton.'

Ebsworthy Tapson did not accept the decision of the court and appealed to the Arches Court of Canterbury. On 19 June 1767, the appeal was disallowed with costs awarded against Tapson. From a bill of expenses on behalf of Newton we see the costs amounted to £38.3s. The court did, however, tax the bill, which resulted in a reduced figure of £26.6s.8d. On top of this amount would have been Tapson's own expenses. In all it seems to have been a princely sum to pay in order to establish a right to a particular seat in the church, especially when already in possession of seats in right of other estates. A century later of course, the church was reseated, thus putting an end to this argument once and for all.

SOURCES

Birkett, P., *A Short History of The Rights of Common Upon the Forest of Dartmoor and the Commons of Devonshire.*

Coate, M., *Cornwall in the Great Civil War and Interregnum 1642–1660.*

Cotton, R.W., *Barnstaple During The Great Civil War 1642–1646.*

Devon and Cornwall Notes and Queries. Vol. XXIX.

Devon Record Office: 2205A.

     189M.

     2750A.

     1292M.

Diocesan Records Faculties 1.

Q/S 128 Maimed Soldiers (16).

Hansford, Worth R., *Worth's Dartmoor* (1988 Edition).

Pollock and Maitland, *History of English Law.*

Richardson, J., *The Local Historian's Encyclopaedia.*

Rowe, S. Rev., *A Perambulation of Dartmoor* (1985 Edition).

Sir Ralph Hopton's Campaign in The West.

Transactions of the Devonshire Association 1889.

West Country Studies Library.

CHA/1905/BRA6-BRO1 (Bridestowe).

❧ *Special Events* ❧

Left: *The village folk at a flag bedecked West Bridge dressed in their finery anticipating the arrival of the Prince and Princess of Wales, 1909.*
(Alan Pearn)

Right: *Presentation to Elsie and Ernie Barkell on their retirement from Bridestowe Post Office in 1957, by Lt. Col. Calmady-Hamlyn, Chairman of the Parish Council. Ernie was appointed Sub Postmaster in 1938 in succession to his Aunt Emily Howard, who had held the office since 1902. Elsie took over in 1960. Other villagers include Alan Owen, Cecil Mortimore, Vince Northcott, Marion Knight, Janet Mills, Violet Mortimore.*
(Howard Barkell)

Left: *Presentation of British Empire Medal to Jim Barkell by Leslie Sweet, Head Postmaster, Okehampton c.1965. Apart from war service Jim was a Postman all his working life. Others in picture, left to right: Mary Barkell, Amy Barkell, Archie Crocker, Jim Huxtable, Cynthia Hamilton, Doreen Ellacott.*
(Howard Barkell)

Special Events

Left: *Exmouth Outing.*
(Brian Lavis)

Below: *Bridestowe Summer Fair, 1955.* Horse: *Mrs Northy, Mrs Sam Ball; Shirly Heathman in caravan with Paul Turner at the 'reins'.*
(Sam Ball)

Below: *A grand occasion in the Parish Hall, 1957.*
(Alan Pearn)

❊ *Pastimes* ❊

Above: *Bridestowe Guides outside the Parish Hall with their mascot, 1930s.* Left to right, back row: *Beatrice Stratton, Mable Gale, Winnie Shaddick, Elsie Neill, Beatrice Lugg, Doris Murrin;* middle row: *Molly Hockin, Frances Philpott, Frances Porter, May Porter, Mattie Down, Naomi Ball, Margaret Stratton, Carlo Stratton;* front row: *Frances White, Rhoda Pearce, Elsie Maddaford, Enid Pellow, Florrie Yelland.* (Author)

Right: *Bridestowe Football Team, League Champions 1922/3.* Left to right, back row: *Mrs Pellow, Mrs Birch, Humphrey Ward, John Down, Albert Tickner, Stan Pellow, Lou Voaden, Frank Pike, Jim Barkell, Charlotte Baskerville, Harry Barkell, John Ward, Harry Weeks, Joe Pascoe, F. Cooper, Rennie Barkell;* middle row: *Cock Wilton, Sam Chastey, Sonny Lintern, Gerald Drew, Frank Birch, Jack Weeks;* front row: *Claude Weeks, Reg Ellis, Amos Baskerville, Ern Barkell, Amy Tremlett, Doris Murrin, Dick Baskerville.* (Howard Barkell)

Bottom right: *Bridestowe Cricket Club, 1953.* Left to right, back row: *J. Milford, L. Down, F. Harris, O. Hamilton, ? Wrigh (?), J. Crocker, N. Gale;* front row: *H. Barkell, S. King, Sir Giles Sebright, E. Barkell, G. Martin, ? Bleasdale (?).* (Norman Gale)

❧ *Pastimes* ❧

Left: *Women's Institute in the Parish Hall.* Left to right, standing: *Mrs Mays, Mrs Lake, Mrs Lavis, Mrs Morrish, Mrs Mudge, Mrs Wisdom, Mrs Salter, Mrs Leonard, Mrs Barkell;* seated: *Mrs Harris, Mrs Lethbridge, Mrs Ward, Miss Moyse.* (Howard Barkell)

Below: *Church-of-England's Men's Society quiz, Parish Hall, 1950s.* Left to right, standing: *Frank Harris, Ernie Chapman, Bert Mays, Jack Crocker, Brian Maddaford, Ronald Thompson with Alan Pearn in front, Ross Salmon, Oliver Hamilton with Ernie Barkell in front, Oliver Broady;* seated: *Mrs Hunter, Dolly Marwood, Margaret Gale, Elsie Barkell, Mrs Pugsley, Nellie Milnes, Marcia Heathman, Margaret Voaden, Anne Reidy.* (Howard Barkell)

Right: *Bridestowe Mothers' Union celebrate their 50-year Anniversary, c.1985.* Left to right, back row: *Hilma Lethbridge, Emma Crocker, Mrs Barlow, Mrs Norrish, Sylvia Willcocks, Leah Moyse, ?, ?, Jean Manning, Cynthia Williams;* front row: *Ivy Maddaford, Mrs Holden, Elsie Barkell, Mabel Gale (senior member), Elizabeth Bray.* (Howard Barkell)

❧ *Sports* ❧

Above: *Celebration match for Major Rollestone, he having played 50 years at Bridestowe Cricket Club, 1970s. Major Rollestone is on the left of the wickets shaking hands with the then Captain, Doug Gale.* (Doug Gale)

Below: *Lady Sebright receiving a cheque from the Lord's Taverner Association towards purchasing the cricket ground, 1960. Left to right, back row: Leonard Down, Herbie Pearn, Derek Northcott, Glanville Martin, Ollie Hamilton, Ross Salmon, ?, Jack Crocker; front row: ?, G. Martin, Lady Sebright, Brian Lethbridge, Mrs Lethbridge, Leo Lethbridge.* (Doug Gale)

❊ *Sports* ❊

Right: *Lamerton Foxhounds leaving the White Hart under the Master, Spencer King, c.1955. Whipper-in probably Ken Harris.*
(Howard Barkell)

Below: *Mr B Hartland Worden with his Champion of Champions, Southball Moonstone (bred at Bridestowe), Crufts, 1934.* (Alan Pearn)

CHAMPION OF CHAMPIONS. Mr. B. Hartland Worden's Southball Moonstone (left) with her owner and the cup which she won after being adjudged the best dog in the show at Cruft's. Lorna Countess Howe, one of the judges, described her as as nearly perfect as a dog can be.

Below: *Mr Worden, breeder of Greyhounds c.1934. Picture taken in a field just below the gardens of the Old Rectory House.*
(Alan Pearn)

Below: *Fox and Hounds Tug of War team on horseback, 1900. Left to right: Woodland Landford (Landlord), Wallace Ellis, Mr Palmer, Fred Gay, ?, Fred Screech, Tom Ash, Mr Edwards (Capt).* (Doug Gale)

Top left: *Richard Cann prior to the Second World War. He was killed in action May 1944 and lies buried in Casino War Cemetery, Italy. His name is on the Bridestowe War Memorial.* (Norman Gale)

Top right: *Devons – 1st, 2nd, 3rd, 4th, and 5th Vol. Batts., Bridestowe (probably Vale Down), 1906.* (Doug Gale)

Centre: *Samuel Cann prior to the Second World War. Unlike his brother, he survived.* (Author)

Bottom left: *The War Memorial, Bridestowe.* (Derek Northcott)

Bottom right: *Fred Gay who worked at Great Crandford prior to the First World War.* (Brian Lavis)

SUBSCRIBERS

Donald A. Addison, Fernworthy Farm, Bridestowe, Devon

Tricia Alston

Eddie A. Amhof, Sourton Down, Devon

Mrs M.E. Anderson and Mrs W.M. Middleton (née Barker), Plymouth, Devon

Barbara Anning (née Watts), Mary Tavy, Devon

Katharine Baker, Cambridgeshire

Darron John Baker, Bridestowe, Devon

Mr S.G. Ball, Durley Dene, Bridestowe, Devon

Robert Bampton, Barrington, Cambridgeshire

G. Banfield, Bridestowe and Sourton/now Torrington

Howard Barkell

Jean Barker, Poole Hill, Bridestowe, Devon

Nichola G.F. Bartlett, Bridestowe, Devon

Robert W. and Jeannie M. Bell, Bridestowe, Devon

Mrs Ruth Bird (née Romain)

Joan and Bob Brown, Plymouth, Devon

John A. Burgess, Bridestowe, Devon

K.J. Burrow, Bucks Cross, Devon

Mr and Mrs M. Butler, Bridestowe, Devon

Stephen and Kathryn Byrne, Springfields, Bridestowe, Devon

Joan Calmady-Hamlyn, Leawood, Bridestowe, Devon

Marie Cantwell (née Philpott), Michigan, USA

Mr D.V. Chapman, Bridestowe, Devon

P.S. Congdon

Dorothy Crawford (née Woodman), Okehampton, Devon

Mark J. Crocker, Farnborough, Hampshire

Simon J. Crocker, Yate, Bristol

W. John (Jack) Crocker, Stroud, Gloucestershire

Graham and Jenny Crocker, Bridestowe, Devon

Andrew J. Crocker, Bristol

Sheila and Peter Daniels, Bridestowe, Devon

Dartmoor National Park Authority

Hazel Dawson, Bridestowe, Devon

Mervyn Down, born Little Bidlake, Bridestowe, Devon

Philip Down, born Little Bidlake, Bridestowe, Devon

Margaret and Bill Down, Little Bidlake, Bridestowe, Devon

Keith Down, born Little Bidlake, Bridestowe, Devon

Mrs J. Dunse, The Station House, Bridestowe, Devon

The Elsworthy family

George and Kath Field, Bridestowe, Devon

Sheila A. Ford, Burntisland, Fife, Scotland

Sybil Fry (née Pearn), Radstock

Norman W. Gale, Bridestowe, Devon

Anthony N. Gale, Okehampton, Devon

Douglas A. Gale, Launceston, Cornwall

Mrs Lucy Grant, Coombe Bow

Cdr and Mrs P. Griffiths, Bridestowe, Devon

Rex and Anne Haythornthwaite, Bridestowe, Devon

Roy Heathman, Lifton, Devon

George Andrew Heathman, Tanyard Court, Bridestowe, Devon

Samantha L.W. Herniman, Gloucester

Doreen Hollinshead (née Screech), Okehampton, Devon

Roy and Jill Hughes, Exmouth, Devon

S. Jackson

Andrew R. Janes, Taunton, Somerset

Tony Johnston and Rose Maddaford, Bridestowe, Devon

Phyllis C. Jones, Okehampton, Devon

Joy F. Kearsey, Lechlade, Gloucestershire

Valerie Keates (née Maddaford), Oxford

Harley J. Kitt, Pool House, Bridestowe, Devon

Marilyn Knott (née Jewell), Bridestowe, Devon

Michael Langford, Bridestowe, Devon

G. Lavis, Exmouth, Devon

B.W.J. Lavis, Bridestowe, Devon

Mr Michael Lavis

Miss India Leigh, Crediton, Devon

Master Ranald Leigh, Crediton, Devon

Mrs Laura Leigh (née Calmady-Hamlyn), Crediton, Devon

John F. Leonard, Beara, Bridestowe, Devon

Brian Lethbridge

Bob and Edna Lloyd, Midhurst, Sussex

Diana and John Maclean, Clokes Hill, Watergate, Bridestowe, Devon

Ruth and Brian Maddaford, Bridestowe, Devon

P.S. McMillan, Exmouth, Devonshire

Thomas and Margaret Moore, Lord and Lady of Bridestowe Sanctuary

Thomas Moore of New York, Lord of Bridestowe Sanctuary

Richard and Naomi Nardi, Bridestowe, Devon

Peggy Newnham (née Brooks), Saltash, Cornwall

I. Eleanor Newsome, Brockville, ON, Canada

Gwen Patterson, Penetang, Ontario, Canada

Mrs Diane Pearce, Bridestowe, Devon

Mr and Mrs M.B. Pearce, Bridestowe, Devon

Alan and Babs Pearn, Charfield, Gloucestershire

Mark Worden Pearn, Kingston Upon Thames

Kerry Rae Pearn, Bedford

David, Lynda and Alice Pellow, Hursdon Farm, Sourton

Martin Pellow, Lillicrapp, Sourton, Devon

Ian Perkins, Bratton Clovelly, Devon

Mr and Mrs P.M. Perry, Plymouth, Devon

Grace Phare, Slade Cross, Ottery St Mary, Devon

Jack Philpott, Exmouth, Devon

Mr and Mrs R. Plumridge, Bridestowe, Devon

W.P. Ponsford, Stone Farm, Bridestowe, Devon

David Porter, Bridestowe, Devon

H.G. Purchase M.P.S., Bridestowe, Devon

Mr and Mrs D.W. Puttick, Eastbourne, East Sussex

Janet and Philip Rattenbury, Bridestowe, Devon

Ken Rickard, Lydford, Devon

Gordon and Betty Ruoff, Bridestowe, Devon

H.M. Seymour, Okehampton, Devon

Mr Jules Shuttleworth

Christine Smith, White Cottage, Bridestowe, Devon

Doctor J.C. Speller, Tavistock, Devon

Springfields Residential Home, Bridestowe, Devon

Mr A.H. Spry, Lewdown, Devon

Gill Squires, Bridestowe, Devon

Terry and Jane Sweet, Warmley, Bristol

Audrey Sykes (née Philpott), Murray Bridge, South Australia

Mrs E. Tancock (née Walters), Crediton, Devon

Joan Teeling (née Philpott), Barnstaple, Devon

S. Trewin, Bridestowe/now Lydford

Kath and Ron Tudge

Yvonne and Dick Turpin, Glebe Park, Bridestowe, Devon

Mr G. Waldron, Plymouth, Devon

John F.W. Walling, Newton Abbot, Devon

Charles W. Walters, Lifton, Devon

Terry J. Watt, Kirkcaldy, Fife

John Watts, Newton Abbot, Devon

Marc Watts, Exford, Somerset

John and Wendy Watts, Bridestowe, Devon

Anne Westlake (née Jewell), Lewdown, Devon

Mr and Mrs J.V. Wheller, Diggaport House, Bridestowe, Devon

Mr P.D. Whitcomb, Salisbury, Wiltshire

The Whiteley family, Bridestowe, Devon

John and Vera Whiting, Bridestowe, Devon

Jennifer A. Wooldridge, Folly Gate

Ian and Chris Woolley, The Retreat, Bridestowe, Devon

Margaret J. Yeo (née Barker), Lifton, Devon

FURTHER TITLES

Titles from the Series

Forthcoming

For details of any of the above titles or if you are
interested in writing your own history, please contact:
Commissioning Editor Community Histories, Halsgrove
House, Lower Moor Way, Tiverton Business Park,
Tiverton, Devon EX16 6SS, England;
email: naomic@halsgrove.com

In order to include as many historic photographs as
possible in this volume, a printed index is not included.
However, the Community History Series is indexed by
Genuki. For further information and indexes to
volumes in the series, please visit:
http://www.cs.ncl.uk/genuki/DEV/indexingproject.html